HOW TO BUY
AND SELL
YOUR HOME

HAMLYN HELP YOURSELF GUIDE

HOW TO BUY AND SELL YOUR HOME

MICHAEL STOCK

HAMLYN

First published in 1989 by
the Hamlyn Publishing Group Limited,
a division of the Octopus Publishing Group,
Michelin House, 81 Fulham Road,
London SW3 6RB

ISBN 0 600 566 374

Printed and bound in Great Britain by
The Guernsey Press Co. Ltd., Guernsey, Channel Islands.

Contents

Introduction 9

Step by Step Guide to Buying Your Home 10

Basic Decisions 14
How much can you afford?
Your buying potential: a checklist
Buying a new house
NHBC protection scheme
Pros and cons of buying a new house
Buying a nearly new house
Buying an older house
Freehold and leasehold
Buying a flat or maisonette
Buying a mobile home
Right to buy tenants
Leasehold tenants with a right to buy
Buying the freehold of a flat
Shared ownership

Choosing your Home 29
Where to look
Surroundings
Position
The interior
The exterior
The neighbours
Leading questions
Checklist: is this the right property?
Viewing a flat
Fixtures and fittings
Making an offer

Buying at auction
Buying by tender

The Professionals   44
Estate agents
Solicitors' property centres
Surveyors and valuers
Solicitors
Other conveyancers
Building societies
The ombudsman
Other lenders
Mortgage brokers

Raising a Mortgage   56
Applying for a mortgage
Types of mortgage
True interest rates
Tax relief
100 per cent loans
Mortgage indemnity policy
Topping up loans
Mortgages for 'right to buy' tenants
Shared ownership
Older borrowers
Mortgage conditions
Mortgage refused
Bridging loans
Mortgage default policy

The Legal Nuts and Bolts   68
Doing your own conveyancing
Checking title
The draft contract
Preliminary enquiries and searches

Exchange of contracts
Insurance
Completion
Joint ownership
House purchase in Scotland

Selling your Home   80
Setting a price
Selling through an agent
Selling at auction
Do-it-yourself selling
Buyers' first impressions
Showing the house
The offer
Before contracts are exchanged
Selling in Scotland

Moving and After   93
Before the move: action checklist
Choosing removers
Insurance for the move
DIY removals
Smoothing the move
Improving your new home
Making changes
Finding a builder

A to Z of Problems and Solutions   106
Animals
Blight notices
Chains
Compulsory purchase
Contract races
Council tenants and the right to buy
Debt

Divorce and separation
Electricity
Gas
Gazumping
Insurance
Mobile homes
Mortgages
Neighbours
New houses
Nuisance from public development
Offers
Planning permission
Refuse
Service charges
Squatters
Trees
Wood
Working from home

Useful Addresses   125

Introduction

House purchase in an expensive business and it pays to know your way around: as a buyer, knowing how to inspect a property can save you from laying out good money on a bad buy, and as a seller, knowing how to show your home to the best advantage can add a sizeable amount to the price – or even save you an estate agent's bill. A good understanding of the range of mortgages available and the legal side of the transaction and of the workings of estate agents, surveyors and builders will help you to get the best out of the professionals involved.

This book takes you through all the major steps of buying and selling, telling you how to avoid the pitfalls and make sure that you end up with the right home at the right price and can move into it with confidence and pleasure. If you hit a snag – anything from gazumping and contract races to neighbour disputes or failure to get planning permission for the extension – or you need to complain about the service you get from the people who are supposed to be helping you, then the A to Z of Problems and Solutions on page 106 will tell you how to cope.

1

Step by Step Guide to Buying Your Home

As a brief guide for beginners, this chapter outlines the major steps along the way to completing a successful purchase. It may sound easy but there are plenty of pitfalls for the unwary along the way and in the more detailed information given over the next five chapters, you can find out how to identify and avoid them.

Step 1

Decide if you can afford to buy or to trade up if you already own a property. The expenses of buying and moving are high and you will need enough money left over from your mortgage repayments to run and maintain your property, so it is important not to over-stretch yourself.

Talk to potential lenders to get an idea of the amount they might advance and the types of properties they are willing to lend on. Building societies and banks have a great deal of free literature on mortgages and house purchase, so take advantage of their offers.

Talk to the other professionals involved – solicitors or other conveyancers, surveyors and estate agents – to get an idea of all the costs involved in the transaction. Draw up a careful budget and decide whether to buy on your own or jointly.

Step 2

Consider the relative merits of housing within your price range:

decide on the type and location of the property. Assess the market by reading the property columns of newspapers and visiting local estate agents.

If you have a property to sell in a buyer's market, it may be wise to put it on the market first. If your search is unsuccessful you can withdraw it and at least you will have formed an idea of how saleable it is. Make sure that your arrangement with the estate agent is on a 'no sale, no fee' basis.

Step 3

View likely properties. Be selective: unless you really enjoy peeping into other people's cupboards, trailing round one unsuitable property after another is a depressing experience. Don't ignore houses that seem just above your price range. It is just possible that the vendor needs to make a quick sale and will be open to offers.

Talk to friends and acquaintances who live in areas that might be suitable; they might know of someone who is about to put a house on the market and would be glad to consider a private sale. Register with several agents and keep chivvying them to make sure you get up-to-date information. If you talk to them about a possible mortgage (whether you intend to arrange your loan through them or not) you may find that they are more eager to be helpful.

Step 4

Once you have found the right house, make an offer, 'subject to contract', to the seller or his agent. You may be asked to put down a deposit with the agent or the seller's solicitor as a sign of good faith. In a seller's market, the owner may have several offers to choose from; in a buyer's market, purchasers often make offers below the asking price on several properties and then go ahead on the best deal.

Step 5

Notify your conveyancer, giving the address of the property, the name of the vendor and particulars of his estate agent and solicitor.

In a buoyant housing market, you will probably wait until this stage to put your own house on the market.

Step 6

Return to the building society or bank manager and fill in the appropriate forms to apply for a mortgage. If you have made no arrangements until now, estate agents or solicitors can sometimes be a useful way of fixing a mortgage but check if they are registered to give independent financial advice.

The lenders have to be satisfied that the property offers sufficient security for the amount of the loan so they will arrange for a valuation and you have to pay for it, whether you go through with the purchase or not. The valuation is not a survey, but many lenders offer a more thorough assessment for an extra fee. You will need to decide whether to take advantage of one of these schemes, or to commission your own surveyor or to rely on your own judgement of the property.

If the property needs extensive work, investigate the possibility of improvement or repair grants.

Step 7

Unless the valuation report is unfavourable, the lender will make a formal 'offer of advance', stating the amount of the loan, the period over which it must be repaid and the rate of interest you will be charged. In a flat market, 90-100 per cent mortgages are thin on the ground; if you get one, you will pay a higher rate of interest.

Step 8

By now, legal work on conveyancing will be under way. Your conveyancer will ensure that proper title is obtained, arrange the necessary registration of the title, check on the existence of any restrictive covenants, enquire about any planned developments that might affect the value of the property, draw up a contract of sale and so on. The scope of the standard enquiries is very limited, so be prepared to do some leg work yourself (see Chapter 6, page 67)

12

If you are selling as well as buying it is important to make sure that the contracts for both are exchanged on the same day. If there are any problems on the sale and you cannot bear the thought of losing the new house, check with your bank manager that you will be able to arrange a bridging loan if necessary. Either side can pull out, right up to exchange of contracts; in a seller's market, contract races and gazumping flourish (see Chapter 9, page 106).

Step 9

Once the searches and legal enquiries have been completed, your conveyancer arranges the exchange of contracts. Now both sides are committed. You will be expected to put down a deposit, which will be forfeited if you do not go through with the deal. Traditionally this was 10 per cent of the purchase price but raising that amount of cash can be a problem, so try to negotiate a reduction. You are now responsible for insurance on your purchase.

On exchange of contracts, the final completion date will be set. If you are a seller as well as a buyer, make sure that the completion dates on both properties link as closely as possible.

Arrange for your removal to your new property.

Step 10

Completion. Your conveyancer arranges for payment of the balance of money for the property and the vendor's solicitor hands over the legal document transferring 'title' to you. The legal documents are usually kept by the building society or bank. The property has now changed ownership.

Make arrangements to collect the keys to your new property and move in (see Chapter 8, on page 93 for advice on smoothing the move).

N.B. The procedure for home purchase in Scotland is quite different, as explained in Chapter 6, on page 77.

2

Basic Decisions

Old hands at the property market, including some estate agents, will say that buying is not right for everyone and should not be seen as a guaranteed road to riches. Certainly you cannot count on constant price rises: you might buy a studio flat at the top of the market with all sorts of classy fixtures and fittings included in the price, then find yourself seriously out of pocket when selling in difficult times. In the short term, prices have been known to go down as well as up.

The best approach for most people is to see their first purchase as buying a 'home' rather than simply as an investment. At the beginning the rewards may seem far away: you are at the mercy of fluctuating interest rates, you have all the expense and responsibility for repairs and maintenance and your outgoings may be three times as much as you would pay in rent. It is only as the years pass, inflation raises rents and the real value of mortgage payments goes down that the owner-occupier begins to reap the benefits. Also, if the past is anything to go by, given enough time property prices do tend to outstrip inflation.

When the market is rising, the attractions of home ownership seem obvious; new buyers rush in, desperate to get a foot on the housing ladder while they can still afford it. But canny first-time buyers will do better when the market is flat and may be falling. A buyer's market means that you can expect to knock a fair bit off the asking price but even more important, you will have choice, you can take your time and not be rushed into a panic purchase you might regret later. On top of that you will find that everyone loves you: sellers, lenders, even solicitors and estate agents can seem quite human!

How much can you afford?

The loan
Lenders differ in the amount they are willing to offer to the same borrower, and lending policies differ from time to time, so it makes sense to shop around before you start touring prospective houses. There is little point in falling in love with a £50,000 house only to find that, on your salary, no one will lend you more than £30,000.

Lenders will offer you a multiple of your income; this may be two or three times (occasionally three and a half times) your gross annual earnings. With a couple who are both earning, they will lend a multiple of both incomes. One lender might offer three times the higher income, plus the amount of the second income, so that in the case of one partner earning £12,000 and the other partner £8,000, the loan would be £44,000. Another lender might offer twice the joint income, so that the loan would be £40,000. When interest rates are high, the multiples tend to be lower because the societies know that borrowers will have more difficulty in finding the repayments. Some, but not all, lenders will take into account overtime, bonuses and commission, providing you can show that they are regular.

At this early stage, you will only be asking for a loan figure 'in principle'; that actual amount will always depend on the valuation of the property you hope to buy, and most lenders will only advance a loan up to 75-80 per cent of the full purchase price. Make enquiries about the type of property your lender would be reluctant to consider: you may set your heart on a 100 year old cottage, a flat with a short lease or a house with sitting tenants in the basement, only to find that your lender considers it a bad risk and no loan is forthcoming. See Chapters 4 and 5, on pages 44 and 56, for more details on lenders and mortgages.

Other expenses
Deciding how much you can afford is not as simple as adding the amount of the loan to the amount of your savings; there are other costs involved. Some are unavoidable, some can be cut by doing the work yourself, but most home buyers have to find a substantial amount of cash.

If you are buying a home without already having a property to sell, you should allow for costs as follows:

Solicitor's fees: There is no fixed scale of charges for conveyancing but reckon on ½ to ¾ per cent of the purchase price; 1 per cent would be on the expensive side. Remember to add VAT to any quote the solicitor gives.

Valuation fee: You will have to pay for the lender's valuation before they offer you a loan and, even if you do not go ahead with the purchase, this cost will have to be met. Costs vary, so check in advance on the scales used by your lender and allow for VAT.

Survey fee: If you commission an independent surveyor for a full structural survey, the charge will be high. It is considerably less expensive if you can arrange to combine the valuation and survey. Remember to add VAT.

Land registry fees: Payable each time a property is purchased. There is a sliding scale of charges according to the price of the property. VAT is not payable on land registry fees.

Stamp duty: A government tax that must be paid on any house bought for over £30,000. This is 1 per cent of the total purchase price.

Indemnity guarantee: If the loan exceeds a certain percentage of the purchase price – usually 75 or 80 per cent – the lender will probably require a guarantee for the extra from an insurance company. The lender and the insurance company agree on the premium, which you then have to pay.

Lender's legal fees: You also have to pay the lender's solicitor's fee. This will be lower in cases where the solicitor acts for both lender and borrower. Add VAT.

Removal costs: Remember to add the costs of insurance for breakages in transit to removal charges.

If you are selling a property at the same time you must also allow for:

Solicitor's fees: Usually ½ to 1 per cent of the selling price.

Estate agent's fees: No fixed scale; charges can be from 1½ per cent to 3 per cent of the selling price and are subject to VAT.

Your buying potential: a checklist

If you are buying only
Amount of loan 'in principle':   £......

Expenses:
Solicitor's fees   £......
Valuation fees   £......
Surveyor's fees   £......
Indemnity guarantee   £......
Land registry fee   £......
Stamp duty   £......
Lender's legal fees   £......
Removal costs   £......
       Total   £......

Available cash   £......
Subtract total expenses   £......

Add to amount of loan to arrive at total possible
purchase price   £......

If you are selling one property and buying another
Estimated selling price   £......
Outstanding mortgage repayment   £......

Net receipts for house   £......

Expenses
Solicitor's fees (buying)   £......
Solicitor's fees (selling)   £......
Estate agent's fees   £......
Valuation fee   £......
Surveyor's fee   £......
Indemnity guarantee   £......
Land registry fee   £......
Stamp duty   £......
Lender's legal fees   £......
Removal costs   £......
       Total   £......

Assets
Net receipts for house   £......
Extra cash available   £......
       Total   £......

Subtract expenses as above   £......

Add remaining assets to loan to arrive at total
possible purchase price   £......

Buying a new house

Houses are often advertised for sale before they are built and if a
site is considered desirable, you may have to stake your claim
before the foundations are laid. You can keep in touch with new
developments through specialist magazines like *What House* and
Home Finder, obtainable in most newsagents.

Once you are interested in a particular site, gather as much
information as possible on the builders or developers involved.
One phase of the site may already be completed, or they may have
developed another site in the neighbourhood: talk to people who
have bought the homes and find out if they sing their praises or list
complaints. Ask if their houses were ready when promised, if they
have had any problems with the property and if so, was the builder
helpful and prompt in putting them right?

If you are choosing your house on the basis of a floor plan and an
artist's drawing, make sure that you know the exact dimensions of
each room. They can look deceptively large on a plan, so pace them
out in a similar sized house belonging to a friend or in your present
home. Draw up a scale plan and mark in your furniture so that you
can be sure it will fit. Visit the site – even if it is only a sea of mud at
present – and check the surroundings carefully to make sure that
your home will not be backing straight onto the council rubbish tip
or looking across a school playground. Make sure you know how
close the next house will be; how large the garden will be and
whether you will be closely overlooked.

The price

If you reserve a house that has yet to be built, make sure that the
price will be stable and that if there are any delays in completion,
the rising costs of building materials will not be passed on to you.
Some builders ask for payment in stages: perhaps when the foundations are laid, when the roof goes on, when the plastering is
completed and so on. Though your lenders will probably agree to

advance the money in stages, it will cost you extra in fees each time they have to send a surveyor to inspect the house and you will be paying out on loans long before the house is any use to you. If you do enter into this type of agreement, make certain that the stages in the builder's contract correspond exactly with those in the mortgage offer.

You will seldom be able to haggle over the price of a new house but you can make sure that you know exactly what is included. Show houses on site can be very deceptive; they include all sorts of fittings that may cost you extra, from the towel rails to the garage.

Many builders offer incentives to encourage you to buy. They include:

★ Discount for early completion; a price reduction if you exchange contracts within a set number of weeks. This can be a good deal if you have no house to sell but you must be absolutely certain that this is the house for you.

★ Part exchange scheme, for those with a house to sell: the builder buys your present house so that you avoid the uncertainty of waiting for a buyer. You will usually receive 8 to 10 per cent less than your house would fetch on the open market, but it may be worth considering if you judge that your house will be hard to sell in the current climate.

★ Expenses paid scheme: you have the chance to add your legal costs to your mortgage, which can be a help to first time buyers, when extra cash is hard to find.

★ Free insurance, lasting two or three years, to cover your mortgage repayments in case you are made redundant.

★ Free contents insurance for the first year.

★ Free security system.

NHBC protection scheme

All houses constructed by builders registered with the National House-Building Council are covered by the NHBC's ten-year new homes warranty, and most building societies and banks would refuse a loan for a new house without this warranty. It is not a guarantee and it does not cover normal wear and tear or free you from the need to carry out ordinary repairs. The cover offered is as follows:

After exchange of contracts but before the 10 year notice has been issued: Cover up to £10,000 against the builder's failure to complete the house, for loss of deposit or expenses in completing the work.

Years one and two: The builder must put right any defects arising from failure to meet the NHBC requirements.

Years three to ten: Insurance cover against major structural damage caused by defects in the structure, subsidence or heave.

Pros and cons of buying a new house

Pros

NHBC 10-year warranty normally included.

Mortgages should present no difficulty.

No major repairs needed for several years.

Extras like kitchen appliances or carpets may be included.

Normally well-insulated and economical to run.

You may get some choice of bathroom or kitchen fittings or decoration.

If the house is not yet completed you may be able to ask for changes to suit your personal needs: position of cupboards, height of kitchen work surfaces, etc. (though you may have to pay extra).

Ready to move into, with no major spring-clean necessary, no holes in the wall to patch.

Cons

You may have to buy without seeing it complete.

Delays may occur in building.

You may be living on a building site for months or years, before the whole estate is finished and re-selling during this time may present problems.

There may be teething troubles: plaster may crack as it dries out and new houses suffer badly with condensation.

The house will need all sorts of fixtures and fittings: curtain rails, door bell, towel holders etc.

Local transport may not be laid on for some time; local shops may not open until long after the estate is built.

You often have to create a garden from scratch.

Buying a nearly new house

There are advantages in buying a house built two or three years before. It will normally cost you less than an identical new house nearby; the previous owners will have had to sort out all the teething troubles and any obvious defects should have surfaced by now. The house will still be covered by the NHBC warranty but it is important not to rely on this as an excuse to dispense with a survey and save the fee. The NHBC protection will not cover defects that should reasonably have been revealed by a survey or those the previous owner knew about. If there are defects, use them as a lever to negotiate a reduction in the price.

Buying an older house

You will probably get more for your money, in terms of size and number of rooms, if you buy an older property. The disadvantage is, of course, that maintenance costs will probably be much higher. Buying a house that is in need of 'doing up' can be a good investment, particularly if you are do-it-yourself experts, but remember that you will be living with the mess and discomfort for a long period. Some local authorities give grants for improving and renovating the property (see Chapter 8, on page 99) and when you do eventually sell, you could make a very handsome profit. Before you make this type of purchase, check that you meet the conditions for grants and make sure you have a clear idea of how much you would have to find for the improvements you have in mind.

If you plan alterations, it is important to check whether or not the building is 'listed' or is in a conservation area. The Department of the Environment compiles lists of buildings of special historical or architectural interest and if your house is included, then you will have to obtain 'listed building consent', in addition to planning permission, for any changes you want to make and there will be strict limits on what you are allowed to do. However, grants may be available for repairing or restoring aspects of historic or architectural interest.

If your house is in a conservation area, you are unlikely to get permission to alter its external appearance – unless, of course, this helps to restore its original character. If you do get permission, you will probably find financial assistance is forthcoming. Remember that all trees within a conservation area automatically come under protection orders.

Freehold and leasehold

When you buy a freehold property you become the permanent owner of the house and the ground on which it stands. Leasehold property stands on ground belonging to a landlord and you own the property for the duration of the lease. While the lease is yours you pay a small ground rent each year to the owner of the freehold. You may also be liable for maintenance charges (for instance, for road repairs on a private estate) and there may be restrictions on the use of the house.

Most leases are originally granted for 99 years and the value of the lease depends on how long it has left to run. For the first 25 years or so, the fact that a property is leasehold will probably affect its value very little, but after that it will gradually decline in value. Lenders will not usually advance a loan on properties with a lease of less than 50 or 55 years (the 25 years of the mortgage plus 25 or 30 extra years).

Buying a flat or maisonette

Most flats in England and Wales are leasehold; in fact it is difficult to get a mortgage on a freehold flat because lenders are worried about who pays the bill if structural repairs are necessary. Lenders who used to be reluctant to advance loans on conversions are usually willing to consider them now, providing they are structurally sound and self-contained.

Though you can haggle over the price of a flat, there is no room for negotiation over the provisions of the lease. You will normally have to pay an annual charge to cover the maintenance of the building, the upkeep of communal areas, gardening etc. and you will have little or no control over the amount you have to pay. On the plus side, you do not have the responsibility of finding builders and decorators or digging the garden.

The lease will also impose restrictions, designed to protect the property and the rights of the other leaseholders: for instance, you may not be allowed to sublet, the landlord may have the right to enter your flat for periodic inspection, you may not be allowed to hang out washing and so on.

In Scotland, long leases are rare and most flats are owned on 'feudal tenure', as are houses. For all practical purposes the buyer (or the 'feuar') is the absolute owner and buys a share of the ground, the garden and the communal areas as well. The deeds will set out the basis for apportioning maintenance and repair charges and there will be various restrictions, as with a lease, which you must accept. For more detail on buying property in Scotland, see Chapter 6, page 77.

Buying a mobile home

If funds are tight, a mobile home might seem like a good, cheap alternative to a house or flat but you need to be aware of the pitfalls. A mobile home is a depreciating asset and as such, you will have to take a loan rather than a mortgage. You will need to find a suitable site and make sure that it is properly licensed, as many sites are only licensed for holiday homes which must be vacated for a specified month every year. You will have to pay rent to the site owner, probably reviewed annually; the site owner will have the right to 'vet' any prospective purchaser when you sell (though he cannot withhold consent unreasonably) and you will have to pay him a commission on the sale. Of course, this only applies if the home stays where it is but 'mobile' homes, in spite of their name, are not easily moved.

Right to buy tenants

You have a right to buy if
★ You are a 'secure' tenant of a local council, a new town development corporation and some housing associations (so long as they are not charities).

★ You have been a tenant of a 'right to buy' landlord for at least two years.

★ Your house or flat is a separate dwelling and you occupy it as your main home.

The exceptions include:

★ Housing designed or meant for the elderly, the physically or mentally disabled.

★ Tenancies where the home goes with the job – for instance, school caretakers or fire authority employees provided by their employers with housing near the job.

★ Tenancies on land acquired by the council for development.

★ Temporary tenancies given to students, those who move into an area to take up a job offer, and the homeless who are given a tenancy while enquiries about their status are proceeding.

★ Business and licensed tenancies.

★ Those who were originally 'squatters' and have been given a licence to occupy the premises.

If you are interested in buying, the first step is to ask your landlord for the Right to Buy Claim Form (form RTB1). If you have difficulty in obtaining one, write to the Department of the Environment, FREEPOST 1988, Burgess Hill, West Sussex RH15 8QY.

Full details of 'right to buy' landlords and the rules governing sales are given in the booklet *Your right to buy your home. A guide for council, new town and housing association tenants*, obtainable from council offices and Citizens' Advice Bureaux.

Is it worth buying?

Buying your council house *can* be a very good deal because you are entitled to a discount of up to £35,000 on the purchase price. The amount of the discount depends on how long you have been a public sector tenant – though you can count in any time you were married to a public sector tenant or the time you spent in armed forces accommodation.

The council works out the market value of your home and, if the price is too high, you have a right to appeal to the district valuer (for details, see Chapter 9, on page 109). When buying the house you are entitled to a basic discount of 32 per cent if you have been a tenant for two years, then an additional one per cent for each extra year, up to a maximum of 60 per cent after 30 years.

This does not mean that you can buy your home then put it on the market the next week and make a killing. Though you can sell whenever you like, you need to stay for a full three years to get the benefit of the discount. If you sell within the first year, you have to pay back the lot; in the second year you pay back two thirds; in the third year you pay back one third.

If you live on an estate where many tenants are buying their homes, sprucing them up and adding handsome doors and bay windows, or in a desirable area near open country or a town with good job prospects, then you may be buying a bargain that will appreciate in value and allow you plenty of freedom of manoeuvre when you eventually decide to move. On the other hand, if you live on a large estate where every house looks the same and few of the tenants are likely to become owners, or in an employment black spot, you may be buying a property that will be difficult – even impossible – to sell in the future.

You will need to add up the costs of the purchase (see section on 'How much can you afford?' on page 15) and also make a careful comparison of the costs of renting and buying. Remember that, in addition to the mortgage repayments, you will have to pay for building and mortgage protection insurance, repairs and maintenance. If you can afford to buy and are convinced that the house will be a good investment, then the extra costs of owning your home should certainly be worthwhile. If you can afford to buy but you cannot count on your house increasing in value (the views of local estate agents may be worth having), then you need to base your decision on your own circumstances. How long are you, or the members of your family, likely to need the house? After all, you will have paid off your mortgage in 25 years, whereas rent goes on for ever! (For details on obtaining a mortgage, see Chapter 5 on page 56).

Buying a council flat
Tenants of flats or maisonettes can usually buy a long lease, normally 125 years and get an even bigger discount than house tenants: 44 per cent after two years, rising by 2 per cent a year up to a maximum of 70 per cent after 15 years.

Though the landlord will still be responsible for the upkeep of the building and the exterior of your flat and probably the lighting and cleaning of the stairways and passages, you will have to pay a share of the costs. These vary widely from landlord to landlord and will escalate over the years. If you live in a block of flats where the passages are always filthy and the lifts scrawled with graffiti, you would be wise to think very hard: when you want to sell, will the common areas of the flats discourage possible purchasers before they even see your beautifully decorated living room?

Leasehold tenants with a right to buy

If you have a leasehold house, you may be entitled to buy the freehold. You will only qualify if:

★ The original lease was granted for more than 21 years (regardless of how long it has to run).

★ You occupy the house as your main residence and you have been living there as the owner of the lease for at least three years, or for periods of time over the last 10 years that add up to three years.

★ The rateable value of the house is below £1,500 in Greater London, £750 elsewhere.

★ The ground rent was less than two thirds of the rateable value when the lease was granted (or on 23 March 1965 if the lease was granted before that).

You begin by giving notice to the landlord that you wish to take up your rights under the Leasehold Reform Act 1967 to buy the freehold. Most landlords resent the legislation and you may find youself involved in trouble and expense in trying to establish a 'fair' price. You will need a surveyor's valuation of the house, then the length of the unexpired lease must be taken into account. The longer the lease, the less you will have to pay.

If you are unable to agree a price with the landlord you may have to refer the matter to the Lands Tribunal for arbitration. Legal costs soon mount up, so you need to weigh up the merits of fighting for what you consider a fair price against paying several thousand pounds more and settling the matter quickly. Compare the prices of leasehold and freehold houses in your area and judge how much the freehold will add to your resale value.

Buying the freehold of a flat

Leaseholders of flats do not have the same statutory rights as house leaseholders but if you have a flat in a small block or a converted house, you might consider joining with the other tenants to buy the freehold. The best plan is to form a limited company, so that the company owns the freehold and each tenant has a new, long lease. The price is, of course, negotiable but reckon on up to 10 times the total ground rent for the flats.

If you are constantly battling with an unwilling landlord over repairs or the passages are always grubby and unlit because he does not carry out his responsibilities properly, this can be a better solution than moving. If you have your eye on the appreciation, remember to take into account the costs of setting up the company, buying the freehold, annual auditing of the company accounts and so on.

Short leasehold flats are less valuable now that the tenancy rights of leaseholders have been reduced. The old law was that the occupier became a protected tenant with good tenure rights and low rent liability, so that landlords often granted another lease quite cheaply because they were saddled with a sitting tenant. The law now says that the occupier stays on as an 'assured tenant', paying a market rent. The landlord has less incentive for granting a cheap lease – which is all the more reason for leaseholders to buy the freehold if possible.

Shared ownership

If you cannot afford to buy your home outright, another possibility is a shared ownership scheme, offered through housing associations and financed by the Housing Corporation. This means that you buy part of your home (it can be as little as 25 per cent in some schemes; others have a higher minimum share) and rent the rest from the housing association. You can increase your share later, as you can afford it, and eventually you own the whole property. Regional offices of the Housing Corporation can tell you more about it.

The scheme has been very popular but availability is strictly limited. It is aimed at those who cannot afford to buy a home in any other way; local authority or housing association tenants, or those on waiting lists, get priority. To begin with, you get a 99 year lease but when you make it to full ownership you will get the freehold – or a new long lease if the property is a flat. Up to four people can become joint owners.

The rent for the share you do not own will be assessed by the rent officer or housing association and will take into account what, as an owner-occupier, you will have to pay for repairs and maintenance, so it will be less than if you were a tenant.

Some local authorities run similar schemes and 'right to buy' tenants can choose this option, paying half the normal purchase price for a half share in the property and paying rent at half the normal rate on the other half. Ask your local housing officer for details.

3

Choosing Your Home

Time and trouble taken in the early stages of viewing properties and making your choice will repay you many times over. It will save you money in surveys that reveal lists of expensive faults or bills that keep you poor for years. It can also save you the heartache of buying what you think is your dream home, only to find you loathe the neighbourhood, the rooms are dark and depressing and you can only sell at a loss.

Every estate agent knows that a balmy spring day, with the birds singing and the smell of freshly mown grass in the front garden can sell many a house that has been on the market all winter. Surface impressions can be deceptive, especially for novices, who tend to stand in the middle of the room, glancing round admiringly while feeling too diffident to look behind the furniture for damp patches or examine the skirting boards for woodworm. The first survival tip for househunters going from one property to another is to make a checklist from the following sections, picking out the features that matter most to you. Then as you view each home, mark down the pros and cons and make sure you know the answers to all the crucial questions before you enter into negotiations.

Where to look

Location will be one of the most important factors in your choice of house; it will also be one of the main factors in determining the price you have to pay. As your job is paying for the house, getting to work easily will be one of your priorities but you will pay considerably more for houses near to reliable commuter transport.

When you are deciding on suitable areas for your search, remember both the time and costs involved in commuting: it might be worth paying more for your house and spending less, year after year, in train fares. If you decide that three hours travelling time a day is just bearable, remember the delays that will occur in bad weather. If winter commuting means four or five hours travel a day, is it still acceptable? If public transport is non-existent, you may find that you need a second, or even third car in the family. Balance these extra costs against the saving you can make on purchase prices in the area.

In a flat or falling market, popular areas hold their prices better than others, so consider whether you want to play safe or try for a bargain that may show more appreciation when the market picks up.

Surroundings

Never buy a house without giving careful thought to its resale value. You may not mind the smell from the pig farm down the road or the noise from the trains passing the bottom of your garden but they are likely to limit the appreciation on your property and mean that, in a difficult market, you would have to sell cheap or not at all.

If the area is on its way up in the world, then your property is likely to appreciate along with it. Signs that a district is improving are plenty of decorators hard at work, structural alterations under way in a large number of houses, new shops opening up, flourishing local activities and pressure groups. Look at the notice boards in the public library and read the local paper; this will give you a feel for what is happening in the area.

A house in an area that is going down is a much riskier buy. The tell-tale signs of an area that is sinking are untended gardens, rubbish littering open spaces, houses boarded up and rows of doorbells on larger houses, indicating multiple occupation. If there are a large number of properties on the market or the prices are low compared with nearby districts, the reasons need investigation.

You will have to weigh up what is most important to you in the immediate area: easy access to public transport, shops within walking distance, nearby parks or playgrounds, local sports facilities. If you have children, you will want to know that the house is within the catchment area of a good school. If you don't have children, bear in mind that prices in the catchment area of the best school in the county may well be higher than those a few streets away.

Position

When you consider the position of the house itself, you will want to know if it is far enough away from any sources of noise and nuisance.

* A school playground nearby will cause obvious problems; a school at the other end of the road may mean children streaming past your house twice a day, throwing their crisp packets into your garden.
* A nearby pub may mean noise at night, problems with parked cars and drinkers sitting on your wall on a summer evening.
* Proximity to the corner shop, a sports field, public library or church can mean a line of parked cars outside your property, not to mention slamming doors and revving engines.
* Road junctions or traffic lights nearby can mean extra noise from stopping, starting and gear changing. Look for residential roads used as short cuts by rush hour traffic or daily parking lots for commuters.
* A view over the park can be delightful but remember the noise at weekends and school holidays; a view over the golf course may be more peaceful but are balls likely to fly through the window?
* Church bells can wreck the peace of Sunday mornings.
* Local businesses can produce smells, noise and rubbish: look out for restaurants and takeaways, garages and car repair works, kennels, factories or warehouses, farms, etc.

The direction in which the house faces can make an enormous difference in terms of light and warmth. South or west facing rooms will get all available sunshine; very pleasant for sun-lovers but it can make bedrooms too warm and stuffy and if you want to protect your furnishings from fading, you may find yourself pulling the curtains across for much of the day. North facing rooms can be cold and dark in winter so beware of north facing kitchens if you spend much of the day there, or if this is where the family normally eat. East facing rooms get the sun in the morning, which can be pleasant for bedrooms and breakfast rooms. Rooms facing north-west or north-east will get direct sunlight in summer but not in winter, when you may need it most; south-west rooms get the benefit of sun in the late afternoon, which may be when most of the family are at home to enjoy it.

A hilltop situation can give you good views but remember that you may have to climb the hill with heavy bags of shopping and that icy weather may turn it into an imitation ski slope. A house on the lower slopes of hilly ground may be subject to damp as fog and mist descend regularly, or even to flooding.

You will also need to look at the position of the house in relation to its neighbours: is there sufficient privacy or do you stare into your neighbours' windows as they stare into yours? A forest of shrubs and trees may give a secluded air but they will also shut out the light. Normally it is unwise to have a large tree within less than its own height of the house, though there are mature trees and mature houses living happily side by side. Poplar trees planted on clay soil are the worst villains: their roots suck moisture from the soil, which then shrinks, with damaging results to your house.

The interior

It is impossible to ignore the overall impression the house gives. If it is warm and welcoming, smartly decorated with attractive furnishings and coffee brewing in the kitchen, it will be far more tempting than an empty house in sore need of decoration. But remember that once the seller's furniture has gone, his pictures have come down, leaving marks on the wallpaper and there are ugly holes where his shelves once were, the house will look very different.

First impressions
First of all you will want to check that you could be comfortable in the house:

★ The rooms must be large enough for your furniture – but not large enough to dwarf it. Always check the measurements yourself, rather than relying on the information in estate agents' handouts.

★ The layout of the rooms must fit your needs. An open plan living and dining room can be useful if you need to keep half an eye on toddlers at all times but means that other members of the family have little privacy.

★ The kitchen should be conveniently laid out with sufficient storage space for your needs, and adequately ventilated. If you want to eat there, check that it is large enough. Is there an outside door with easy access to the garden and dustbin?

★ If some of your appliances (freezer, washing machine, etc.) have to go in the garage, are electricity and water laid on?

★ How is the house heated? If it has central heating, does this also heat the water?

★ The garage should be large enough to take your car (never take it for granted). If there is no garage, check on the parking position. Is there room to park in the drive or put up a car port? If you have to park in the street, is there plenty of room; do you have to pay a residents' parking charge? Remember that insurance companies charge extra for cars without garages.

★ Houses in first-rate decorative order command higher prices but you need to consider whether you would want to live with the previous owner's taste in wallpaper for long enough to get your money's worth. It does mean that you can move in without mess or upheaval; on the other hand cosmetic changes are comparatively inexpensive. Some owners decorate before selling to push up the price; others are covering up problems, so take special care when inspecting newly decorated rooms (see below).

★ Check the view from the main rooms. Do you look out onto well-tended gardens, a tree-lined street, a neighbour's caravan or a row of parked cars? Remember that a view over open spaces can become a view over a new housing estate.

★ The garden should suit your preferences. Check on the amount of sun it gets, how easy it will be to maintain, whether it is safe for children to play in (will you be able to see them easily from the house?), is it secluded enough for sunbathing?

Close inspection

Once you have decided that the house is worth considering, you will want to carry out a much closer inspection. Work round systematically room by room, not forgetting the loft, checking that everything works, noting any problem areas (anything that will obviously cost money or needs further investigation by a surveyor).

★ Minor cracks in plaster are usually nothing to worry about but long diagonal cracks (especially if they have been filled in and opened up again), cracks you can trace on both sides of the wall or a crack which starts on the ceiling and runs down the wall, should be taken seriously.

★ Damp may show up as stains above the skirting or near the ceiling, loose wallpaper, bubbling or powdery plaster or rotting woodwork (dry rotted wood may crumble at a touch). Ceiling stains may be a sign of missing tiles on the roof, leaky pipes or radiators or simply a past flood from an overflowing bath so note the position carefully. Pools of water on windowsills are more likely to be the result of condensation.

★ Floors should be firm; try a heavy-footed walk across each room and be suspicious if all the ornaments rattle. If it is possible to turn back the edge of the carpet to look at the floor by outside doors or up to a bay window, then do so: these are prime spots for rot. Check that floor tiles or wood block floors are in good condition.

★ Cracked or crinkly skirting boards can be an indication of rot or woodworm. Little round holes in the skirting boards or fresh piles of dust nearby show that woodworm is hard at work.

★ Round pin electric sockets mean that the wiring is outdated and will need replacing (an expensive operation). If it has already been rewired, was this done professionally or as a DIY job?

★ Check that the plumbing is modern: lead or iron pipes will need replacing. Test the water pressure, upstairs and down, by turning on the taps and flush the loo to make sure it works properly. You should be able to tell if the plumbing is particularly noisy.

★ If the window frames are wood, make sure they are sound; check for rust on steel frames. Modern aluminium window frames do not corrode or need maintenance.

★ If there is central heating, make sure that it is in working order. Ask to see the servicing contract and check when it was installed and if any parts have been replaced recently.

★ If the windows are double glazed, look out for signs of damp between the panes; this will mean that they are badly sealed.

★ In the loft, make sure that pipes and water tank are well lagged. Check for signs of water penetration, particularly if you can see any glimpses of light through the roof (note the approximate position so that you can check outside for loose tiles, etc.).

The exterior

Experienced buyers usually take along a pair of binoculars to help them inspect the outside of the house.

⋆ The walls should be straight with no lean and no bulges (you can judge this best by squinting along the line of the wall).

⋆ Zig-zag cracking round windows or doors may be a sign of subsidence but if the cracks were obviously filled in some time ago and have not opened up again, there should be no cause for worry.

⋆ Pointing between the bricks and on chimneystacks should be smooth and full, without cracks or gaps.

⋆ Doors and windows should fit well; rain will soon penetrate any gaps and cause damp and rot problems.

⋆ Any missing roof tiles should be noted; check inside for resulting damp. If the house has a flat roof, it will need careful inspection as the only remedy for a flat roof in bad repair is replacement. Depressions that hold puddles of water are a danger sign.

⋆ Broken guttering and rusty pipes can mean that water pours down the side of the house causing damp problems inside, so look for damage or green marks on the walls.

⋆ If there is cement rendering on the walls note the condition carefully as maintenance can be expensive.

⋆ If the house is old, check that there is a damp course.

The neighbours

You can put little faith in the vendors' description of the neighbours: the chances are they will tell you that they are very pleasant, minding their own business but always ready to help in a crisis. You could try probing further – how long have they been neighbours, have there been any disputes between them, do they mix socially – but you can only use your own judgement on the truthfulness of the answers. Of course, the people next door may move next month but the likelihood is that they will stay for some time and your life will be more comfortable if you can get along with them.

Check on the facts: approximate ages, number of children, number of pets and so on. If you are looking for a quiet retirement home, you are unlikely to welcome three small children and two large dogs in the next door garden; on the other hand if you have a young family, you may find the elderly couple next door full of complaints. If there are party walls, make sure that you make a visit when the family next door is likely to be gathered: can you hear their stereo, their raised voices or their barking dog? Once you have decided that you are seriously interested in the property, knock on their door, ask a few questions about the district and make your own assessment.

Leading questions

Drawbacks: The vendor is unlikely to volunteer details of any drawbacks in the property but he is under a legal obligation to answer direct questions about it truthfully, so be ruthless and ask if the nearby river has ever overflowed, if he knows of any proposed development scheme that might affect the property or if he has ever had a problem with dry rot.

Restrictive covenants: These are most likely to be found in the case of leasehold houses but it is always wise to check.

Maintenance charges: On private estates, in particular, there could be charges for road repairs or the maintenance of communal garden areas.

Planning permission: Has planning permission ever been applied for and if it was refused, what was the reason? If you are thinking of alterations and extensions, ask about similar work which may have been done in the neighbourhood: you should get a feel for the attitude of the local authority towards planning permission.

Running costs: Ask to see gas and electricity bills.

Improvements: If any improvements have been carried out on the property, find out when they were done, who carried out the work and if it is still under guarantee. You might take the opportunity to find out the names of reliable local builders.

Market history: Find out how long the house has been on the market and if there have been any other offers. If so, why was the offer not accepted or, if it was accepted, why did the deal fall through? Even if the seller does not tell you the whole story, you will probably be able to read between the lines and judge whether you are in a strong bargaining position or not.

Checklist: is this the right property?

* Is the property freehold or leasehold?
* If it is leasehold, how long does the lease have to run; what is the ground rent?
* What is the rateable value or, after April 1990, what is the amount of poll tax per head in the area?
* What are the service and maintenance charges?
* Will you have vacant possession on completion?
* Are there any rights of way for others over your property, at any time?
* Does the property have enough space to meet your needs and if not, is there space for alterations and extensions?
* Are there any restrictive covenants on the property?
* Are there any local authority restrictions: e.g. listed buildings, conservation areas, tree preservation orders?
* Are the plumbing and electrical systems modern?
* If the house was built within the last 10 years, does it have the NHBC warranty?
* Which fixtures and fittings are included in the price, and which are available at an extra cost?
* Is there mains drainage and if not, what costs are involved?
* Is there central heating: if so, is it in good order and has it been regularly serviced?
* If improvements have been carried out (e.g. double glazing, cavity wall insulation) do the guarantees still apply?
* What are the average running costs of the property: rates, water rates, heating costs, etc.?
* Are there any local problems (noise, smells, etc.) that might affect your comfort – and your resale value?
* What are the exact boundaries of the property?
* Is there adequate parking for your family and for visitors?

Viewing a flat

Outside
* The state of the building as a whole will give you a good idea of the standards maintained by the landlord. Remember that when

you come to sell, a run-down building will affect the resale value of the best kept flat. Are the passages clean and well-decorated, do the lifts run smoothly?

★ As you enter the building, note the security system, if any. Does the entryphone work well? If there is no entryphone, is the door left open for anyone to come in, or do flat-dwellers have to come down to the front door to greet every visitor?

★ If you will be living anywhere above the third floor, you will need a lift – even if you prefer the stairs, your older visitors and those with small children will not. Lifts break down from time to time, so two lifts are better than one.

★ If there is a communal garden, is it well kept or neglected? Is it large enough for a number of residents to use at the same time?

★ You will need to know that you can park your car without driving all round the neighbourhood to find a space. If the flat comes with a 'car space', is that space numbered and reserved for you? If not, are there sufficient spaces for every flat? Where will your visitors park? Is there somewhere convenient to park for loading and unloading?

★ When you arrive at the flat itself, watch out for nearby lifts or rubbish chutes. The flats nearest to the stairs may also be noisy.

★ Notice whether the front door is in a quiet corner (burglars able to work at their leisure) or opposite other doors (neighbours able to hear every visitor arrive).

★ Remember that ground floor and basement flats may be dark with little or no view, near to sources of nuisance like dustbins, garages and entrances. Top floor flats (usually more expensive) will be quieter, with no overhead noise and a better outlook. Disadvantages may be stairs to climb and larger heating bills.

★ Check on fire-fighting equipment and the escape route in case of fire. Would you be able to get down the stairs easily? Is there a second fire exit, preferably separated from the stairs by fire-proof doors that are kept closed?

Inside

★ Make sure that the layout of the flat is convenient. Do the rooms lead off a hall or do you have to walk through the living room to reach the kitchen or bedroom? Will the children be trying to sleep on the other side of the wall where the television stands?

★ Check the configuration of the flats above and below, as well as on either side. Is your bedroom under the living room of the flat above or is next door's loo on the other side of your bedroom wall?

⋆ The windows in the flat may all face one way, which can mean that the kitchen and bedroom are far too hot in a south-facing flat or that all the rooms face north and are chilly and dark.

⋆ If the windows are not reversible for easy cleaning you will want to know about arrangements for window cleaning in the block.

⋆ Check on storage space in the flat and the availability of extra space elsewhere in the building. Remember that you may need somewhere to put a pram, bicycle, etc.

⋆ Both kitchen and bathroom should have good ventilation. Are you likely to suffer from cooking smells in the main room?

⋆ Investigate the arrangements for rubbish disposal. Is there a chute or do you have to take your rubbish down to the dustbins? If the latter, do you have your own dustbin? Is the dustbin area clean?

⋆ It is not easy to gauge the amount of noise that will travel through the walls but it is worth taking time to listen. Spend a while in each room with the door and windows shut (ask the seller to turn off the radio!) and see if you can hear sounds from the other flats. Walk heavily across the floors: if they creak and boom, you can reckon that you will suffer from similar noise from the flat above.

Questions to ask

⋆ Is the block administered by a landlord, by managing agents or by a residents' association? Landlords who live on the premises can cause you extra hassle; if managing agents are involved, their charges must be paid on top of the costs of maintenance; residents' associations may be run by one or two strong-minded individuals, capable of pushing through their ideas.

⋆ What are the maintenance/service charges and what do they cover? Are they shared equally between the flats? Ask to see the bills for the past few years, so that you can see how fast they are rising.

⋆ Does each flat organize its own heating or is there a heating system for the block? If the latter, do you have individual control over your heating and over the costs?

⋆ What restrictive covenants are there on the flat?

⋆ When was the exterior last painted and when is decoration due again? This can entail a big increase in the maintenance bill for a particular year.

★ Do you have access to a garden? If so, how easy is that access and are there restrictions on the use of the garden? Who looks after it?

Fixtures and fittings

Once you decide that you want to buy the property, but before you decide on the amount of your offer, go round with the owner and check on the items that will be included in the sale. Some of the items may become bargaining points when you come to fix a price: for instance, you might raise your offer if carpets and curtains were included, or the seller might take a lower figure if the kitchen appliances were not included after all.

Checklist of fixtures and fittings:
bathroom cabinet
bathroom fittings: towel rails, toilet roll holder, etc.
bathroom heater
built-in bedroom furniture
carpets and underlay
curtains
curtain tracks and fittings
door bell
electric storage heaters
fitted fires: gas or electric
fitted mirrors
garden shed
garden plants, bushes, trees
garden furniture
greenhouse
immersion heater
kitchen appliances
kitchen cupboards
shelves
television aerial
light fittings
water softener
window blinds

Making an offer

Most vendors put the highest price they dare ask on their property and will not be dismayed to receive an offer below the asking price. How much less you can offer while still being considered a serious purchaser, is a matter for judgement. You will be in a good bargaining position if the vendor has to move in a hurry because of a change of job or a divorce or a previous deal falling through when he was just about to sign the contract on a new property. The time of year is also relevant: those who are selling in the holiday months of July and August or the run up to Christmas will probably be anxious for a quick sale. A vendor who is 'trading up' or moving for a change of scene after retirement is more likely to hold out for the asking price.

You can make the offer direct to the seller or keep the whole thing at arm's length by dealing through the estate agent. The advantage of the direct approach is that you may get a better idea of the vendor's sticking point and do a little on-the-spot haggling. On the other hand, the estate agent will be experienced in convincing clients to accept a realistic offer, rather than sticking out for the top price and risking disappointment. Emphasize any bargaining edge you might have as a first-time buyer with a mortgage at your fingertips, a cash buyer, or someone whose own house sale is only waiting for signature on the contract.

Confirm your offer in writing to the estate agent but make sure that you add the words SUBJECT TO CONTRACT AND SURVEY. You are then free to withdraw from the deal later if you change your mind for any reason. If your offer is accepted, you may be asked for a deposit (perhaps £100 or £200), which is paid either to the agent or the seller's solicitor. This is simply a token of good faith as it will be refunded in full if either party withdraws later and you should make sure that you get a receipt saying that the deposit was paid 'subject to contract and survey'.

If the vendor is making a private sale, rather than using an estate agent, then you confirm your offer to him, specifying anything that the price includes (e.g. carpets, curtains and kitchen appliances). Any deposit must be made to his solicitor along with a letter saying that it is paid to him 'as stakeholder, subject to contract and survey'. Never send a cheque direct to the vendor.

The procedure is different in Scotland, where an offer constitutes a firm contract (See Chapter 6, page 77).

Buying at auction

Once a house is 'knocked down' to you at auction your bid is legally binding; you have to pay 10 per cent deposit right away and complete within 28 days, otherwise you will lose your deposit and could be sued for any losses incurred by the vendor. This means that you have to do all the work on the transaction beforehand, as though your offer had already been accepted: you need a firm mortgage offer (with a bridging loan for the 10 per cent deposit if necessary) and your solicitor will need to make all the usual searches. If you are having a survey, this too must be done in advance.

You need to do all your homework on local prices so that you have a good idea of what the property should fetch; then decide on your price and stick to it. The main danger with bidding at auctions is that you may be carried away and bid more than you can afford. If the particulars of the auction state 'unless previously sold' you might try an offer before the auction, as the vendor is prepared to negotiate privately if the price is right. On the other hand if it says 'sold by order of executors' or 'sold by order of trustees' then there are legal reasons why the property must be sold at auction and making an offer might act to your disadvantage in influencing the sellers to raise the reserve price.

Properties offered for sale 'subject to reserve price' will be withdrawn if that price is not met. The agent will not tell you what that reserve price is but it is worth putting in some effort in persuading him to give you a rough guideline, so that you do not waste money pursuing a house that is out of your financial reach.

Buying by tender

Tenders are seldom used in selling private houses but you may meet them when unusual properties are involved, or when a number of offers have been received. There are different types of tender so make sure that you are clear about the terms.

Closed tenders: You have to submit your offer (possibly with a cheque for a deposit) in a sealed envelope to the seller's agents by a specified date when all the offers are opened. This works like an auction, except that you do not have the advantage of hearing the other bids before making yours: if your offer is accepted, the contract is binding and you are expected to complete within 28 days.

Open tenders: These have to be submitted by a certain date but they can be made subject to contract and survey so the deal proceeds like an ordinary house sale and both sides have room for manoeuvre.

4

The Professionals

House purchase usually involves a wide variety of professional help. Experienced house buyers may do a good deal of the work themselves but for most of us, each stage of the process – finding a house, checking its condition, financing the purchase, transferring ownership – will involve experienced advisors. For novices, it is essential to know the difference between sole agencies and sole selling rights, valuations and surveys, solicitors and licensed conveyancers. Asking the right questions and choosing reputable members of professional organizations will minimize the chances of problems and disputes but you also need to know where to go if you feel let down, overcharged or even swindled.

Estate agents

Agents have proliferated in the high street over the past few years. Some are qualified and belong to reputable professional associations with their own codes of conduct (see page 47). Others put up a sign and launch into the market because the enormous rises in house prices over the past two decades have made it a highly profitable business. This does not automatically mean that they give a poor service but there are some cowboys among them.

Over the past 18 months many large chains have sprung up, with building societies, banks and other financial institutions buying up the independent estate agents. There have been complaints that the new-style agencies sell houses like used cars, with a hard sell approach and youthful negotiators who know nothing about the structure of the buildings.

Buying

As a buyer you will obviously make full use of all the estate agents in the neighbourhood. They will supply details of suitable properties on their books (and often plenty of unsuitable ones as well!) and arrange for you to view. Members of the National Association of Estate Agents operate a National Homelink Scheme for clients who are moving to another area; your local agent contacts the Homelink member in the new location, who sends you particulars from his books.

Never rely on the particulars given in the estate agents' handouts: L-shaped rooms may well be measured at their widest point and the 'double bedroom' may not be large enough to take a double bed *and* leave you room to stand behind it.

The buyer pays no fee to the agents so their duty is to get the best price for the seller, though you may find yourself dealing with an agent who will reveal the lowest price the seller will take, in order to make a quick deal (this will not be the agent you choose to sell *your* property). Agents can often help with mortgage arrangements. Some will be tied to one financial organization, so you will need to shop around to see if a better deal is on offer elsewhere. Others have independent brokers working in their offices and offer a range of financial packages. You are under no obligation to arrange your mortgage through the agents who are selling the property, so you should resist any form of pressure.

In some cities there are relocation services who will search for suitable properties and produce short lists for viewing. The charges are around 1-2 per cent but they can be useful for returning expatriots or high-speed company moves.

If you pay a deposit to an agent once your offer on a property is accepted, make sure that he belongs to one of the professional associations with an indemnity scheme to protect clients from fraud (see page 47). Better still, decline to pay a deposit at this stage, as it does not act as a guarantee that you will go through with a purchase, or that the property is reserved for you. If the agent or the seller want some show of good faith, it should be enough to demonstrate that you are laying out money for valuation, survey or searches by your solicitor.

Selling

Commission rates vary so you should always check in advance and make sure that commission is only payable if the agent sells the property. You are lucky if you find an agent who only takes 1½ per cent of the purchase price (providing he does the job properly); if the agent asks for more than 3½ per cent, shop around. Remember that, though an extra ½ per cent may not sound much, it will mean an extra £300 on a £60,000 house. Ask about extra charges for advertising and 'For Sale' boards and make sure that the agreement is put in writing.

There are several methods of selling through agents:

Multiple agency: You place the property with several agents and the agent who sells the house gets the commission.

Sole agency: You place the sale in the hands of a single estate agent. The commission he charges should be less, probably about 2 per cent. In theory, the agent will be willing to put more time and effort into selling your property and you do not risk being hurried into a sale by agents who are competing for the commission. The agent will probably want to tie you down to a period of three or even six months; if possible, it is better to keep your options open, then you can change agents if you feel the first one is not doing a good job.

Joint sole agents: Two or more agents act together and agree to share the commission when either makes a sale.

Sole selling rights: A single estate agent handles the property and you have to pay commission, even if you finally negotiate the sale without any help from him. This system has little to commend it from the seller's point of view.

You may decide to use the agent who is handling the house you are hoping to buy; he certainly has an extra incentive for fixing a sale but he might be tempted to talk you into taking a lower price, to hurry the deal along. If you are selling and buying in the same area, choose the agent who impressed you as most efficient when dealing with you as a buyer. This will not necessarily be the agent who had the house you wanted on his books but the one who took notice of the specifications you gave him and sent the details of suitable properties, not just a pack of handouts for everything on sale at the time.

There are rogues in the property business, so beware of agents who do not have your house on their books but who arrive on your doorstep with a keen prospective buyer in tow. The agent may well contact you with a good offer, which will only be available if you transfer your business to the new agent. The offer will probably be withdrawn soon after the transfer but the agent has collected extra business. If your agent has offered a particularly low commission rate, make sure that you are not talked into selling at a low price: such agents are sometimes 'shopping' for their friends and family. You also need to be cautious about agents who put letters through your door saying that they specialize in properties like yours (check that out for yourself) or that they have buyers waiting for houses in your neighbourhood (they may just be trying to pull in more clients). Ask the agent for details in writing of charges, terms and the service to be provided. (For details of selling without the help of an agent, see Chapter 7, page 85)

Complaints
Serious complaints about estate agents should be referred to the local Trading Standards Department which has the ability to ban them from trading if they are guilty of serious misconduct. You should also complain to the professional association of the agents involved (if they belong to one). The National Association of Estate Agents, the Incorporated Society of Valuers and Auctioneers and the Royal Institution of Chartered Surveyors all have codes of conduct and indemnity schemes to assist clients who suffer loss if an agent behaves fraudulently.

Solicitors' property centres

These centres are a new way of selling property in England and Wales, though they dominate the property market in Scotland (see Chapter 6, page 77). They are usually run by several firms of local solicitors and one of the aims is to cut the length of time taken by the house-buying process. While property centre staff work on marketing the house, just as agents have always done, the solicitor is able to begin the conveyancing without to-ing and fro-ing with agents.

You should always ask for a quote in advance and check exactly what is included in the package: the bill usually includes legal fees and commission, with expenses added as an extra and VAT charged on top.

Surveyors and valuers

Once you have applied for a mortgage on your chosen property, the lender will arrange for a valuation survey. This is a very limited report, entirely for the benefit of the lenders, so that they can ensure that, if you default on your mortgage, they will get their money back from the sale of the house. If the valuer discovers major problems, he may decide that the house is worth less than the price you are being asked to pay, so the loan will be refused. Alternatively, the lender may withhold part of the loan until the problems have been put right and, if you do not have the ready cash, this will involve you in extra expense in the form of a bridging loan. Lenders will normally let you see the findings of the valuation survey but you should not rely on the report to point out all the defects of the house. It is up to you to satisfy yourself; you can rely on your own judgement or commission an independent survey. It will save you money if you arrange for the valuation and survey to be done by the same person.

Opinion is sharply divided among experienced house-buyers on the value of a survey, between those who consider that only the foolhardy would make such a large purchase without expert advice on the condition of the property and those who feel that a survey is not a guarantee and in most cases will be limited by practical considerations: for instance, if the floors are covered by fitted carpets, a surveyor is unlikely to reveal anything that could not be discovered by the careful inspection of an informed buyer. Certainly a surveyor is unlikely to be able to take up the floorboards to examine the condition of the timbers or the electrical wiring.

Structural survey

This is a detailed technical inspection and report on the condition of the property and should be carried out by a qualified surveyor or architect. The extent of the inspection and the fee should be agreed with the surveyor in advance: it would normally cover foundations, walls, roof, floors, plumbing and electrics, windows, drains, chimneys, outbuildings and so on. In the case of a flat, it should cover the whole building, not just the flat itself, as you will be liable for steep maintenance charges if there are any major defects.

This type of survey is expensive and the majority of home buyers do without one, though this could be false economy if you are buying an old or 'problem' property. In any case the surveyor should be able to give some estimate of what any necessary remedial work should cost and this could be used to negotiate a lower price with the seller – especially when the market in property is slow. The seller of a 'difficult' property sometimes commissions an independent survey of the house to reassure prospective buyers.

House (flat) buyers' report
Members of the Royal Institution of Chartered Surveyors and the Incorporated Society of Valuers and Auctioneers offer a report that comes halfway between a valuation and a full survey, both in cost and thoroughness. They make it clear that this is not suitable for very large houses (over 200 sq metres) or for period properties (built before 1930).

These reports are limited to visible defects and hedged about with exclusion clauses but you may feel, particularly if you are a first-time buyer, that it is worthwhile to have the property inspected by a trained eye that might spot telltale signs of trouble.

Complaints
If your surveyor fails to report on a defect he should have noticed, then he is liable to pay for having it put right. Of course, what he should have noticed will be limited by the exclusion clauses in the report, so read them carefully. The first thing to do, if you find yourself faced with a repair bill and feel that your surveyor has been negligent, is to contact him and lay out your evidence – you may find that he will pay compensation, even though he does not admit liability. If you make no progress, then take legal advice on making a claim against him. But being negligent is not the same as making a mistake; you will have to show that he did not exercise the level of skill that you were entitled to expect from a qualified professional.

In the case of a building society valuation, the surveyor's contract is with the lender, not the buyer. But if, for instance, the valuation reveals no major fault with the house then, a few months later, your damp course fails then, providing you have done no work on the property to contribute towards the problem, you could have a case against the valuer.

Surveyors sometimes try to limit their liability for negligence or breach of contract by putting wide disclaimers in the contract but, in law, this will not usually override the general duty to take reasonable care.

If you have a complaint against a chartered surveyor you should contact the professional body, the Royal Institution of Chartered Surveyors. The Institution can discipline members but cannot compensate you.

Solicitors

Now that solicitors no longer have a monopoly over conveyancing and they are allowed to advertise their services, some solicitors have dramatically reduced their prices. It should be easy enough to find specialist low-cost conveyancing solicitors; some charge a flat fee, rather than a percentage of the purchase price. However, some buyers do report that taking the cheapest quotation can mean a poor level of service. The best way to find a good solicitor is to ask around amongst friends and colleagues and choose someone who did a good job for them. You can cut costs by using the same solicitor the building society or bank is using for their legal work on the deal; you can get in touch through your local manager.

Always ask for an estimate at the outset. The Law Society provides forms for solicitors in England and Wales to give written estimates of charges for conveyancing; these should set out all the costs and charges.

Complaints

Complaints about your solicitor's work should go first to him and then, if you receive no satisfactory explanation, to the senior partner in the firm. If that does not bring satisfactory results, you can take your complaint to the Solicitor's Complaints Bureau, set up by the Law Society with an investigation committee with a majority of lay-persons. They can investigate complaints about delays, failure to deal with your money properly, shoddy work and so on. They have disciplinary powers but cannot order a solicitor to pay compensation. If your claim is over negligence, the Bureau can arrange an hour's free consultation with another solicitor, who will advise you on how to take the matter further. (See Useful Addresses, on page 128).

If the bill from your solicitor is far bigger than you expected and you feel that you have been overcharged, do not pay it. Instead, tell your solicitor to apply for a 'remuneration certificate'. This means that a Law Society panel will look at the charges and the work they cover and consider whether they are fair or not. The remuneration certificate issued by the panel will say whether or not they think that the bill should be reduced and if so, by how much. You do not have to pay for this service but if the bill is not reduced you do have to pay interest on it from the time it was submitted. In Scotland, the system is different: you can have your bill submitted for 'taxation' by the Auditor of the Court of Session but you do have to pay for this – and, unlike the Law Society, the Auditor can raise the bill as well as reducing it.

Other conveyancers

Conveyancing firms who will handle the transfer of property, often at a lower price than solicitors will charge, may be run by solicitors' ex-clerks who have a good deal of practical experience without the paper qualifications. If you are thinking of using such a firm, choose a member of the Council of Licensed Conveyancers or the National Association of Conveyancers. Members must have five years' experience and are covered by professional indemnity insurance and are fidelity bonded, so that you would get your money back in case of fraud.

The Law Society takes a dim view of 'unqualified' people poaching the preserves of solicitors but their most useful service has probably been to force solicitors into competing on cost. You need to keep in mind that licensed conveyancers do not have the expertise to cope if things go wrong and might have to call in solicitors anyway, with resulting higher bills – but then, solicitors will also charge extra for unravelling complications. Another disadvantage is that a solicitor acting for the building society alone will charge higher fees, so you need to find out all the costs involved before you can make a useful comparison.

Building societies

Building societies are governed by the Building Societies Act 1986, which states that they exist for the purpose of making loans to members from the funds subscribed by members. They are the first port of call for the majority of home-buyers looking for a mortgage loan. Most building societies will give preference to those who are already saving with them and though this hardly matters when mortgages are plentiful, it could make a real difference to your chances as a first-time buyer when there are more would-be borrowers than there is money to lend. But a building society account is no guarantee of a loan, so before you start saving with a society (or better still, two societies) study their literature and make sure that their mortgage terms cover your situation. Extra competition has meant that they offer packages specially tailored for different sectors of the market but even now you may find the smaller societies are more flexible than the big national ones. Some societies are tying themselves to one insurance company to provide endowments so, if this is the type of mortgage you are considering (see Chapter 5, page 58), you should compare terms with other institutions.

The Ombudsman

If you have a complaint against a building society and the society has failed to deal with it, you can refer it for independent review by the Building Societies Ombudsman. You first have to go through the society's internal complaints procedure: putting the problem to the local branch manager then, if necessary, to the head office (most societies have a leaflet setting out their procedure; ask at your local office). If you are still dissatisfied, you can contact the Ombudsman's office for a complaints form. (See Useful Addresses, page 126).

   If, after investigation, he finds your complaint justified, the Ombudsman has the authority to direct the society to take whatever steps he thinks necessary: this includes paying compensation of up to £100,000. You normally have up to 28 days to accept the Ombudsman's ruling but if you do not accept, his decision does not affect your legal rights. In any case, you do not pay for his intervention.

Other lenders

Banks: Banks have been increasingly active in the mortgage business in recent years and all the large high street banks offer mortgages, together with the less well known foreign banks. Their interest rates tend to stay fairly close to those of building societies but they sometimes use higher multiples of income so that you can get a bigger loan and they may be more amenable to granting a loan 'in principle', which puts you in a much stronger position when negotiating with vendors.

The disadvantage is that they may charge a 'setting up fee', though this is less common when competition is brisk. The bank may expect you to open a current account with them, if you are not already a customer, or may restrict loans to those who have already held a current account for six months or more.

If you have a complaint which is not settled at branch level, refer it to the area manager and then to the bank's head office. If you are still dissatisfied, you can apply to the Banking Ombudsman. The Ombudsman cannot deal with complaints over the decision of whether or not to grant a loan but he can deal with maladministration in reaching or implementing a loan decision. You can accept or reject the Ombudsman's decision; if you accept, you cannot take any further action (see Useful Addresses, page 125).

Builders: A builder or property company with new houses to sell may have a package arrangement with a building society. This may save you a good deal of leg work, the rates may be advantageous and it may enable you to jump the queue when mortgages are in short supply. There may even be extra incentives, such as 100 per cent mortgages or low interest rates for the first year. Obviously you should know where the loan comes from and the full details of interest rates etc. before you commit yourself. Remember that the builder may be adding the cost of these extra incentives to the price of the house.

Employers: Some firms offer low interest loans to their staff as part of the perks; this applies especially to those working for banks, insurance companies and building societies. Check the terms carefully – these schemes are not called 'golden handcuffs' for nothing. Will you have to repay the loan if you leave the firm or will the interest rates shoot up?

Local authorities: Local authorities should be able to supply mortgages for tenants with the right to buy their council properties. However, availability varies from one authority to another; you would be wise to apply early in the financial year.

Insurance companies: Some offer assurance-linked loans and will require you to take one of their policies. These can be more expensive than loans from other sources, so check carefully. The best way of making contact with insurance companies, if you cannot finance your purchase elsewhere or you are looking for a top-up loan, is through an independent mortgage broker.

Mortgage brokers

Mortgage brokers are middlemen: they do not lend money themselves but they can arrange loans from other institutions; they are particularly useful in times of mortgage famine, as they will know who still has money to lend. You can usually find a broker from the For Sale advertisements in the local paper. Under the Financial Services Act these middlemen are legally obliged to declare themselves as 'tied agents' or 'independent'. Avoid tied agents, who are in the business of selling the products of a single company. An independent broker should be able to offer a range of specially tailored packages to suit the requirements of an individual borrower.

If you take a mortgage linked to an endowment policy, pension plan or unit trust plan with an insurance policy, you will not have to pay for the broker's services, as his commission comes from the company. On a repayment mortgage he will charge a fee, so find out all the figures involved before you take a decision. Make sure you know what the fee is and consider whether it would be worth your while to pay, rather than taking an endowment mortgage (see Chapter 5, page 58). Make sure that the broker gives you written quotations and study the figures carefully. It makes sense to take advice from more than one broker and compare the packages they offer.

Consult a mortgage broker who is also an insurance broker and whose firm is listed with the Insurance Brokers' Registration Council or belongs to the Financial Intermediaries, Managers and Brokers Regulatory Association (FIMBRA), which has a code of conduct for its members and can investigate complaints. Brokers are licensed by the Office of Fair Trading, so if you have complaints about their business conduct, you can refer them to the local office. Under the Financial Services Act, independent brokers can be held responsible for arranging loans that were in their own interest rather than that of the customer.

5

Raising a Mortgage

Few house-buyers are lucky enough to be able to finance their purchase without a mortgage but there is no 'right' type of mortgage for everyone. As a first-time buyer, your priority may be to minimize your repayments in the first difficult years; as an older or second-time buyer, the lump sum available at the end of an insurance-linked mortgage may be the deciding factor. Whatever your circumstances, never take the first offer, from whatever source; get alternative quotations and compare them carefully.

Applying for a mortgage

Before you can hope to make a choice between offers, the lenders will want to make certain that you are a reasonable risk. Some lenders ask you to fill in detailed forms, others may want a personal interview. Apart from details of the property you want to buy and your current mortgage details you will be required to give a good deal of personal information:

Name, date of birth, address, how long you have lived at that address (if it is not very long, details of previous residence).

Marital status; relationship to anyone with whom you are taking a joint mortgage.

Your credit record, including any county court judgements against you.

Any regular payments you are making already: e.g. hire purchase, insurance, maintenance, etc.

Your job, name and address of your employer, length of employment and previous job if you have not been there very long (if you

are self-employed, the name and address of your accountant).
Income from your job including regular overtime and bonuses, and income from all other sources.
Income of spouse (whether it is a joint mortgage or not).

Types of mortgage

Repayment mortgage
This is the simplest type of mortgage: each monthly payment pays the interest on the loan and also repays some of the capital. The amount you pay will depend on the size of the loan, the length of the mortgage and the current rate of interest.

Level repayment mortgages. Many building societies only offer this type of repayment mortgage, repaid with a level monthly sum throughout the term of the mortgage, assuming that the level of interest remains the same. In fact, of course, interest rates will vary and you should take this into account when calculating how much you can afford. In the early years of the mortgage, the lion's share of the payment goes in interest but as you gradually pay back the capital, the interest decreases so that towards the end of the loan period, only a small share of each payment is interest.

Deferred repayment (gross profile) mortgages. Some banks and building societies offer this type of mortgage because it can help buyers who are stretching themselves to the limit to get on the housing ladder. The tax relief is not averaged out over the period of the loan so repayments start off lower than with the level repayment system. As the amount of interest decreases over the years the amount of tax relief drops so your payments increase. Some lenders adjust the payments annually, others monthly. Over the whole period of the mortgage you will pay more but this may be worthwhile if it eases the financial burden in the early years when cash is short.

Repayment mortgages are more flexible than insurance linked loans. If you get into difficulties you can normally extend the period of the mortgage without increasing the repayments, or perhaps agree with the lender that you pay the interest charges only for a time. The disadvantages are that there is no built-in life cover so you will need to take out a separate policy, and that when the loan is finally paid off there is no cash surplus, as is the case with other types of mortgage. If you move house, you have to pay off the loan and begin again with a new mortgage.

Mortgage protection policy. When you choose a repayment mortgage, it makes sense to take out a policy that would pay off the mortgage and protect your family home if you were to die before the repayments are completed; if two earners have a joint mortgage, then they can take out a joint policy that will pay out on the death of either of them. The cost will depend on the age, sex and health of the people involved and the size of the loan but a mortgage protection policy should be inexpensive, so check around and compare prices.

Endowment mortgages

The majority of borrowers currently take endowment based loans. With this type of mortgage you pay interest only on the loan. You also pay premiums on an endowment life insurance policy which, when it matures, pays off the loan and may leave you an additional nest-egg. Both your home and the insurance policy act as security against the loan. If you die before it is paid, the policy covers the mortgage, so you will not need a mortgage protection policy as well.

Non-profit endowment mortgage. The proceeds of the policy will be just enough to pay off the loan. There is little to recommend this type of loan; you would be better off with a repayment mortgage plus a mortgage protection policy.

With profits endowment mortgage. The policy will pay off the loan but in addition you receive bonuses from the company, so that you can expect a good-sized lump sum as well. Premiums are expensive (you are participating in a savings scheme as well as paying off your loan) and the amount you receive at the end depends entirely on the performance of the company.

Low cost with profits endowment. This is the most popular form of endowment mortgage. It costs much less than the full with profits scheme because it does not *guarantee* to pay off the loan when it matures. But the insurance company has worked out that, with the addition of bonuses over the years, it should not only cover the loan but leave you with something over. If the proceeds of the policy, with bonuses, came to less than the size of the loan, you would have to find the difference – but this risk is very small.

Low start, low cost with profits policy. This is basically the same policy as above but the premiums are lower for the first few years, when it is more difficult to find the money, then rise later.

Buyers moving from one property to another may be less worried about monthly payments than first-time buyers and better able to cope with rising interest rates, so an endowment policy, with its element of saving and the security of owning your own house at the end of it, could make sense. When you sell your house, you pay off the loan from the proceeds but keep the endowment policy to cover the loan on your new property. If you are taking a bigger loan, you can increase the policy or take a second policy to cover the extra amount.

The disadvantage is that, if you get into difficulties over the payments, you have fewer alternatives; you will probably have to convert the policy into a repayment mortgage and cash in the policy to help pay off the capital of the loan.

When you are checking out the figures, remember that the bonus figures projected by the company will not be converted into cash in hand for 25 years, when their real purchasing power is likely to be much less. In 1984 the Chancellor abolished tax relief on new life assurance policies so the premiums no longer qualify for tax relief.

Unit-linked mortgages

These carry far more risks than other schemes. They are available mainly through insurance companies who will invest your money in shares, property, etc. The value of your policy depends on how those investments perform. If they perform poorly, you could end up with less money than you have paid in (or, if your policy guarantees to pay off your mortgage, you could be faced with a rise in monthly payments). This type of policy was popular when stock market prices were rising regularly but since the stock market crash, they have been treated with more caution.

Pension plan mortgages

These are available to the self-employed and to those without occupational pension schemes and are similar to endowment schemes. You pay only interest during the life of the loan but the mortgage is linked to a pension plan, so that on retirement a lump sum pays off the capital and provides you with a pension on the remainder. You will have to take out a term insurance policy to pay off the loan if you die early.

They are particularly attractive to those on higher rates of tax, as tax relief is given on both interest and pension contributions. Housebuyers under 25 or 30 will probably find it difficult to get this type of mortgage; most companies feel that retirement is too far in the future.

True interest rates

Lenders have various different methods of working out mortgage payments and this can make it difficult for the borrower to make reliable comparisons between the terms offered. To give you an overall picture of the cost of your loan, the lender is obliged to quote another rate known as the APR (Annual Percentage Rate). This takes account of one-off charges like valuation and legal fees, as well as the way interest is calculated and is supposed to reflect the true cost of borrowing. The APR is normally higher than the quoted rate of interest: for instance a quoted rate of 12.75 might be 13.3 per cent APR.

Most building societies calculate the interest owed only once a year and then divide it into equal monthly amounts. Banks tend to calculate interest on a monthly basis, so the APR is lower.

Tax relief

Tax relief is given on mortgage interest payments at the highest rate of tax you pay but only up to a £30,000 loan. If the loan is higher than this, you will get tax relief on the first £30,000 but you pay the full interest rate on the remainder. Before 1 August 1988, buyers with a joint mortgage (apart from married couples) were allowed tax relief on up to £30,000 per person but this tax loophole has now been closed and the £30,000 limit applies to the property rather than the people involved. You are only allowed tax relief on your only, or main home (though you can still claim tax relief if you rent out your home while you are working abroad).

Basic tax relief is given at source under MIRAS (Mortgage Interest Relief at Source) scheme; if you are on a higher rate of tax, the extra tax relief will be given by adjusting your Notice of Coding or, if you are self-employed, in your tax assessment.

100 per cent loans

A more flexible attitude to 100 per cent loans has emerged over the past few years because house prices have escalated to such a level that even a small percentage deposit means a large amount of cash savings. However, lenders are still very cautious, as they find borrowers are less likely to default when they have invested some of their own money in the property, even if it is only 5 per cent of the purchase price. If you are offered such a loan, expect to pay a higher rate of interest and check the redemption clauses: some lenders charge 1 per cent of the outstanding loan if it is redeemed within the first couple of years, for any reason other than the sale of the property.

You are most likely to be offered a 100 per cent mortgage on a new house or when you are buying a property for less than the lender's valuation (a rare occurrence!). Lenders may also be sympathetic to those who have had no chance to save yet but have the prospect of high earnings in the future.

Most applicants are first-time buyers, as those with a foot on the property ladder can usually find a deposit for a second or third time purchase. Lenders are suspicious of second-time buyers asking for 100 per cent mortgages. If these buyers are holding back profits made on the first house to buy new carpets for the second or finance a second car, then they are using mortgage money (on which they have obtained tax relief) as a cheap way of borrowing for luxuries and this is not encouraged. However, lenders may consider a second-time buyer if they can put up a good case: for instance, if a new job means moving to an area with higher property prices or if a person is moving after a divorce and losing extra cash in the settlement.

Mortgage indemnity policy

Most lenders who give loans of over 75 per cent will insist that you pay for an insurance policy that guarantees to pay back the balance of the loan if they have to repossess the property and sell it for less than the outstanding balance of the mortgage. It gets progressively more expensive as the proportion of the loan rises to 80 per cent, 85 per cent and so on. In most cases the cost will be added to the amount of the loan so that you can pay it off in monthly instalments but on the highest percentages you might be asked to pay immediately.

Topping up loans

If the mortgage you are offered is not enough, you may be able to arrange an extra loan from an insurance company to top it up. The rate of interest is likely to be higher than that on the main loan and some insurance companies may insist that you take out an insurance policy on the amount lent by the building society, as well as the top-up amount, so that the whole deal is very expensive.

Not all lenders allow these extra loans, as they think that they have reckoned up the maximum amount you can afford to pay when making their original calculation. It is, in any case, something you should think about seriously: can you really afford all the repayments or would you be better off looking for a cheaper property?

Mortgages for 'right to buy' tenants

Tenants with a right to buy also have a right to a mortgage from their landlords. The multiple is usually 2½ times annual gross income and, depending on your income, the landlord must lend you 100 per cent of the purchase price. If you are over 60, the amount of the loan may be lower. Remember that you may be able to borrow more cheaply from a building society or bank and that they may be willing to lend a larger sum.

If you wish to apply for a mortgage from your landlord, you must complete form RTB4, which will have arrived along with your section 125 notice (the document which sets the price of your house). You must return this to your landlord within 3 months of receiving the section 125 notice. If you have applied for an independent valuation of the property, because you feel that the landlord has set too high a price, then you must return the form within three months of receiving the second valuation.

When you eventually sell your house or flat, the buyers will have no right to a mortgage from the landlord, so it makes sense to check with local building societies to see if they would be willing to lend on the type of property you are thinking of buying, even if you finance your purchase another way. If it is very hard to raise a mortgage on the property, it may affect the resale value.

Shared ownership

Lenders normally treat two single people who want to become joint owners in much the same way as a married couple, for the purposes of a mortgage. If two couples (or four friends) want to buy a property together, finding a loan will probably take a little longer but you may be able to find a lender who will take account of four incomes. If one partner in the deal later wants to move on, the remaining owners can buy out the extra share by increasing their mortgage or find someone to take on that share (subject to approval by the lender). If you are thinking of shared ownership, it is essential to have a legal agreement drawn up, so that everyone knows where they stand.

Older borrowers

Financing a move can be a problem for pensioners with little or no capital apart from their home. Legal fees and moving can eat up savings or take an unwelcome slice out of the selling price of that home. If, for instance, you want to move to a property of roughly the same value in one of the new retirement home developments, it might be worth considering mortgaging part of the new property and putting the money into a protected annuity which will generate enough to pay off the mortgage. The investment can be protected by insurance which will yield a lump sum when it matures.

Another possibility is a small interest only mortgage, granted by some lenders, with the capital being repaid out of the estate when the owner dies. The type of scheme where the lender contributes up to 50 per cent of the purchase price in return for a 'life interest' needs very careful consideration before you commit yourself. Under this arrangement, you occupy the property until your death, or until it is sold; then it belongs to the lender. This may be an option if you have no family and do not want to leave the property to anyone in particular but it may also mean that if you can no longer look after yourself and have to go into a residential home, you will have no home to sell and therefore no capital to generate any income you may need.

Some housing associations run leasehold sheltered housing schemes, where you can buy 70 per cent of your home with the remaining 30 per cent covered by government subsidy. If you want to sell, you get back 70 per cent of the market price, less a charge for administrative costs.

Fact sheets on *Housing schemes for elderly people where a capital sum is required* and *Raising an income from your home* are available from Age Concern, 60 Pitcairn Road, Mitcham, Surrey CR4 3LL. (Enclose a large stamped addressed envelope.)

Mortgage conditions

Your mortgage will have some conditions attached. These may include:
* Undertaking certain repairs within a given period.
* Insuring the property, possibly with one of several specified companies.
* Not letting all or part of your home without permission from the lender.
* Informing the lender about any local authority plans that might affect the value of the property.

★ Informing the lender of any alterations you plan to make to the property.

Mortgage refused

If your mortgage application is turned down, you should find out the reason. It may be personal (you are too young, too old, your income is too low, your job is too uncertain) or related to the property (poor condition, short lease) or economic (no money available to lend at present). If you have been saving with the society who turns you down, try writing to the regional manager, saying that you plan to take your money somewhere else; it might mean that the society is willing to take another look.

Whatever the reason, shop around; in most cases you will find that another lender will offer a mortgage. *What Mortgage* magazine (price £1.20, available through newsagents) carries an up-to-date chart detailing lending policies and interest rates of individual banks, building societies and insurance companies. However, if you have tried several lenders and the answer is always negative, consider whether the property is really a good buy or whether you can really afford the commitment of a mortgage in your current circumstances. If you believe that your mortgage was turned down because of prejudice of some kind, then you should make use of the complaints procedure and, if necessary, contact the Building Societies Ombudsman (see Useful Addresses, page 126).

If you feel that a bad credit reference is the reason for refusal, you have the legal right to check on details held by the credit reference agencies. Ask for the name and address of any credit reference agency used to check your financial standing. You can then contact them and obtain a copy of your file. If an entry turns out to be incorrect, you can ask them to alter it.

Bridging loans

If you synchronize the sale of your property perfectly with the purchase of the new one, you will never need to know about bridging loans. They are best avoided because they mean that you are, in effect, paying two mortgages at the same time. However, if things do not run that smoothly, you may have to apply to your bank manager (some building societies also grant bridging loans) to tide you over financially.

Closed bridging. This is fairly easy to arrange and not too painful. It applies when you have exchanged contracts on the house you are selling but the purchase will not have been completed by the time you need to complete on the new property. You know when you will get the money and the bank knows when the loan will be repaid, so you are taking no risks and you can calculate exactly what the loan will cost you. Interest rates are usually about two per cent above the base rate and there may be a setting up fee.

Open-ended bridging. This is hard to come by and can cost you a great deal of money. You could find yourself in this position if your buyer drops out at the last moment and you cannot bear to lose the new house or you are certain that it is only a matter of time before your buyer completes but the seller refuses to wait any longer. The danger is that you cannot know how long the loan may run and what the eventual cost will be. As though that was not bad enough, you have no guarantee that your first property will sell at the asking price, so you could end up with a shortfall.

The interest rate will be high – three to five per cent above the base rate – and you will probably have to pay a high setting up fee, too. You may find that the fee is payable even if your buyer suddenly comes through with the contract and you do not take up the loan. The bank may insist on full structural surveys on both properties, at several hundred pounds a time, as a condition of the loan.

You are entitled to tax relief on a bridging loan, in addition to that on your existing mortgage, and some lenders will defer the interest payment until your sale is completed, so that you can pay the money out of the capital. But many advisors say that if you need a bridging loan you cannot – by definition – afford it.

Mortgage default policy

When you first take out your mortgage you can take out a policy that would cover your mortgage payments if you were ill or out of work and unable to meet them. But the premiums are quite high and the policy usually only covers 12 months or at most two years. The terms should be carefully checked. Do they cover redundancy as well as illness, and what would be the position if you took voluntary redundancy? Do they cover your type of employment or do they exclude self-employed or part-time work?

6

The Legal Nuts and Bolts

After the excitement of finding the house and making the offer, comes a long and sometimes anxious waiting period while the legal work of conveyancing gets under way. Until the contracts are exchanged you have no legal right to the house; the seller could change his mind or sell to a higher bidder. Legal wheels can move slowly and local authority wheels even more slowly, so the average time between offer and completion is three months. If you are involved in a chain of buyers and sellers, it can take much longer.

Contracts should not be exchanged until after:
* The draft contract has been thoroughly checked and amended as necessary.
* The legal title of the property has been checked.
* The preliminary enquiries have been answered.
* The local searches are completed.
* The mortgage loan is confirmed and the deposit is available.

Doing your own conveyancing

A minority of house buyers handle their own conveyancing, with the help of a step-by-step manual such as *Bradshaw's Guide to House Buying, Selling and Conveyancing for All* (Castle Books, price £6.95). You need to weigh the time and trouble you will have to take against the saving involved; there is less financial advantage in DIY now that cheaper conveyancing is on offer. The professionals warn that there are many snags lying in wait for the DIY conveyancer and that if anything goes wrong, you may end up paying for legal help anyway. Remember that while you can claim compensation from a solicitor who neglects to do his work properly, you cannot claim from yourself if you make a hash of things.

Most experienced hands advise against attempting your own conveyancing in the following cases:

★ When you are buying an unregistered house.

★ When you are buying a new house (registering the first title is more complicated than a transfer).

★ When the property is not a self-contained house (all sorts of extra problems can arise).

★ When you are buying in Scotland (see page 77).

Checking title

First of all, it is necessary to check that the seller owns the property and has the right to sell it. This is simple and straightforward in the case of registered land. Most private properties in England and Wales are registered, and this means that the Land Registry records the details of who owns what and whether anyone but the seller has a legal interest in the property you plan to buy.

If the property is unregistered your conveyancer will need to check back through at least 15 years of transactions affecting the title. If the house is in an area of compulsory registration your conveyancer will register the title once you become the owner.

The draft contract

The seller's conveyancer will draw up a draft contract, assuming that no major snags will be revealed by the searches. This will probably be in a standard format but that does not mean that you can safely forget the whole thing and leave it to the legal eagles. Your conveyancer has never seen the property; you have. If you have carried out a detailed inspection, as recommended in Chapter 3, page 29, you should be able to brief him thoroughly and identify any problem areas that need further investigation.

Make sure you read the draft contract carefully and discuss the following points:

★ *Fixtures and fittings*. Conveyancers use standard forms asking the seller to list items included and excluded, as well as those for sale separately. Check each item against your own list (see Chapter 3, page 40) and make sure that nothing has been omitted.

★ *Boundaries.* You should know where the exact boundaries of the property lie; who owns the walls and fences and whether any restrictions exist on their height or type. There is usually less room for dispute in the town than in the country but there is no substitute for checking yourself: ask to see the plans and check that they match up with what you can see for yourself. Check that the walls and fences are where the plan says they are and that the garage is within your own clear boundaries. Make sure you know who owns which fence and if there is any confusion, talk to both the seller and the neighbours and see if their views on ownership differ. If you see a badly neglected fence on an otherwise well-cared for property, it just might be the subject of a neighbour's dispute. In that case, you will have to gauge whether it would be easy to move the offending fence (preferably at the seller's expense) or whether you will be buying years of trouble along with your new house.

★ *Rights of way.* Your conveyancer will need to check on any rights of way through your property; a right of way can come about if there is an ancient footpath across the land or if your neighbour has been using your garden as a short cut for the past 20 years without hindrance. If you have to approach your house or your garage along an unmade road or a piece of rough ground you will need to know that you have the right to do so. If maintaining your property will mean going onto your neighbour's land (for instance to paint a side window or to repair the edge of the roof), is this right granted in the deeds and if not, has there ever been any trouble getting permission? Country properties, in particular, can be subject to some very strange rights of way, so need specially careful checking.

★ *Alterations and additions.* If the previous owner has made any alterations or additions to the property, let your conveyancer know about them so that he can check whether planning permission or building regulation approval was obtained, rather than relying on a general answer given by the seller in the preliminary enquiries. You don't want to buy your dream house only to find you have to knock part of it down because the necessary permission was never given! You will need to know if any improvements grants have been made as these can restrict the right to sell to anyone but an owner occupier.

★ *Marital disputes.* If you got any whiff of any divorce or separation in the air when you were talking to the seller, your conveyancer should know about it. He can check whether a claim has been registered on the house (see Chapter 9, page 110) and, if the property is owned by only one spouse, it might be wise to have written consent to the sale from the other partner.

★ *Tenants and other occupiers.* If you saw evidence of more than one family living in the property, if there was more than one doorbell, or one room looked as though it was occupied as a bedsitter, tell your conveyancer so that he can ensure that no tenants are likely to be sitting tight on completion day.

★ *Promises made.* If the seller has promised to have any remedial work done on the property or produce any guarantees on work already done, have this written into the contract.

Preliminary enquiries and searches

It is probably safe to say that in almost every case, the preliminary enquiries and searches reveal less than you, the buyer, think they do. What happens is that a list of preliminary enquiries (listed on a standard form with space for extras) goes to the seller's solicitor. Though there is a disclaimer on the form that says the vendor does not guarantee that the replies are accurate, you would still have a claim over any deliberate misrepresentation that caused you loss later. The seller and his solicitor know this very well, so the replies are usually extremely vague, along the lines of 'not to the seller's knowledge' and 'please rely on your own survey'. Hence the importance of further investigation, as described previously.

One of the questions in the preliminary enquiries covers disputes with neighbours but sellers rarely admit to anything amiss. Always make time to have a word with the neighbours during your early inspection; they will usually be glad to see the people who could be moving in next door and any problems will soon emerge.

The local searches (also a set of standard questions) are designed to give the planning history of the particular property you intend to buy and check that nothing is likely to affect its value (including any planning infringements; a motorway scheduled to pass through the back garden; a compulsory purchase order). However, the search will not reveal:

* Planning applications from the neighbours.
* Any scheme not yet far enough advanced to be included in the land charges register, even if it is a road widening scheme that could take the front garden, or a flyover on a level with the bedroom window.
* Any plans for development down the road.

Making your own enquiries
If you want to be sure that the bulldozers will not be roaring past your new house in a few months time, you will need to take matters into your own hands. You can do useful preliminary work by chatting to the landlord of the nearest pub or the news editor of the local paper or calling in at the Citizens' Advice Bureau. Armed with any hints you pick up about the possible ring road that has been argued over for years or the controversial supermarket development that is awaiting planning permission and might bring a never-ending string of shoppers' cars past the door, go to the planning office and ask to see the planning applications *both approved and pending*. Of course, the proposal to build a housing estate on the fields that give the living room that splendid open aspect may not go through – but could you live with them if they did?

Delays in searches
The length of time taken by local authority searches, as the paperwork is passed from one department to another in a leisurely manner, is now notorious. Ten weeks to process a search is quite common and in some London areas it can be as long as 20 weeks.

If you want to be certain of tying up the deal within a reasonable time, you might offer an exchange of contracts 'subject to search'. In a buoyant market, the seller is unlikely to agree: it means that he has to take his house off the market and forgo any change of an improved offer, even if completion is still months away, while the buyer can back out over any little problem revealed by the searches. However, in a flat market a seller who is pretty confident of the result of the searches might be willing to make the commitment. An alternative is taking out insurance: there is now a policy that will allow a sale to go ahead and guarantees to cover the cost of any depreciation the property suffers as a result of an adverse entry in the search. The cost depends on how long has elapsed since the last local search was made on the property. Ask your conveyancer for details but make sure you know what is covered: though the policy will give protection in the case of serious problems, it may not cover you if a relatively minor matter is discovered.

Exchange of contracts

Once contracts are exchanged both buyer and seller are legally bound, so it must be done simultaneously or you risk being left without a home or with two properties to pay for and no capital to pay with. The buyer's conveyancer will normally send a signed but undated contract to the seller's conveyancer, who sends him the seller's signed contract. Then the two conveyancers will agree (probably by phone) on inserting the date to make the transaction valid. Neither side can then back out without penalty.

The deposit. On exchange, the buyer will be expected to put down a deposit. Traditionally this is 10 per cent of the purchase price but with house prices now so high this is a considerable amount of money, so you might try to negotiate for a 5 per cent deposit or less – especially if you can argue that you are getting a 95 per cent mortgage! If you have already paid a deposit when making the offer, this should be deducted from the amount you are expected to put down on exchange of contracts.

Many buyers, faced with producing a deposit of several thousand pounds before they have the proceeds of their own house sale or mortgage money, will need a bridging loan for the deposit but this will normally be no problem, providing contracts have been exchanged on the buyer's house or the mortgage has been agreed. Beware of solicitors who try to slip in a clause saying that the seller is authorized to use your deposit as a deposit on his proposed purchase. Once it has been used by the seller, it will be very difficult to get your money back if the deal turns sour. Insist that it is paid to the solicitor as stakeholder instead.

Solicitors should pass on to the buyer any interest the deposit earns while in the special clients' account, though this will be at a low rate.

Some conveyancers take part in a deposit guarantee scheme whereby an insurance company guarantees to pay a 10 per cent deposit if you fail to complete the deal – and will then take steps to recover the money from you. The amount of the premium depends on the purchase price of the property and the conveyancer may make a charge for arranging the insurance, so check if it will, in the end, turn out cheaper than a loan. You will also need to check whether the seller will accept a deposit guarantee instead of a cheque; he is under no obligation to do so.

Insurance

Once contracts are exchanged, the buyer is responsible for insuring the property, even though the seller is still living there. This is essential because if the property burned down tomorrow, you would still be liable for the full purchase price, even though you owned only a few charred remains. Some lenders insist that you insure with one of their recommended insurance companies and will often handle the insurance for you. Others will allow you to choose your own insurer, so that you can shop around for a cheaper policy, providing the lender is satisfied that it gives adequate cover. Watch out for lenders who charge a fee if you reject their insurer for one of your own choice! If your lender does arrange your insurance, check whether the premium will be added to your mortgage repayments or paid direct to them annually.

Whether you are arranging insurance through your lender or independently, read the policy and make sure you know what is covered and what is excluded; ask for clarification in writing on any obscure points. The policy should cover a standard set of risks: fire, lightning, explosion, earthquake, storm, flood, vandalism, subsidence, landslides, falling trees and burst pipes. It will not, of course, cover your home against deterioration and regular maintenance will always be your responsibility. It should also cover your legal liability towards third parties: if, for instance, your television aerial is blown down on top of your neighbour's car.

Many policies include cover for alternative accommodation if you have to move out of your home while repairs are carried out. This is essential if you have no kindly relatives who could house you in case of emergency but check how much would be payable, especially if you live in an area where any temporary accommodation would be very costly. If your new home has large picture windows or a number of glass doors, it might be useful to choose a policy that specifically covers window and door glass.

You may be insuring for a sum well above the purchase price of your house because you are insuring against the cost of rebuilding, including architects' and surveyors' fees, demolition and site clearance costs. Most insurers increase the insurance cover automatically each year as the cost of rebuilding goes up – and, of course, your premium will increase, too. Make sure that you are never under-insured. You should always let your insurers know if you have carried out any alterations or extensions that would add to the value of your home, so that they can adjust the policy (and the premium) accordingly. If you have made £5000 worth of improvements in a house insured for £50,000 and have not told your insurers, then the worst happens and your house is destroyed, they could cut the amount they pay out by 10 per cent.

Completion

Completion is the time when the buyer's conveyancer hands over the cheque for the balance of the purchase price, the seller's solicitor hands over the documents transferring title and the legal ownership passes from seller to buyer. The date for completion will be in the contract: it usually takes place 28 days after exchange of contracts but there is no reason why the time should not be longer, if it suits both parties, or shorter, to save interest on loans. Never agree to a completion date until you are certain that you can meet it; remember that all the various payments (insurance premiums, solicitor's fees, stamp duty, etc.) must be met at that time, so check that the money will be available. You don't have to be there in person for completion; normally your conveyancer will ring to tell you that all the formalities have been completed. The deeds will be handed over by the seller's conveyancer along with the title but if you are buying on a mortgage, they will be passed on to the lender as security against the loan. After completion, the transfer and mortgage will be registered at the Land Registry.

Failure to complete

Once you reach this stage of the proceedings you are legally obligated to go ahead, even if disaster strikes and you lose your job in the meantime. If you do not produce the money for the sale on completion day, the seller's conveyancer will serve a 'Notice to Complete' which normally gives you 16 days to complete before further action is taken. If you still do not come up with the money you may lose part or all of your deposit; you will have to pay a high interest rate on the remainder of the money owing until you do pay up (the interest rate will be laid down in the contract) and you may be liable for damages if the seller (or even other people in the chain) suffer loss because of your failure to complete.

Where a long chain of vendors and purchasers is involved, failure to complete may be for purely logistical reasons: the tail end transactions cannot be completed before the end of banking hours, so that the money cannot change hands. In this case the conveyancers will usually agree on a formula that allows the money to be held over until the next morning.

Joint ownership

When you are buying jointly with another person, whether you are related or not, you can choose one of two ways to hold the property:

Joint tenancy. This means that neither party can sell without the agreement of the other and when one owner dies, the other automatically becomes sole owner. This is usually only suitable when a husband and wife are buying together and a joint tenancy can be ended (if, for instance, they have marital problems and are thinking of going their own ways) by one partner giving written 'notice of severance'. It then becomes a tenancy in common. In the days when estate duty would have meant paying death duties on half the house, it was the method normally recommended by solicitors but now death duties are no longer payable on legacies between husband and wife.

Tenancy in common. This means that either owner can dispose of their share of the property as they wish, either during their lifetime or on their death. It is the normal method of holding property for joint owners who are not married; it is also the method to choose if you want to leave your share in the property to anyone but your co-owner.

A proper agreement is a 'must' for co-habitees and other sharers: it is called a 'declaration of trust' and deals with who has a legal share in the property and the amount of that share. For an experienced conveyancer this is a simple job which should add little, if anything, to the price.

House purchase in Scotland

In Scotland, most property is sold through solicitors (though estate agents are increasing their share of the market) and buyers can obtain particulars from individual firms of estate agents or from solicitors' property centres. The centres will have particulars of property from all the solicitors in the area and, as with estate agents in the rest of the country, there is no charge to buyers. If you are interested in a particular house or flat you will be referred to the solicitor who is selling it and he will charge a commission on the sale. A list of property centres can be obtained from the Law Society of Scotland.

There are no set charges for conveyancing, so you should get an estimate of fees before you ask a solicitor to act for you. Do-it-yourself conveyancing is not recommended in Scotland.

Offers

The asking price is usually only a starting figure, though sometimes a property may be offered at a fixed price for a quick sale. Normally the seller is looking for 'offers over' a certain amount and houses often sell for considerably more than the price originally listed. If the market is buoyant or the house is very desirable so that the seller expects several offers, he will set a closing date. If the market is flat and there is no time limit on offers, you might put in a low bid and set a time limit yourself; you can sometimes get a good buy this way.

You can negotiate orally with the seller over the price, or the fixtures and fittings included, but once the offer is made in writing it is binding. This means that you must arrange your mortgage and any necessary surveys before you make an offer. It is very rare for an offer to be accepted 'subject to survey' in Scotland. It is made formally through your solicitor and will be quite a long document, specifying 'date of entry' (when you want to move in) and listing the conditions on which the offer is made. These are usually legal matters concerning title and the absence of planning proposals that might adversely affect the property.

Once the seller accepts in writing, through his solicitor, you are both legally committed. The advantage of this system is that the whole business is very swift and you do not have to worry about gazumping. One big disadvantage is that you have to spend money on a building society valuation and your own survey before you know if your offer is accepted, though if you find out from the seller that other people are interested in making offers, you may be able to negotiate with a surveyor to act for more than one prospective buyer at the same time, with a reduced fee for each one. A second disadvantage is that it is very difficult to pitch your offer just right and there is no way of finding out what the other bids might be. Your solicitor's advice is important here; he will know the local market and advise you on a price. At the time of your offer, you may include any extras you want to buy, at what price: this might swing the deal your way if there is another offer of around the same price without the extra inducement.

Missives

When your offer has been accepted, things usually move quite fast and you will usually be moving into your new home within a few weeks. The seller's solicitor normally instigates the local authority enquiries, so this cuts down delays considerably. When the various legal enquiries have been made, the two solicitors will exchange 'missives'; this is equivalent to exchange of contracts in England and Wales. The buyer is responsible for insuring the property from the day when the missives are exchanged.

The settlement

After the exchange of missives, your solicitor will handle the preparation of the disposition (the document that transfers the title of the property) and other formalities. In the Scottish system it is not necessary to put down a 10 per cent deposit when the contracts are exchanged. The full price is payable 'on settlement', or completion, when your solicitor will receive the title deeds, including the disposition in your favour. Your solicitor will then register the disposition with the Land Registry of Scotland or (in areas where title registration has not been introduced) in a property register dating from 1617, known as the Sasine Register. Stamp duty is payable, as well as Land Registry or Sasines Register charge.

7

Selling Your Home

The best time for selling your home is, traditionally, spring or early summer when gardens look their best and the sun (you hope) sparkles on fresh paintwork and before the minds of potential buyers turn to their summer holidays. However, the state of the property market also depends on the availability of mortgages and the level of interest rates and a house that would have had buyers queuing two deep down the path six months ago may suddenly become hard to sell.

Unless you have to sell at a particular time, because you are moving your job or you need to find a smaller place to cut costs, you will need to keep an eye on current trends in the market. When you have a property to sell, a buyer's market may mean that you get less for your property but, in turn, you pay less for your new home. This can be an advantage if you are trading up in an area where the more expensive properties are harder to sell and prices drop more sharply than those at the cheaper end. On the other hand, if your home has disadvantages (it backs onto the railway line or has one good-sized bedroom and one cubbyhole), you would be well advised to wait for an up-turn in the market, so that you can take your pick from buyers desperate for a foot on the housing ladder.

The best laid plans can sometimes go astray because, once you have entered into negotiations for your new home, your timetable will be governed by the need to synchronize your sale and purchase. Unless you can move in with friends or family for a while, or your employer will finance temporary accommodation, you will not want to sign away your present home before you are certain of getting the next one. Likewise, unless you are in the happy position of having large amounts of available capital, you will not want to contract to buy another property before your sale is assured.

Setting a price

Many sellers rely on estate agents to set a price on their home; agents should have a good feel for the movement of the market in your area and be able to advise accordingly. If you ask one agent to price your home, ask two others as well; you may find their recommendations vary widely. Make it clear that you are not, at this stage, asking them to sell the property. They may ask for a fee for this service, in which case you may want to try other agents who will do it in the hope of getting your business. Bear in mind that most people are inclined to choose the agent who puts the highest price on their home but he is not necessarily the most reliable and businesslike.

You will already have a good idea of what your home will fetch from studying the property columns of the papers and handouts from the agents. You can get a more accurate picture if you view one or two similar properties already on offer. When you do this, be honest with yourself: is the position of your house more or less attractive, how does the state of decoration compare, are the rooms as spacious, light and well-decorated? Of course, the asking price of a property is not necessarily the purchase price and you will want to know what similar properties in your neighbourhood have fetched over the past few months. If a 'Sold' board has disappeared recently, ask the owner or the agent about the final price; they will usually be willing to tell you when they know your reason for asking. But take into account any changes in the market since then: are properties selling like hot cakes or are there 'For Sale' boards in every street? Beware of 'fishermen's tales' about enormous prices told in the pub or supermarket checkout queue; many sellers think their home is uniquely valuable, only to have face reality when the offers fail to materialize.

Never price by totting up what you need to buy the new house, plus putting in the new kitchen and bathroom and re-carpeting throughout. If you can't afford all that by selling your present home at a realistic price, then perhaps you can't afford to move! It may be a good idea to set the asking price about two per cent higher than the price you expect to get, as buyers like to feel that they have something knocked off. But don't set it so high (just in *case* you get lucky) that you miss a serious buyer who does not want to play haggling games. Once you have decided on a price, make it look less by the oldest marketing trick in the book: £5995 looks far more reasonable than £6000!

Selling through an agent

One of the first decisions you have to make is whether or not to use an estate agent and, for most people, this resolves itself into a choice of spending money (probably at least £1200 on a £60,000 house) and putting a great deal of time and energy into master-minding the deal themselves. If you decide to sell through agents, read Chapter 4 (page 44) for advice on how to choose the right firm.

What an agent will do
★ Advise on a selling price (see above).
★ Measure your home and draw up a list of particulars. Make sure they know about any extras – a brand new central heating boiler, guarantees from wood treatment firms, complete rewiring, cavity wall insulation and so on.
★ Take photographs for publicity purposes. Check when this is happening so that you can give the front door a wash and replenish the hanging baskets.
★ Put up a 'For Sale' board. You are not obliged to have a board, so if you do not want one, make this clear to the agent at the outset. Some sellers feel that a board maximizes their chances of attracting buyers (agents reckon that 30 per cent of enquiries come as a result of seeing boards); others think that any serious purchaser will tour the local agents anyway. Remember that if you are using several agents and they all put up boards, it can look as though you have a problem property on your hands and undermine your bargaining position.
★ Produce typed details of the property to hand out to prospective buyers. Not all agents submit these to the seller but you might want to check that room measurements are correct and that any fixtures and fittings listed are meant to be included in the purchase price. You could even tidy up the the language and weed out any notorious estate agents' euphemisms like 'bijou' which everyone knows means tiny and cramped, or 'individual decor', which prob-ably means they think your wallpaper is hideous.

* Advertise your property in their windows and in newspapers. Check at the outset whether or not there is an extra charge for advertising; it can be very expensive.
* Arrange for prospective buyers to view and show them round the property. If you employ agents, you can choose whether to do all the showing round yourself or leave it to them. If you leave a key with the agent, make sure that he lets you know every time he plans to show someone round and that he never gives viewers the key to look round on their own, even if you have moved out and left the house empty.
* Negotiate the selling price. Some buyers may prefer to make their offer direct to you and this can have its advantages, as you can negotiate on the spot. However, if you dislike the idea of any bargaining, simply ask them to make any offer formally, through the agent. It can be a mistake to disclose your rock bottom price to the agent, who might pass it on to the buyer in the hope of concluding a quick deal.

The pros and cons of using an agent
Pros
* They are in touch with large numbers of buyers, both locally and from further afield.
* They will be able to advertise more widely, including in local property magazines financed by a number of agents.
* You do not have the embarrassment of showing round potential buyers and negotiating prices.
* They can give help in obtaining mortgages to buyers who might otherwise have difficulty in arranging finances.

Cons
* The cost; 2 or 3 per cent of the purchase price with VAT added on top.
* A procession of people who look at everything the agent has to show, whether they are seriously interested or not.
* Some buyers may be put off by the smooth talk or hard sell of agents; they know that they are salesmen with a job to do.
* Buyers may be unsure of where they stand if they do the negotiating at one remove, through an agent. They are well aware that the price has to allow for estate agents' commission, so they

might feel they are getting a better deal with a private sale; they might also feel that they have to act more promptly.

Selling at auction

You might consider selling your home at auction if you are fairly certain that it will be much in demand, so that competitive bidding will drive the price higher, or if it is a really unusual property (a converted windmill or oast house, for instance) so that it is impossible to price it accurately. Most firms of estate agents are also auctioneers so they will be able to advise you over whether you might benefit from this form of sale.

A single agent will handle arrangements for publicity and sale; commission will usually be 2½ per cent of the purchase price. You will also have to pay advertising costs so agree on a budget at the outset and make sure you know what is included. Look out for hidden costs, for instance the hire of a hotel room for the auction itself. This method of selling is a gamble; it will cost you extra, so will only be worthwhile if you get a really good sale price.

The property will be advertised about six weeks beforehand and you should make sure that this is on the basis of 'unless previously sold by private treaty'. Then you can withdraw it if you get an offer you feel you cannot refuse.

If the sale arouses a healthy interest among buyers, you will have to be prepared for valuers and surveyors coming to examine the property but this will give you some idea of the state of the market and may influence the 'reserve price' you decide to put on the property, after taking the auctioneer's advice. If the bidding does not reach this figure at the auction, the property will be withdrawn. You will then be expected to pay a fee instead of commission and you may find that you have to withdraw your home from the market for the time being, as buyers are unlikely to offer more than the top auction price.

Once the auctioneer's hammer has fallen on a bid, the contract is signed immediately and the successful bidder pays a deposit there and then. Completion usually takes place within four weeks, so you must be ready to move and give the buyer vacant possession at that time.

Do-it-yourself selling

Enthusiasts recommend the DIY method for those who like to feel they have control of the situation and it can be particularly successful when the market is buoyant. After all, you know your home better than anyone else and you have more of a stake in the sale than any estate agent.

There are some security problems about selling this way as you will have to display your phone number and show people round yourself, so it is probably unsuitable for elderly couples or women living alone. In any case, it is sensible to ask anyone who phones for their name and number, so that you can phone back with an appointment. Keep a chain on the door, so that you can talk to strangers who arrive unannounced without letting them in. If you are alone in the house when they arrive you can make an appointment for later, when you can have someone with you, or ask them to come back in 10 minutes, so that you can ask a neighbour to come in. Any genuine house-hunter will understand you taking sensible precautions. Remember that estate agents are far from guaranteed protection: there is nothing to stop clients giving them false names and addresses or using their visit with the agent to 'case' the property for a break-in, and once the particulars of the house are circulating, you may well have strangers turning up on the doorstep anyway.

For sale board
You will need to spread the word as quickly as possible, so a 'For Sale' board is a good idea. DIY shops often sell suitable notices, so make sure they are attached to a good strong post, firmly anchored in the garden or attached to the fence. You can say 'Apply Within' or give your phone number or both.

Advertisements
Remember that only 10 per cent of buyers look beyond a 10 mile radius of their present home, so the local papers are probably the best place to advertise. Don't be talked into running your advert for 10 days for a special price; take at the most two nights in the first week, then if you need to continue advertising, you might consider re-arranging your wording. It may be worth advertising in the far more expensive nationals at the weekends if your home is in the top

price bracket or if you live in an area where people are looking for second homes.

Never scorn the window of a local shop; the grapevine may pass on the news to interested friends and family from further afield. If there is a property shop of the kind that displays your details for a set charge, it will probably be worth using. Don't confuse this type of property shop with the solicitors' property centres which work rather like estate agents and charge commission on sales.

You can use a whole range of abbreviations to save money on your advertisement on the grounds that prospective buyers will know exactly what you mean but as one of the secrets of a successful private sale is to make your home stand out from the crowd, it is usually better to pay for a longer, properly worded description to attract the eye, rather than relying on 'des res 3 bed lux bth'. You can still use the more obvious abbreviations like FH for freehold or CH for central heating without spoiling the effect.

Your advertisement should begin with the location of the property and end with the price; in between you should give basic information about the number of rooms, garage and garden, plus any tempting extras. For instance, your display advertisement might run:

BECKRIDGE

Detached, double-fronted house, large sitting room with rural view, separate dining room, 3 bedrooms, one with shower-room en suite, newly refitted kitchen, bathroom, separate WC. Gas central heating, double glazing throughout. Well-stocked garden, double garage.

£95,000 Freehold

Tel: . . . . . .

or your classified advertisement might say:

COPTOWN. 3 bedroom end of terrace house, through sitting/dining room, fully fitted kitchen, bathroom. Small garden, carport. In quiet situation, near shops and school, station 5 minutes walk. Curtains and carpets included. £60,000. Tel . . . . . . (evenings)

Preparing the particulars

You will need a typed list of particulars, similar to those given out by agents. Try to borrow a friend's word processor to run them out, or have them typed and photocopied at a duplicating agency. At the top of each sheet, fix a colour photo of your home, taken on a sunny day.

Your list should include:
* Full address.
* Price.
* Freehold or leasehold (if leasehold, say how long the lease has to run).
* Details of each room, including measurements, fitted cupboards or shelving, telephone points and power points, fireplaces or radiators, wall lights or decorative features, windows and which direction they face. In the kitchen, mention fitted units, plumbing for dishwasher and washing machine, extractor fan. In the bathroom, mention fittings like towel rails, wall cabinet, type of shower.
* Type of central heating and approximate annual costs of running it.
* Mains services connected to the property.
* Details of garden (size and type) and outside buildings: garage, greenhouse, toolshed, coal shed.
* Rateable value and rates payable (while applicable); any service and maintenance charges.
* Description of the neighbourhood, availability of transport, schools and shops.
* Any other selling points like views, recent modernization, guarantees on work done, planning permission obtained.
* A disclaimer to the effect: 'These particulars are believed to be correct but do not constitute any sort of contract or offer.'

Prepare a full list of fixtures and fittings included in the sale (see Chapter 3, page 40) and another list of any items you would be willing to sell for a fee to be negotiated.

Buyers' first impressions

The feeling prospective buyers get as they first arrive at your home is very important. You can never sell a house on deception: any serious potential purchaser will want to visit several times, then it has to pass the building society valuation and, possibly, a survey. But anyone who comes to view will know very quickly whether this is a home they might want to live in and those first impressions can overcome a multitude of minor snags revealed later. It is well worth taking trouble to display your house to the best advantage:

★ Mow the lawn, trim the hedges and weed the flowerbeds (at least at the front). Cut back any overhanging trees and shrubs that can drip rain on visitors standing on the doorstep.

★ If your front garden is bare, invest in a couple of tubs of flowers or a hanging basket.

★ Sweep the path and remove the oil-stains. If your car usually stands in the drive, park it somewhere else for the time being; the drive will look far more spacious without it.

★ Clean the windows and wash the front door. If your knocker and letter box are old and rusty, replace them.

★ Have any cracked window panes replaced and get the curtains washed.

★ Attend to any dripping taps, drawers that stick and loose handles on doors and cupboards. Little things like that give the impression of a poorly maintained home; if everything in full view works well, buyers are more likely to assume that all the important things are in good order, too.

★ Clear out the old newspapers and all the rubbish that has been accumulating for years and take it to the tip now, instead of waiting for moving day. The less cluttered the rooms, the bigger they look. The same applies to cupboards: they look far more roomy if they are neat and tidy.

★ Large scale redecoration is probably a mistake; surveyors always suspect that you are covering over the cracks and damp patches and buyers may feel that they are paying extra for a decoration scheme they would not have chosen. On the other hand, if you feel that some rooms look shabby, a coat of fresh paint can do wonders. If your house is likely to be a first buy for a young couple, they would probably prefer to pay less and do it up themselves but if it is the type of property bought by older people, they will probably be looking for a house in good decorative order and be prepared to pay a premium.

★ Make sure that the house smells pleasant. Air it thoroughly every day and avoid cooking pungent dishes like curry or opening a tin of cat food just before viewers arrive. Too much air freshener leads to suspicions that you are trying to hide something, and baking bread or heating vanilla pods under the grill is a bit obvious but an occasional vase of fresh flowers or the aroma of freshly brewed coffee in the kitchen gives your home a welcoming feel.

★ Make sure there is plenty of light; on a dull day, turn the lights on and in the evenings have plenty of lamps in strategic places. Open doors to rooms off halls and landings to give a light, roomy impression.

★ Keep dogs well out of the way; many people are nervous of them and may hurry away before they have had a thorough look round. A sleeping or purring cat can make a room look cosy, so long as they are not the type to sharpen their claws on strangers' legs.

Showing the house

If you are showing viewers round the house yourself, rather than leaving it to the agents, aim at being pleasant and helpful without being overfriendly or giving a hard sell – both are likely to put them off. Let them walk into a room first while you stay in the doorway, at least at first; three or more people in the middle of a small room makes it feel pokey. Be prepared to point out any good points, like the view or the cupboard space but don't chatter on all the time; allow them to look, to picture their furniture in the rooms and to think. After you have taken them round, give them the chance to have another look on their own; this works well with couples who are longing for the chance to discuss the pros and cons privately. Obviously it is wise to put away any objects of value safely before you show any strangers round your home.

Have bills for gas and electricity and maintenance charges (if any) ready to show, to give an idea of running costs. Draw attention to the excellent bus service from the end of the road, the nearby parks and play areas for children, good schools in the area, commuting distance to the nearest town and so on.

You are not obliged to tell them about any disadvantages that your home may have (though some old hands find a 'total honesty' approach very effective) but if you are asked a direct question you must answer truthfully, or you could be open to a charge of misrepresentation. If you are unsure of the answer to any question, it is safer to say 'I don't know'.

The offer

You do not have to negotiate over the price of your house; if the market is on your side or you are under no pressure to move, simply say that the asking price is the price you want. Alternatively, you might say that you are willing to discuss an offer providing the buyer is in a position to proceed quickly. Of course, if you have to complete your own purchase within a month or lose it, or if you have been foolhardy enough to take out a bridging loan, you may not have many choices open to you. In this case, it is important not to let the buyer know that you are hard pressed or the offer will drop fast.

If you see more than one offer on the horizon, you might be in the happy position of choosing between buyers. Obviously you hope that the people who have fallen in love with your home have the cash in the bank or are first-time buyers with a mortgage guarantee in their pockets but most sellers are not that lucky. Once you are negotiating seriously, you should find out as much as you can about your buyers' position: do they have a house to sell? (If so, has it been on the market for long?); do they have the promise of a mortgage 'in principle'; how big a mortgage do they need? Unless the economic climate means that there is an abundance of mortgage money, beware of anyone needing a mortgage over 85 per cent; they are usually hard to come by. If they are already in a chain, find out how long it is and, if possible, who else is involved: if you discover that the other end of the chain is a run-down, woodworm-infested terrace in an employment blackspot, you might be better off taking a lower offer from someone else.

If you are selling through agents, they will arrange confirmation of the offer and forward the details to your solicitor. If you are selling privately, make sure that the buyer confirms any verbal offer in writing and that you accept in writing, giving the name and address of the conveyancer who is instructed to proceed with the legal arrangements on your behalf. Pass on to your conveyancer details of the buyer's full name and address, work and home phone numbers, the name and address of his conveyancer and copies of the offer and your letter of acceptance. After that, the legal work goes ahead as with any other sale.

Before contracts are exchanged

Some sellers take their house off the market as soon as an offer is accepted, as though they had already made a sale. But nothing is guaranteed until contracts are exchanged, so it is much safer to keep showing it to house-hunters who are genuinely interested. You can be quite open with your buyers about this; tell them that you need to protect your rear in case his purchase falls through. Of course, you may get a better offer and it is quite legal to accept it, even if your buyer has already spent money on surveys and searches. However, even if your conscience does not prick at these tactics, you need to be careful: a buyer who is about to conclude his own sale and sign a contract can be a better bet than a buyer with a better offer and a house that is not even on the market! You should certainly never accept a higher offer without giving the first buyer a chance to match it. If you have other buyers interested at about the same price, tell them that they will have first refusal if current negotiations fall through, then set a time limit within which contracts must be exchanged.

Take care over the following:
* Don't accept a contract subject to searches, survey or anything else. It will tie your hands while the buyer finds it easy to back out.
* If you agree to do any remedial work before contracts are exchanged, get an indemnity from the buyer (ask your solicitor to prepare a suitable form of words) so that, if the sale falls through for any reason, he will cover the costs.
* Never let the buyers move in before completion; if the full purchase price is not forthcoming you will have all the trouble of getting them out. If you have already moved out and you release the key so that they can measure up for carpets and so on, make sure that they sign an undertaking that this is only for viewing purposes.

Selling in Scotland

In Scotland you can sell through solicitors, through estate agents or by private sale (see Chapter 6, page 77). Whatever method you choose you should alert your solicitor at the outset as he will begin the local authority searches, so that there is no holdup later.

You should set your asking price rather like a reserve price at an auction, at the lowest price you would accept (or even below). Offers, usually well above the asking price, will be made through your solicitor and you should certainly never accept an offer in writing without consulting him. You can set a closing date for offers but don't rush, you will probably get a much better price if you take your time. Remember that once the legal process is in motion, house purchase in Scotland is very speedy, compared to the rest of Britain. If several buyers put in offers, you may choose the highest or you may take into account other factors, such as the price for extras or the proposed date of entry.

When married couples are not joint owners of the property, Scottish law requires that the non-owner gives permission before the sale takes place.

There are many advantages to the Scottish system but it does make it much harder to tie up sale and purchase simultaneously. It is quite usual for the seller to move into temporary accommodation after concluding the sale and before finding somewhere to buy. This is because, once you make an offer to buy, you have to be ready to proceed (for details on buying, see Chapter 6, page 77).

8

Moving and After

Once your purchase is completed your solicitor should confirm the time when you can pick up the keys and move in. If the seller is moving out on completion day, this will often be around midday but may be later if several transactions are involved, so you will need to co-ordinate your move accordingly. Moving is an art in itself and things will go more smoothly if you make a careful plan of action in advance.

Of course, taking possession of your new home may only be the beginning of your plans. You may already have checked out the possibility of improving or altering the new property; now you need to get down to the nitty-gritty of finding builders, obtaining the necessary permission or applying for grants.

Before the move: action checklist

Gas and electricity. Notify the board in your present area that you are moving out and give them the name of the new owner. Make a formal application for taking over the supply at your new address. Arrange for the meters to be read before you move out, giving as much notice as you can, and ensure that the same arrangements have been made at your new home. You will probably need a fitter to disconnect appliances at your old home and reconnect them at the new one; you will need to give seven working days notice.

Mail. Unless you want to rely on notifying everyone who is likely to write to you of your change of address and asking the new owners to send on any letters that slip through the net, you can pay a fee to have your mail redirected. Ask for a form at the post office and send it off at least a week before you move; you can arrange the service for one month, three months or a year.

Insurance. If you are moving into a home of your own for the first time you will need to take out insurance to cover the contents. Make sure that the cover is index-linked, so that it keeps up with inflation. Remember that valuable items are covered only up to a certain value; you may have to pay an additional premium to insure them adequately. If you already have contents insurance, make sure that you adjust your cover if you are buying new furniture and appliances. You will need to notify your car insurance company of your change of address. The premium may alter if you are moving to a different area.

Phone. Check if the previous owners will be taking their phones with them, so that you will have to buy or rent new ones. Notify your local telephone area at least a week ahead that you are leaving: give them the date of your move and ask for the bill up to that date to be sent to your new address. Apply to take over the phone at your new home. You can arrange for your calls to be redirected but the quarterly charge for this service is quite high.

Rates/community charge. You are responsible for the rates on your old home up to completion date, then they are the responsibility of the new owner and you are responsible for those on your new home. From April 1990 the community charge, or poll tax, replaces rates (in Scotland the community charge was introduced in April 1989). This is a flat rate charge which does not relate to the size of your property, so if you are moving within the same local authority, the tax per head will remain the same but it may differ if you are moving to another area. You should notify your local authority of the date of your move.

TV and video rental. Contact your rental company in good time and find out if you can take your TV and video (and possibly have your account transferred to another branch) or whether you will need to return them and take out a new agreement in another area. If you do take them with you, check that your insurance covers them in transit.

Questions for the seller. Well before you move in, you should ask:
* Where are the fuse boxes, meters and mains switches?
* Where are the water stopcocks?
* How does the central heating system work; how do you light the pilot light and set the programmer? When was it last serviced and is

there a service contract? How old is the system? Is there a handbook?

★ When is refuse collected; do you have to put bins or sacks in a specified place?

★ What are the names and addresses of electricians, plumbers, window cleaners and decorators used and found satisfactory?

Measuring up. Arrange a convenient time with the seller, or the agent in the case of an empty house. Draw a rough plan of each room and mark the measurements on it, taking special care to mark alcoves and recesses. If the seller is taking curtain rails, measure for new ones.

Plants. Garden plants are part of the fixtures, unless you have made special arrangements with your buyer, but those in pots and tubs, on the patio or in the greenhouse, are not. You will need to check that they are included in the removers' estimate (see below) or the removal men may refuse to take them on the day. In any case, they may be too heavy to move in their tubs. Water them well, then wrap the root ball, packed with as much soil as possible, in a piece of sacking and put the whole plant into a black polythene bag.

Pets. They should never be sent in the removal van, so you must make arrangements to transport them separately. If you have particularly nervous animals, ask your vet about tranquillizers.

★ Make sure that you have a suitable carrier for cats; you can obtain a cardboard carrier quite cheaply from a pet shop (get the carton in advance and get the cat used to being shut inside for short periods).

★ Birds can travel in their cages with the cover over the top but if you don't have room for the cage in your car, prepare a box with airholes.

★ It is dangerous to transport fish in their bowls or tanks. They can be carried in clean plastic bags filled with fresh or salt water and sealed, leaving enough air above the water. The bags should then be placed in a strong polystyrene container which can be sealed, so that they will not be subject to rapid temperature changes. Check with your pet shop on keeping the correct water temperature for tropical fish.

Junk. This is the moment to get rid of all the junk that has built up over the years. Be ruthless: weed out all the childrens' old toys, all those out-of-fashion clothes, all the electrical appliances that no longer work. If you can't bear to throw them all away, take them to a car boot sale!

Choosing removers

Everyone seems to have a tale to tell about removers who turn up late or not at all or who leave three piece suites out in the rain while they go for lunch but choosing a reliable professional firm should steer you round the horrors. Personal recommendation is best but failing that, make sure that the firm belongs to the British Association of Removers, which imposes a code of standards and will take up complaints if you are not satisfied.

When you ring a firm, check that they would be able to arrange a move on the right day, then ask them to send an estimator to give you a quote. The cost of the move will depend on how far you have to go and how much you have to take; it may also vary according to the day of the week. You must be clear about whether or not you want a service that includes packing. If not, then they should supply you with cartons and tea chests. Check whether covers to protect your mattresses and hanging wardrobes for your clothes are included in the deal.

Make sure that the estimator sees exactly what needs to be moved: and that includes the contents of the garden shed, the freezer in the garage and the boxes full of books and toys in the loft. He should also know as much as possible about the conditions at the other end: how near will the van be able to park, is there a long drive, how many floors are there, is the staircase steep or are the doorways narrow? If you are moving to a flat, which floor is it on, are there long passageways to negotiate, and is there a lift big enough to be useful in the move? The more you explain at the outset, the more accurate the estimate will be.

You will not want to take the highest quote but paying too little can be risky for something as important as moving all your possessions. Remember that carpet fitting will not be included in the quote, nor will disconnecting the gas cooker or dismantling the light fittings.

Insurance for the move

Never assume that you are fully covered for the replacement of any items damaged during the move; make enquiries about the cover included in the deal and make sure you know exactly what is covered. Some firms will exclude anything that you have packed yourself (unless, of course, the removal men drop it onto the concrete in front of your eyes) and you may be expected to pay the first part of any claim yourself.

Check with your own insurers to see if your contents insurance covers your possessions during the removal; if not, it may be worth paying an additional premium to extend the cover. You may find that there is a ceiling on the amount payable on any single item and you might want to consider whether it would be safer to take your Ming vase wrapped in blankets in your own car with your fur coat safely locked in the boot.

DIY removals

Hiring a van and moving your furniture yourself will be considerably cheaper but you need health, strength and *at least* two energetic helpers. You need to calculate the costs carefully to make sure the effort is worth the saving. Take into account van hire charge, mileage rate (possibly for more than one trip), insurance, VAT, fuel and feeding your helpers.

When choosing a van, remember that driving a heavy vehicle is very different from driving a car. Though you can legally drive a van up to 7½ tons, laden weight, only experienced drivers should attempt it. Ask the hire firm if you can test drive different sizes of vehicles to see how they handle. Then decide if it would be better to hire a large van and do the whole thing at once, or if (time permitting) you would be better off making two or more trips. Choose a van with some sort of ramp: without one, heaving in your heavy furniture can be extremely difficult, even dangerous. Check out the route to your home and try to avoid narrow roads and difficult junctions.

DIY removers should remember the following
★ What goes in last comes out first, so leave essentials to last.
★ As far as you can, pack room by room; it makes unloading easier.
★ Roll rugs and carpets pattern side in and do not stand furniture on them.

★ Dismantle anything that comes to pieces. It will pack into the van more easily and there is less risk of damage both to yourself and to the furniture: your furniture will weigh far more than you expect, by the time you have carried it down the garden.

★ Empty and defrost the fridge and freezer well in advance; they are not designed for carrying weights. Tape the shelves in place and the doors shut.

★ Use lots of small boxes and cartons rather than a few huge ones. They will be easier to carry and there is less risk of the bottoms falling out.

★ You will reach your new home in much better shape if you remember the golden rule about lifting: keep your back straight and bend your knees, never bend your back.

★ Pack clothes, linen and curtains in large plastic bags, carefully sealed. They will be useful for padding furniture and saving it from dents and scratches.

★ Anchor down as many of your goods and chattels as possible; use strips of cloth or stretchy material on soft furnishings as rope may leave marks.

Smoothing the move

The day before, attend to last minute arrangements:

★ Sort out the keys for the new owner and label them: front door, back door, garage door, etc. They should go into a strong envelope with the buyer's name on it, ready for handing over the next day.

★ Make sure you have a list of phone numbers: the removers, your solicitor and the seller's solicitor, the gas and electricity boards in case fitters do not arrive as promised. Keep some coins for phone boxes in your handbag or pocket, just in case!

★ Make a plan of the location of the new house; mark street names or numbers and landmarks such as churches or pubs, so that the removal men don't waste time cruising about searching for the right place. Give the removers the phone number of your new home, or a friend who will act as contact, so that they can let you know if they are delayed on the journey.

★ Prepare a travel pack with essentials: snacks, flasks for hot drinks and cans of cold beverages, corkscrew and tin-opener, pain-killers, sticking plaster, plenty of tissues, towels and soap.

Before you leave the house on moving day, make sure you:
★ Check every room to see that everything that belongs to you is taken but everything specified in your agreement with the buyer has been left behind.
★ Turn off gas, electricity and water. Even if the new owners are due to arrive within a few hours, take no chances; they could be delayed. If you have not already told them where to find mains switches and stopcocks, leave a note to tell them.
★ Make sure that any instruction booklets for gas or electric appliances, central heating, etc. are left out.
★ Once all the furniture has gone, sweep out. Vacuum carpets, if you are leaving them behind.
★ Leave your new address and phone number.

When you arrive at your new home
★ See that the carpets are protected by druggets or old sheets before everyone begins tramping in and out with dirty shoes.
★ Examine your belongings for dents, scratches, breakages or tears in upholstery as they arrive. If there is any damage take the foreman round with you, point it out and make a list. Ask him to initial it and give him a copy. Then make a prompt claim on the insurance.
★ Make sure that heavy pieces of furniture are placed in the right spot so that you will not have to heave them about later.
★ Check the removal van before it leaves, just in case anything has been left inside.

Improving your new home

When you choose your new home, it may have been with an eye to improvements, and if it needs work to bring it up to modern standards, you may be able to claim a grant from your local authority to help with the cost. Most grants are discretionary, so whether or not you get them depends on the way your authority interprets the regulations and the current availability of funds.

Remember that a grant will never cover the whole cost of the work and you won't get one for improving a second or holiday home. Before you make any firm plans or spend any money you should contact the home improvements officer at your local council to check on the chances of getting a grant and get advice on the most suitable grant to apply for. The council will usually give an indication of whether or not you are likely to get a grant before you buy a property but the application will only be approved after completion.

To be eligible for the main grants, owner-occupiers must own the freehold or have a lease with at least five years still to run and the property must be your only or main home.

Five main types of grants are available for householders:
Intermediate grants. These grants are mandatory, so your local authority must pay them at the maximum rate at which you qualify. They cover putting in standard amenities like a bath, sink, washbasin, inside WC and hot and cold water supply in homes built before 1961. They can also cover repairs carried out at the same time but if adding the new amenities would mean extra work such as, for instance, an extension to house the bathroom, you might be better off applying for an improvement grant.

Improvement grants. These are intended for major improvements and conversions to bring homes built before 1961 up to a good standard. They will only be given if the property meets certain standards and is expected to have a useful life of at least 30 years. They will not be given for enlarging a house by adding an extra bedroom but may be available to help with the cost of converting a house into flats. Home owners have only been eligible for grants for properties below a certain rateable value; check with your authority on limits following the introduction of the poll tax.

Repair grants. These are made for major structural repairs to the roof, walls, floor or foundations of houses and flats built before 1919; like the improvement grant, the repairs grant is subject to rateable value limits. Maintenance work like rewiring or replacing old bathroom suites does not qualify. The property must be capable of being brought up to a reasonable overall standard, once the repairs are done. You cannot apply for a repairs grant *and* an improvement grant. The local authority must give you a repairs grant if you have been served with a repair notice under the 1985 Housing Act; otherwise the grant is discretionary.

Common parts grants. Available to cover the improvement or repair of the shared parts of pre-1961 buildings with one or more flats. Leaseholders of self-contained flats can apply, as well as landlords, and they can do so either as an individual or as a group. As a leaseholder you have to get your landlord's permission for any proposed work and, if several of you apply together, make sure that everyone is committed to paying their share.

Home insulation grants. Householders who receive income support, family credit or housing benefit may be eligible if their home was built before 1976 and if it has less than 30mm of insulation in the loft.

The amount of the grant will depend on the work you plan to do and your own financial position. Sometimes it can be paid in instalments but normally the grant is paid when the work has been completed to the satisfaction of the local authority. A time limit may be imposed, so that if the work is not completed within the time set, the grant will not be paid.

Making changes

If you want to make changes to your home, you may need permission from the planning authorities or building regulations approval.

Planning permission

There are plenty of alterations you can make without needing planning permission but your local authority must approve anything classed as development, and they will want to ensure that it does not affect the interests of the neighbourhood. It is your responsibility to get permission before you begin work so check with your planning department whenever you plan to make changes, just in case. Sometimes permission is needed where you might not expect it, for instance if you want to put up a flagpole or a radio mast.

You apply for planning permission by filling in several copies of forms obtainable from your local authority; you will have to pay a fee. You will also need to supply detailed plans or scale drawings of your proposals. They do not have to be professionally drawn but must be clear and accurate; if you cannot do this yourself you may need to employ an architect or surveyor to draw them up for you. Each application is considered on its merits and will either be granted or refused for a reason which will be given along with the refusal (see Chapter 9, page 120).

You will NOT normally need planning permission in the following cases:

Internal alterations So long as the use of the house is not changed. You can knock down walls or turn a study into a bathroom without permission. You do need permission to convert a house into flats.

Porches. So long as the floor area is not more than two square metres, no part of it is more than three metres high and no part of it is less than two metres from the boundary between your garden and a road or public footpath.

Extensions. Subject to these conditions:

★ The volume of the original house is not increased by whichever is greater: 70 cubic metres or 15 per cent (20 per cent in Scotland) up to a maximum of 115 cubic metres. For terraced houses, this is 50 cubic metres or one-tenth of the original house.

★ It is no higher than the roof of the house.

★ No part of it projects beyond any wall of the house that faces a highway (that may include a service road or footpath).

★ No part of the extension that is within two metres of your boundary is more than four metres high.

★ Not more than half the original garden area is covered.

★ It is not to be used as an independent dwelling. This means that anyone living there must also live as part of your household.

Fences or walls. Providing your wall or fence is not more than one metre high where it marks your boundary with a road used by vehicles or two metres high elsewhere.

Sun lounge or conservatory. Providing it is attached to the house and meets the rules for extensions.

Tool-shed or greenhouse. So long as it is not more than three metres high (four metres if it has a ridged roof) and does not project beyond any wall of the house that faces a highway (that may include footpaths).

Loft conversions. So long as it does not enlarge the house. If it does then the rules for extensions apply.

Garages. If it conforms to the rules for extensions (for garages that come within five metres of the house) or for sheds (for garages more than five metres from the house).

Building regulations

As well as any planning permission necessary, you will probably need building regulations approval for any structural work, alterations or extensions. The regulations cover things like the preparation of the site, weather resistance, heat and sound insulation, safety of the structure, ventilation and waste disposal.

You must give formal notification of your plans, with detailed drawings and an estimate of the cost to the building control department; ask for guidance notes to help you prepare them. The regulations vary in different parts of the UK (for instance, in Scotland electric wiring is included) so it is important to get advice at an early stage. If you are employing a builder, he will probably prepare the application for you but getting the necessary approval is your responsibility. If you begin work without getting approval and that work does not meet with the regulations, you could end up having to tear it all down.

Finding a builder

Personal recommendation is best but make sure that the firm you engage is experienced in the type of work you want done: the one-man-and-a-boy outfit that added next door's porch may not be the right firm to undertake a sizeable extension. You would be well advised to choose a builder who belongs to the Building Employers Confederation or the Federation of Master Builders; both operate schemes to protect clients against bad workmanship; check on the terms before you begin. Beware of cowboys who operate on a strictly cash and nothing in writing basis; they may start out by charging less but it could cost you more in the long run.

First you need to decide exactly what you want done; draw up a detailed list of the work you want included. Approach more than one firm (three is a good average) and ask for quotations. When they arrive, check whether they are quotations or estimates. An estimate is only the contractor's best guess at what the work might cost and the final bill could be quite different. Builders are not always able to give a firm estimate, as they cannot foresee what problems may crop up as they go along, but you can insist that any extra work must be discussed with you before it is done and the additional cost confirmed.

The quotation should set out full details of the work, the materials to be used, what guarantees are offered, and starting and finishing dates for the work. The finishing date may be an estimate but if it is important that it is completed within a set time, you should make this part of the contract. If payments are to be made in stages, each stage of the work should be listed and priced for labour and materials.

Before accepting a quotation, check whether sub-contractors will be used and who is liable if anything goes wrong. Check also that the builder is insured against claims for personal injury or damage to property; otherwise you might find yourself liable if his ladder falls on the milkman or your building work makes chunks of plaster fall out of your neighbour's wall.

When you have decided on which quotation offers the best value for money, confirm the arrangements, dates and prices in writing. Then, once the work is under way, keep a close eye on what is happening (without hanging over the workmens' shoulders) and keep checking against the original specifications. If anything fails to match up, don't wait until the job is completed; ask for an explanation right away.

Complaints

Under the Supply of Goods and Services Act, you have a right to expect that the work will be done with reasonable care and skill, within a reasonable time and for a reasonable price. If your builder has not met these requirements he has broken his contract and you may be able to claim back your money, or at least part of it – though arguments over what is 'reasonable' may only be finally resolved in court. In Scotland the law is different but the material effects are much the same.

If you have a complaint you should take the following steps:

1. Put your complaint to the builder in writing; send the letter by recorded delivery and keep a copy.

2. If the response is unsatisfactory or non-existent, write again setting a date by which you expect matters put right, saying that

otherwise you will take further action. If you have not yet parted with your cheque, withhold payment.

3.   Contact the firm's trade association and give full details. They may be able to lean on the builder or offer an arbitration scheme. Check the terms carefully if you accept such arbitration; you may not be entitled to go ahead with any court action if the decision goes against you.

4.   If you are still making no headway, consider getting a report from an expert (e.g. an architect or surveyor) to substantiate your case over bad workmanship. Inform the builder that you are about to take this step; it might make him more amenable.

5.   As a last resort you can take him to court but before embarking on this make sure that you have a good case and a fair chance of getting your money back. Take advice from a consumer advice centre or Citizen's Advice Bureau or see your solicitor.

9

A to Z of Problems and Solutions

Animals

Trouble with your new neighbours' pets
★ The owner of a dangerous dog can be prosecuted by the local
authority, so try complaining to the environmental health department first. If that doesn't do any good you can take legal action
yourself: apply to the local magistrate's court for a summons.
Sometimes the threat of legal action is enough to make owners take
more care. But remember that a boisterous dog who leaps all over
you and scares the children is not usually reckoned to be dangerous; a dog that snaps and snarls and rips pieces out of your
children's clothes is a different matter.
★ If next door's cat digs lavatories in your flowerbed, there isn't
much you can do about it (except use cat repellant or dot the beds
with small sticks), as owners are not held responsible for what their
cats do.
★ Barking dogs may be enough of a nuisance for the local authority
to take action (sometimes it goes against the byelaws) but if not,
you would have to bring a private prosecution. If an owner ignores
your complaints, serve a 'formal notice', signed by as many other
local residents as possible (at least three), giving him a set time in
which to put the matter right before you take further action.

Blight notices

You can't sell because of the possibility of compulsory purchase
Local authority plans can hang fire for years and no one wants to

buy a home that is right in the way of a possible new motorway, or the site for the new council offices. So long as you can show that you have tried to sell and failed to get an offer at a reasonable market price (or any offer at all) you can force the authority responsible for the scheme to buy in advance by serving them with a blight notice. You must own the freehold or a lease with at least three years left to run and you must have lived in the house for at least six months (or have lived there for six months before moving out and leaving it empty).

If the authority accepts the blight notice you go ahead and negotiate a price, on the same basis as compulsory purchase (see below). If not, they will send you a counter-notice of objection, perhaps saying that the authority only wants part of your property or giving other reasons. You can then go to the Lands Tribunal, an independent body set up to deal with this type of dispute, for a decision but take professional advice first; they can award costs to either side. The counter-notice must be issued within two months or the blight notice takes effect anyway.

Chains

You are caught in a house purchase chain
If you are unlucky, chains can make buying and selling your home a long, dreary business. The owner of the property you are hoping to buy is buying from another owner who is selling to someone else with a house to sell, and so the chain goes on. When one link breaks – a seller changes his mind or a buyer cannot finance the purchase – a whole sequence of related transactions can fall down.

If you must move immediately for some reason or you cannot bear to lose the new home you have lined up and your sale has collapsed at the last minute, there is a last resort solution for the desperate: the chain breaker. Chain breakers are usually attached to estate agents. They will arrange to have your house independently valued and then offer to buy it from you at perhaps 90 per cent of its value (even less if the market is flat). But you stand to lose a good deal of money and you could find that you no longer have enough to complete the new purchase.

Compulsory purchase

There is a compulsory purchase order on your home
When your home is compulsorily purchased, the authority bringing the order must pay you the market price for your property. There is plenty of room for disagreement on the real market price and you should get help from the professionals (solicitor and surveyor) to make sure your interests are protected. If you cannot agree, the case can go to the Lands Tribunal.

You can claim payments for:
* Legal costs of conveyancing for your new home.
* Survey fee.
* Costs of transferring your mortgage or getting a new one.
* Reasonable travel expenses involved in finding a new home.
* Removal expenses and telephone reconnection charges.
* Costs of altering soft furnishings or fixtures and fittings to fit your new home.
* The disturbance and inconvenience caused by having to uproot yourself (you qualify if you have been living in the property as your only, or your main home for at least five years).

Payments do not cover:
* The difference between the market value of your old home and the higher price of the new home you choose.
* The extra legal and other costs incurred on a more expensive home (these would stay at the level of a similarly priced house).

The authority wants to buy only part of your property
In a case where the authority wants to take a slice out of your garden for a new road or other development, you may be able to make them buy the whole of the property if you can show that taking a part will cause 'serious detriment' to what is left. If you and the authority cannot agree, the Lands Tribunal will decide whether all or part should be bought: if, for instance, the scheme will cut down the size of your front garden, you are unlikely to succeed but if it takes the whole of it, leaving your windows staring onto the traffic, you would have a good cause.

When only part of your property is bought you get two forms of compensation
* The value of the land you lose, which will not usually be very

high. The authority should offer new fences or walls as part of the deal.

★ Payment for 'injurious affection'. This is to make up for any loss in the value of your property because of the new works, so that if the price you can sell for drops by 5 or 10 per cent, then compensation from the authority should make up that percentage.

Contract races

The seller tells you: the first to sign gets the house
Sellers who have more than one offer from prospective buyers may send out two or more contracts and tell the would-be buyers that the first one to sign gets the property. The golden rule is never to enter a contract race unless you can be reasonably sure of winning; it may be better to withdraw early, even if you have already spent money on the legal processes, than to risk losing later, when you will face a hefty bill. You might avoid contract races if you make it clear at the time of your offer, that you would immediately withdraw at the merest hint of such an unacceptable practice. Another possibility is the option method described below under Gazumping.

Council tenants and the right to buy

You think your landlord has over-valued your home
If, as a right to buy tenant, you think that the landlord has set the purchase price too high, you can ask for an independent valuation from the district valuer. You must notify the landlord in writing, not later than three months after receiving the notice naming a price (known as the 125 notice) that you want a 'determination of value under section 128 of the Housing Act 1985'.

After that, you have four weeks to put any representations to the district valuer and if you have a report from a surveyor, pointing out the defects of the property, you should send a copy. The district valuer's decision is final.

Note of caution: The district valuer *might* decide that the property is worth more than your landlord was asking in the first place.

Debt

You seem to owe money to everybody

If you have overstretched yourself in buying a home, or suddenly lose your job and can't meet the bills and see yourself getting into debt, the golden rules is to TELL: tell your creditors about your difficulties, tell them you are taking steps to sort things out, tell them that you will let them know your proposals in, say, three weeks' time. In the meantime:

★ Don't be tempted into taking a loan to pay off what you owe; you will only end up with more debts.

★ Take steps to cut your expenditure: reduce your mortgage costs if possible (see page 115), pare down the housekeeping, cut your fuel bill by less waste, destroy your credit cards, trade in your car for a cheaper, more economical vehicle, etc.

★ List essential expenditure, compare it with your income and see how much you can spare each week to rescue the situation.

★ List everything you owe: mortgage and loans, gas and electricity, credit cards, bank overdraft, HP and catalogues.

★ Decide how much you can afford to pay each creditor, on a regular basis. Remember that the most important creditors are your mortgage company, electricity, gas and water boards and local authorities, so they must be dealt with first.

★ Write to each creditor, offering to pay a certain amount on a weekly or monthly basis. Don't try to make it look good by offering more than you can afford to pay; if you fail to keep your promises, creditors may take a harder line.

If a creditor refuses your offer, write and list the other creditors who have accepted. Give details of your total income, your expenditure and the amount you are planning to pay off all round. Creditors are often far more willing to listen if a third party contacts them with all this information so if you are lucky enough to have a money advice centre near you, take your problem there.

Divorce and separation

You and your partner are splitting up and you want to keep your home

When two people buy a property as joint owners, neither can sell the property or raise a mortgage without getting the other's signature, so you do not have to worry about your partner selling your home over your head. However, if the property is in your partner's name, you may need to take steps to safeguard your rights.

If you are married, you should see a solicitor (legal aid is available) and ask him to 'register a charge' on the property. This will stop your spouse from selling the property but it does not stop the lender taking action to repossess because mortgage arrears have built up.

If you are not married, you do not have the same rights over a home that is in your partner's name. But if you have contributed financially or in other ways (doing work that would otherwise have been paid for) you should ask your solicitor to start court proceedings and register a 'pending action'. This will have the effect of preserving the *status quo* until you reach a settlement or the court decides on the merits of your claim.

You and your partner are divorcing; what happens to your home?
The court will decide on the division of property, making their ruling on the basis of the assets and income of the people involved and this can override the existing ownership. The interests of dependent children always come first, so whichever partner has care of the children will normally be entitled to stay in the matrimonial home; where children are not involved, the court might order the sale of the home and the proceeds to be divided between the partners, or the ownership transferred from one partner to the other.

Difficulties with lenders after separation or divorce
After your relationship with your partner has broken down, staying on in your home may mean taking over the mortgage payments – and that, in turn, means negotiating with the lender. Explain the situation, including what legal rights you are claiming over the home. Tell them if you need to reduce the cost of the mortgage and try any of the methods detailed below under Mortgages. If you are not married, you may find that the lender refuses to accept payments from you. In this case, tell them that you are taking legal action to establish your right to a share in the home and keep up the payments (with a careful record of what has been paid and when). This may affect the attitude of the court when it makes its decision.

If the mortgage is already in arrears and the lender is threatening to take action, ask for this to be postponed until any property settlement is made. Start paying instalments so that more arrears do not build up; if you cannot afford the whole amount, pay part of it and explain the reasons.

Electricity

Complaints not dealt with
Any complaint about bills, equipment sold to you or servicing of equipment should go first to your local Electricity Board. You can call at the nearest showroom, or ring the number shown on your bill. If that gets you nowhere, write to the customer services manager at the address at the top of your bill and, if you are still not satisfied, write to your Area Electricity Consultative Council (see the back of your bill for their address). Give exact details of the action taken so far, with dates, and attach copies of any correspondence. If you prefer, you can get in touch with one of the district committee members; their addresses are listed in Electricity Board showrooms.

Bills amazingly high
Of course, you may be using an amazing amount of electricity, but if it is substantially more than in previous quarters for no apparent reason, your meter could be faulty (unfortunately there are far more horrified consumers than faulty meters!). You can ask the Electricity Board to check the meter but they may charge you for this service.

Gas

Complaints not dealt with
For complaints about bills, appliances or services you follow much the same procedure as with the Electricity Board and there is a similar service for checking meters (see above). But if you still feel aggrieved after taking up your complaint at local level, look on the back of your bill for the address of the regional chairman and write giving full details. If, after that, you need more muscle, contact the

Consumers' Council for your region at the address displayed in the showroom. The Gas Consumers' Councils have been set up to represent the interests of customers and are independent of British Gas.

Gazumping

You worry that a higher bidder will snatch the property
The longer the time that elapses between making your offer and signing the contract, the greater the opportunity for gazumping – when the seller accepts a higher offer from another buyer. There are two ways of protecting yourself, so long as you are certain that you can go ahead with the purchase within a set time. Both should be handled through a solicitor:
Precontract deposit agreement. Both parties pay a preliminary deposit of ½ per cent of the purchase price to a stakeholder and sign an agreement to exchange contracts within four weeks. If either one withdraws without good reasons (the reasons must be spelt out in the agreement), the other takes both deposits.
Taking an option. The buyer can pay a straight fee in return for the exclusive right to buy, providing that contracts are exchanged within a set length of time. The agreement must spell out whether or not the fee is finally refundable from the purchase price when the deal goes through. If it is not, it is reasonable for the buyer to set a longer term before contracts must be exchanged.

Insurance

Claims refused or handled badly
If you find yourself deadlocked in an argument with the insurance company and no protests have any effect, find out which trade association they belong to and send all the details to the consumer information department. If you are offered arbitration, make sure of the terms: are you bound by the decision or can you take it further? If the company belongs to the Ombudsman scheme (not all do: it's a useful thing to check when choosing a company) you can take your problem to him (see Useful Addresses on page 125). You

can reject his decision and reserve the right to take the matter to court but if you accept the decision, then it will be binding.

Cover for injury to visitors

You should make sure that cover for 'personal liability' is included in either your buildings or contents insurance. This covers claims from anyone visiting your home (or delivering goods or services) for injury to themselves or their property: for instance, if the babysitter trips over the loose stair carpet and breaks an ankle; if a slate falls off the roof onto the doctor's car; if the next door neighbour gets an electric shock from your kettle.

Mobile Homes

The site owner puts up the rent

Your written agreement will normally say that the site rent, or pitch fee, is to be reviewed on a certain date each year. What usually happens is that the site owner decides on the increase and notifies each owner, then it is up to you to object if he is demanding too much. The typical agreement says that increases can take into account three things:

★ The retail price index: so that an increase in line with inflation would be fair.
★ Any money spent by the owner for the benefit of residents. This is usually taken to refer to improvements to the site; after all, you would expect the owner to maintain the site properly in return for your rent, so if he had let it run down, then had to spend a large amount putting things right, you should not have to pay out more.
★ Any other factors, including legislation, 'applicable to the operation of the park'. New laws that increase the site owner's costs might cause raised rents but past court cases have shown that owners are not allowed to put up your rent just because other rents for similar parks are higher.

The first thing to do, if you think the increase is unfair, is to ask the site owner in writing for an explanation of the reasons. If you are satisfied with the answer, then pay up; if not, then go on paying the old rent. That may persuade the owner to negotiate, especially if a number of owners stick together. However, he may threaten to take you to court to get his money and then you should check your position with the local Citizen's Advice Bureau or housing advice centre.

Mortgages

You can't keep up the payments

If you do not meet your monthly payments, the lender can go to court for a possession order and sell your home to reclaim the amount of the loan. However, most lenders are as anxious as you are to avoid this and you can avert such a disaster by taking prompt action. As soon as you find you cannot pay the full amount of your mortgage, or redundancy is on the horizon and you know you will be unable to pay, let your lender know. Never let arrears build up without any explanation and never take another loan to cover the repayments on the first one or you are on a slippery slope to trouble.

If your problems are short term, you may be able to:

★ Extend the loan term of a repayment mortgage so that your monthly payments are reduced.

★ Pay interest only on a repayment mortgage for a limited time. If your mortgage is new, this will only make a small reduction in your monthly payments, as most of what you are paying is interest. If you have had your mortgage for some time, the reduction will be more worthwhile.

★ Change an endowment mortgage into a repayment mortgage. Your monthly payments will be lower because you are no longer covering the premiums on an insurance policy.

★ If your lender will not change the terms of your endowment mortgage, you may be able to take a new mortgage for the whole amount and pay off your existing lender.

If your problems are long term: the best solution may be to sell your property and buy a cheaper home. If you wait for the lender to take action to repossess your home, it will be sold as speedily as possible, usually at auction, and at a price that will enable the lender to recoup the loan. If you sell it yourself, at the full market price, you stand a chance of making a small profit.

Help from state benefits

★ *Income support*. This benefit is available to people who work less than 24 hours a week and do not earn enough to live on. It takes into account your weekly outgoings and is supposed to bring your income up to the level where you can make ends meet. It will normally pay interest on your mortgage (though it does not cover capital repayments) but, if you are under 60, it pays only half the interest for the first 16 weeks. It may also cover ground rent and certain services charges. You cannot claim income support if you and your partner together have savings of more than £6000 but this does not include the value of your home or any life insurance policies. The amount you get depends on your age, how many dependants you have and how much you have in savings (savings between £3000 and £6000 are taken into account). Ask for leaflet SB1 from DSS offices for full details. You can make a claim on form BS1, available from post offices or, if you are unemployed, form B1 from your unemployment benefit office.

★ *Family credit*. If you have had to switch to a low-paid job since you took your mortgage, you may be eligible for family credit to boost your income. To qualify you must have at least one child under 16 (under 19 if in full-time education) and you or your partner must be working at least 24 hours a week. Self-employed people can claim too but once again, £6000 of savings is the cut-off point. Family credit is usually paid for 26 weeks at a time. Claims are made on form FC1 Family Credit, available from post offices.

The arrears have already built up

If your lender is already threatening to take legal proceedings, it is not too late to rescue the situation. Write to your lender saying that you are making every effort to clear the arrears and asking if it would be possible to make any of the above arrangements for cutting your costs. If your circumstances are about to change for the better (e.g. you have found work in a new/better paid job), spell them out. If you can't find anything hopeful to say along those lines, then offer to have the mortgage interest, plus something towards the arrears, deducted from your benefit each week (contact the DSS about the direct payments scheme).

This should convince your lender that you are making genuine efforts to put things straight but if, instead of co-operation, you get a letter saying that legal action is proceeding, try taking the matter higher up the line by writing to the general manager of the company, attaching a copy of your previous reasonable offer.

Neighbours

Noises from next door
In all disputes with neighbours, a few friendly words in the early days can save months of haggling, but some neighbours don't listen to words, friendly or otherwise. Whether or not you can take action depends on the circumstances: everyone has a right to live normally in their own home, so there is little you can do about the baby who screams all night, the pop music that disturbs your Sunday nap or the loud arguments that rage on the other side of the party wall. However, if the noise is unreasonable – stereos blaring out for hours on end or frequent late night parties disturbing the whole neighbourhood – and your informal complaints make no impact, then contact the environmental health officer at the town hall. If he agrees that the noise is a nuisance, in the legal sense (he will have to hear it for himself, rather than taking your word for it), he can serve a notice telling your neighbours to stop it and take action if they don't obey.

One thing you should never do is turn up *your* stereo to drown the noise or to get your own back; you could end up as the one who commits a nuisance!

Trespassing on your neighbours' land
One of the best reasons for keeping on good terms with your neighbours is that if you need to go onto their land to repair your fence or place a ladder to paint your guttering, you have to get permission from them. Even if there is no other way of doing the repairs, you have no automatic right of entry – unless this is set out in the deeds or you can claim a 'prescriptive right' because the previous owners have been going in, without asking, for at least 20 years (hard to prove).

If you decide to wait until your neighbours are out and then do the work anyway, you might possiblt get away with it, though if you do any damage, your neighbours could sue. They could apply for a court injunction to stop you but this will cost them money and trouble.

Your neighbours plan new buildings
In England and Wales your neighbours don't have to tell you that they are planning new developments, though some local authorities do notify anyone who might be affected; in Scotland neighbours have to tell you before making a planning application. In a conservation area, a notice will be put up on or near the property for at least seven days, outlining the application.

If you know that something is afoot, you need to make any objections quickly; once the local authority has taken a decision, it will be too late. You can inspect the application at the planning department and you may have a valid objection if the proposed work affects your privacy or substantially cuts down the light in your rooms. The fact that your pleasant view will disappear is just bad luck; you have no legal right to pleasant views. If the first you know about it is when work begins, you can check to see if permission was granted; if not, notify the planning department, explain your objections and leave the rest to them.

New houses

Disputes with the builders over defects
When defects show up after a few months in your new home, if it is covered by the NHBC 10 year warranty you hope that the builder will put them right without any fuss. If you give him a reasonable time and he fails to correct the defects, the NHBC can send a field officer to inspect the house (with both the owner and the builder) and if he recommends that work should be done, the builder is required to do it within 30 days. If you are not satisfied you can ask for arbitration, and an independent arbitrator will be appointed. The arbitrator is usually an architect or surveyor and his award has the force of a High Court judgement. But beware: if the arbitration goes against you, you will have to foot the bill.

The builder has gone out of business by the time the defects show
You notify the NHBC, who will arrange for a field inspector to investigate and, if he agrees with your claim, he will make a schedule of remedial work to be carried out. You will be asked to get two quotations for the work and will then be given the go ahead to accept one of them.

Nuisance from public development

Life is unbearable because of works outside your home
If the council is building a new road or a block of flats right next to
your home and you find that the noise and vibration is unbearable,
try claiming for the expenses of moving your family to other
temporary accommodation. Be sure to negotiate with the authority
before you make a move and be ready to show that it is impossible
to stay in your own home while the works are in progress. Involve
your doctor if possible; emphasize the health risks for old or young
members of the family. But don't expect the authority to pay for a
hotel suite; the most you can hope for is the difference between the
reasonable expenses of moving temporarily and what it would have
cost you if you had remained at home.

The completed works reduce the market value of your property
You can claim compensation if nuisance from the new works, once
they come into use, cause a drop in the market value of your home.
It applies to new roads, carriageways or flyovers and road widening; new airports, runways and extension of runways; change of use
of land where public building works give rise to noise, fumes,
smoke, artificial lighting or substances discharged onto your land.

You may qualify if:
★ Depreciation is more than £50 on the valuation date – which is 12
months after the works came into use.
★ You are a freeholder or a leaseholder with at least three years left
to run on the lease.
★ You are an owner-occupier on the date of your claim – and you
owned it before the works were in use. You cannot buy a house six
months after the new road opened and claim after you move in; the
authority will assume that you paid the right market price at the
time.
Disputes over the amount of compensation can go to the Lands
Tribunal but take professional advice first.

You want to sell during the first year
Though claims normally have to wait a year – until what is known as
the valuation date – you can claim if you sell during that year. You
must make a claim after you have exchanged contracts but before

completing the sale. Though your buyer will own the house by the time it is surveyed and valued by the authority, this will make no difference to your claim.

Offers

Your offer on your dream home is refused
This is always disappointing but it would be a mistake to give up – if, that is, you feel that this house is special and you won't find another like it down the road. The seller may be trying for an unrealistic price and he may suddenly wake up to the fact; if you have been outbid, the buyers may be unable to sell their own house, or get snarled up in a chain. Let both seller and agent know that you would still be interested if circumstances changed. Keep an eye on the 'For Sale' board and if it does not change to 'Sold' fairly quickly, ring the agent and check on the state of play. If deal falls through after the seller has found *his* dream house, he may welcome you with open arms.

Planning permission

You are refused planning permission
When the local authority refuses your application they will give reasons. For instance, they may say that your building would spoil the look of the street or your garage would cut visibility at a road junction. You can sometimes rescue the situation by changing your plans slightly (a different design or a change in siting may do it) and applying again. If you re-submit the application within 12 months you do not have to pay a second fee.

You can appeal to the Secretary of State for the Environment if you feel you have a good case to argue against the authority's decision. The inspector who conducts the appeal usually asks both sides to put their case in writing but he may decide on a public enquiry. You do not have to pay for the appeal but you may have to pay for specialist advice to back your argument. A pamphlet called *Planning Appeals – A Guide*, obtainable from the planning office, gives more information.

If the authority fails to give you an answer within eight weeks from the time they get the application, you can go ahead and appeal anyway, just as though they had refused. They may ask you for more time to consider, but you don't have to agree.

You have gone ahead without the necessary permission
The authority may simply ask you to apply for planning permission before you go any further and if it is granted, then you have no more worries. Or they may serve an 'enforcement order', saying that you have to pull down any building that has been put up without permission. You can appeal to the Secretary of State and if you win you can keep the building but if you lose, you can be fined for each day that the building remains.

Refuse

You need to dispose of bulky rubbish
★ If you need to dispose of an old fridge or washing machine before you move, contact your local environmental health department. Most authorities have a collection service for these large household items but don't expect them to be round the day after you phone. In some areas the service is free, in others there will be a small charge.
★ Local authorities are obliged to provide tips where you can dispose of the worn out television, the boxes of rubbish from the attic or even an old car, free of charge. Ask at your local council offices but be prepared for a journey.
★ Some authorities will remove building rubble without charge. If yours isn't one of them and the thought of disposing of it a sackful at a time fills you with dread, you might consider hiring a skip. Some local authorities hire skips themselves; otherwise you can hire from a waste disposal firm, listed in the Yellow Pages. Remember that you must ask the local planning department for permission to put a skip on the road or pavement; some hirers arrange this for you and include it in their charge.

Service charges

You get a large bill for service or maintenance charges on your flat
This is a thorny area and you might find the leaflet issued by the

Department of the Environment called *Service charges for flats – a guide for landlords and tenants* useful. Query bills that seem unreasonable with the landlord and ask for a breakdown and explanation. If you can't agree, you may have to apply to the courts to decide if the charge is fair and reasonable. If they decide that it is not, then they will set a new amount.

In the case of major jobs like painting the whole building or re-roofing, the law requires the landlord to get two estimates for the work and to give details to leaseholders so that they have at least one month to raise queries or objections. If he does not comply he is committing an offence – so let him know that you know what the law says.

You will have far more muscle in negotiating with your landlord if you form a residents' association. The Federation of Private Residents' Associations (see Useful Addresses on page 125) can supply information on setting one up, for a small fee.

Squatters

Strangers move into your home
If you arrive at your new home to find trespassers already in residence or squatters move in when you are away for a time, all you need to do is ask them to leave and, if they refuse, call the police. Never try to evict them forcibly; under the Criminal Law Act 1977 the police have powers to arrest them immediately. If they have caused any damage you can, in theory, claim damages from them but if they are homeless and jobless, it may be a waste of time.

Trees

Branches or roots cause you trouble
If branches from next door's tree overhang your garden you have the right to cut them off, though it will probably save hurt feelings if you talk to your neighbours first. The branches you cut down belong to them, so offer them back. You are unlikely to be able to do much about a tree than blocks some of your light but does not

overhang your property, unless you can agree with your neighbour about getting it thinned out or cut down.

Spreading roots can cause damage to drains and take moisture from the soil – clay soil in particular – so that it contracts and affects the house foundations. Your building insurance will probably cover this so you should claim on your policy, in which case your insurance company may well claim against your neighbour's insurance.

Wood

Your home is under attack from woodworm, dry rot or wet rot
★ *Woodworm.* Tiny circular holes in the skirting board or in the wood around sinks, baths and loos can be an indication that the hungry little beetles are at work. Signs are most obvious between May and September.
★ *Wet rot.* Can be found anywhere that moisture collects, like the corners of window frames or anywhere there has been a persistent leak.
★ *Dry rot.* Flourishes in damp, unventilated conditions and spreads with alarming rapidity, so speedy treatment is essential.
Do-it-yourself remedies are available for woodworm and wet rot which can be effective if you take action soon enough. Dry rot is a job for the experts and you may need professional help in dealing with wet rot and woodworm, too. Choose a firm which is a member of the British Wood Preserving Association; they all give a guarantee that will be honoured even if the firm goes out of business. Estimates are free and prices vary quite a bit, so get several quotes and compare them.

Working from home

You want to start a business from your front room
No one is likely to object if you are writing a book, dressmaking on your sewing machine or throwing pots. However, if it is something that would affect your neighbours or mean a 'material' change of use – a boarding kennels, a guest house, a carpentry shop or a

warehouse in the garage – then you would need planning permission.

Other local authority departments may also have to be involved: if you want to set up as a child minder, the social services will need to approve the premises, and if you begin a catering service, providing lunches for offices or laying on wedding receptions, the health inspector will want to see your kitchen.

Useful Addresses

Association of British Insurers
Aldermary House
Queen Street
London EC4N 1TT

Association of Licensed Conveyancers
200-201 High Street
Exeter EX4 3EB

Banking Ombudsman
Citadel House
5-11 Fetter Lane
London EC4A 1BR

British Association of Removers
279 Gray's Inn Road
London WC1X 8SY

British Insurance and Investment Brokers Association
BIBA House
14 Bevis Marks
London EC3A 7NT

British Wood Preserving Association
150 Southampton Row
London WC1B 5AL

Building Employers Confederation
82 New Cavendish Street
London W1M 8AD

Building Societies Association
3 Savile Row
London W1X 1AF

Building Societies Ombudsman
35-37 Grosvenor Gardens
London SW1X 7AW

Corporation of Insurance and Financial Advisors
6-7 Leapale Road
Guildford
Surrey GU1 4JX

Council of Licensed Conveyancers
Golden Cross House
Duncannon Street
London WC2N 4JF

Department of the Environment
2 Marsham Street
London SW1

Federation of Master Builders
33 John Street
London WC1N 2BB

Federation of Private Residents' Association
11 Dartmouth Street
London SW11H 9BL

FIMBRA (Financial Intermediaries, Managers and Brokers Regulatory Association)
Hertsmere House
Marsh Wall
London E14 9RW

Gas Consumers' Council
18 Great Marlborough Street
London W1V 1AF

Incorporated Association of Architects and Surveyors
Jubilee House
Billingbrook Road
Weston Favell
Northampton NN3 4NW

Incorporated Society of Valuers and Auctioneers
3 Cadogan Gate
London SW1X 0AS

Insurance Ombudsman Bureau
31 Southampton Row
London WC1B 5HJ

Land Registry
32 Lincoln's Inn Fields
London WC2A 3PH

Law Society
113 Chancery Lance
London WC2A 1PL

Law Society of Scotland
26 Drumsheugh Gardens
Edinburgh EH3 7YR

Local Government Ombudsman
Commission for Local Administration in England
21 Queen Anne's Gate
London SW1H 9BU

National Association of Conveyancers
44 London Road
Kingston upon Thames
Surrey KT2 6QF

National Association of Estate Agents
Arbon House
21 Jury Street
Warwick CV34 4EH

National House Building Council
(Registered Office, Conciliation and Insurance Deparment)
Chiltern Avenue
Amersham
Bucks. HP6 5AP

NHBC London Information Office
58 Portland Place
London W1N 4BU

Office of Fair Trading
Field House
15-25 Breams Buildings
London EC4A 1PR

Royal Institute of British Architects
66 Portland Place
London W1N 4AD

Royal Institution of Chartered Surveyors
12 Great George Street
London SW1P 3AD
Scottish address: 7 Manor Place
Edinburgh EH3 7DN

Solicitors Complaints Bureau
Portland House
Stag Place
London SW1E 5BL

Middlethorpe Hall in Yorkshire

Eastwell Manor, near Ashford in Kent

Bishopstrow House in Wiltshire

Llangoed Hall in Powys

Maiden Newton House, near Dorchester
Ettington Park, near Stratford-upon-Avon

Gravetye Manor in West Sussex

Cannizaro House, Wimbledon Common, London

Kildrummy Castle in Aberdeenshire

Chewton Glen in Hampshire

Hanbury Manor, near Ware in Hertfordshire

Longueville Manor, on Jersey, Channel Islands

lemented by the sumptuous plastered ceiling. Four painted crests stand out from the ornate raised surface which features nine coronets and a frieze of winged cherubs. From the large windows you get a lovely view of the fountain in the centre of the lawn just in front of the main garden area.

The proprietors describe dining at Rookery Hall as 'entirely twentieth century' with the emphasis on quality raw materials to produce original dishes inspired by classical foundations. One of Head Chef Christopher Phillip's favourite starters is a Galantine made from the Gressingham Duck, with a mosaic of vegetables and marinated duck foie gras. This is served with a lightly spiced onion and ginger marmalade accompanied by a dice of beetroot bound in an orange flavoured oil. A worthy main course recommendation from the excellent à la carte menu is a succulent Saddle of Wild Hare with braised baby vegetables and a lightly Poivrade Sauce spiked with Blackcurrants. Another favourite is a Cannon of Leicestershire Lamb served with a crisp Pastry Tartlet of Asparagus and Artichoke on a Tomato Sauce flavoured with Basil. Whatever your choice, each dish has its own special selection of vegetables to complement it.

Following a £3.6 million expansion programme, there are now forty-five bedrooms, all furnished to the very highest standards and offering those pleasing little extras like a bowl of fruit, some quality toiletries and a few freshly baked cookies that cost so little but make the difference between a good hotel and an outstanding hotel. Fifteen of the extra bedrooms are in the refurbished Georgian stable block: a further twenty-one bedrooms have been created in an entirely new wing.

Croquet, tennis, coarse fishing and an endless number of ways to explore the natural beauty of the surrounding area are all available. Nearby attractions are outlined in a booklet which awaits all guests in their room, but some of the more popular are the city of Chester just twenty miles away (and North Wales just beyond), and the towns of Northwich and Crewe.

52

STAPLEFORD PARK

Address Melton Mowbray, Leicestershire LE14 2EF
Tel: 057 284 522 Fax: 057 284 651

Nearest town Melton Mowbray
Directions From the M1, take the Loughborough
exit (junction 23) and follow signs to Melton
Mowbray. Driving straight through Melton
Mowbray, follow the B676 for four miles, then turn
right at the signpost for Stapleford. From the A1,
turn off at the Colsterworth roundabout on to the
B676, signposted Melton Mowbray. Drive about ten
miles, through the village of Saxby, then turn left
to Stapleford. The entrance to Stapleford Park is on
the left.
Open throughout the year.
Price for dinner, with wine, bed and breakfast for
two – over £150.
Credit cards All major credit cards accepted.
*Children under ten by prior arrangement. The hotel is
not suitable for the disabled. Pets and horses can be
accommodated.*
Overall mark out of ten 9

Easily reached by road or rail link, Stapleford Park is situated in rural Leicestershire, between the A1 and the M1. Despite its ease of access, however, Stapleford Park is in no way a noisy or disturbed location: set within its generous 500 acres of parkland, the hotel is an idyllic oasis of peace and quiet, ideally situated for touring the heart (some would say the soul) of England.

First mentioned in the Domesday Book, the current Stapleford Park – a Grade I listed building – dates back to the sixteenth century. Owned by a succession of earls of Harborough, it passed into the hands of one John Gretton, in 1894. He substantially altered the house in the Elizabethan style and added a stable block. Shortly afterwards, Edward, Prince of Wales, showed an interest in purchasing the property as a country retreat. However, his formidable mother Queen Victoria forbade this on the grounds that he would be 'corrupted by the company of the local hunting society'! So Stapleford never became a royal retreat, and was purchased on a whim by an American, Bob Payton, in 1988.

Most expensive restorations of hotels are undertaken by large conglomerates backed by financial institutions, the conference market being the primary objective. Not so Stapleford Park. Had Bob Payton and his wife Wendy known that restoration and modernization would eventually cost them £4.5 million, they might never have embarked on the scheme. Fortunately, they rose to the challenge. Painstakingly completed to a very high standard, the hotel – its exterior being a somewhat eclectic architectural *mélange*, the interior a sometimes theatrical but always welcoming home – exudes luxury, with the odd touch of whimsey. The Paytons' philosophy is simple: 'Nineteenth-century hospitality backed up by twenty-first-century technology . . . We bet the former is easier to deliver than the latter.'

Part of Stapleford Park's individuality springs from the 'signature' rooms: its thirty guest rooms were each designed by famous names including Wedgwood, Tiffany and Crabtree & Evelyn. While the hotel sports the air of a Victorian gentleman's lodge, individual touches, such as a mural of the Paytons' dog in the front hall, ensure that it doesn't fall back on stereotype.

The Paytons' love of – and pride in – the place, bring about an informal feel which pervades the entire house. They take great care to pay individual attention to every guest. From enthusiastic staff through to the provision of teddy bears for lonely children, the whole impression is of them taking a genuine pleasure in accommodating you and making you feel at home. For example, strict dress rules for the (non-smoking) dining room are not *de rigueur*, although smart style is in order. The room contrasts simple white linen and Wedgwood china with elaborate Grinling Gibbons carvings which adorn the walls. Stapleford Park's cuisine is one of the less spectacular aspects of the hotel, although it is reasonably priced at less than £25 per person for a three-course meal with wine. While dinner is traditional English with an occasional American touch, breakfast is served in the American-Continental style and is exemplary, with its home-made muffins, blueberry jam and fresh bread.

The bedrooms – all with en suite facilities – come in five grades, starting with de luxe at £85, ranging through superb, premier and outstanding, to the suites at £200–£325. With their own distinctive designer atmosphere, all rooms contain every conceivable amenity required to make for a very comfortable stay.

The full title of the hotel is Stapleford Park Country House Hotel and Sporting Estate: certainly a wide range of outdoor pursuits (especially equestrian) are available within the grounds. Nearby Melton Mowbray has been regarded as the traditional home of fox hunting for over two hundred years, and the estate maintains strong links with the Leicestershire Hunting Society. Carriage driving and riding lessons are also both available, but bring your own riding hat. For those after a different kind of quarry, there are two lakes offering fishing, and other sports include clay pigeon shooting and game shooting (the latter on request), and there is also tennis and croquet. The hotel is well placed for exploring Leicestershire's many places of historical and cultural interest, including Belton House, Belvoir Castle and Burghley House.

East Anglia

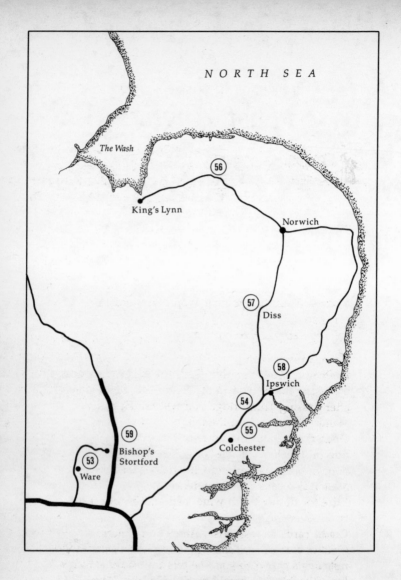

East Anglia

53 Hanbury Manor
54 Hintlesham Hall
55 Maison Talbooth
56 The Old Rectory

57 Salisbury House
58 Seckford Hall
59 Whitehall

HANBURY MANOR

Address Thundridge, near Ware, Hertfordshire
SG12 0SD
Tel: 0920 487722 Fax: 0920 487692

Nearest town Ware.
Directions From London, leave the M25 at junction
25, taking the A10 north through Ware. Immediately
after passing Thundridge you will see Hanbury
Manor signposted on the left.
Open throughout the year.
Special breaks available for golf, beauty,
honeymoons, Easter and Christmas. Hanbury
Manor also caters for conferences.
Price for dinner, with wine, bed and breakfast for
two – over £200.
Credit cards Access, Visa, Amex and Diners.
Children are welcomed although they are not allowed in the
restaurants after 6.30 p.m.; no pets are allowed although
kennelling can be arranged nearby. Hanbury Manor does
provide for the disabled; there is a specially converted
bedroom and most of the public rooms are easily accessible.
Overall mark out of ten 9

In summer 1990 Hanbury Manor opened its doors to guests, after a staggering £24 million development by Rockresorts Inc, a US-based hotel chain. Such investment here and elsewhere in this country indicates the healthy state in which the exclusive end of the British Country House Hotel industry finds itself today.

Originally recorded in the Domesday Book as belonging to the Bishop of Bayeux, the estate became the property of the Hanbury family in 1781. It was the Hanburys who built the present Jacobean-style mansion, later converting some forty acres of the complete estate (currently occupying two hundred acres) into a pinetum and a series of lakes, ponds and gardens; the Rose Garden, the Garden of Remembrance and the intriguing Secret Garden. These Victorian glories were painstakingly recreated during the conversion of the property, as exemplified in the manor's stunningly restored Walled Garden. The latter includes two magnificent greenhouses with a large collection of peach trees, orchids, potted plants and grapevines. Hanbury Manor has most recently been used as a girls' convent school.

Within the sensitively renovated exterior of the manor, with its diamond-patterned brickwork and tall, Jacobean-style chimneys, there is a splendidly restored interior. The open fireplace, panelled walls, beamed ceiling and exposed floor of the Oak Hall create an immediate impression of warmth. There are seventy-one bedrooms in the main house, and a further twenty-seven in the Garden Court, a short stroll away. Most bedrooms enjoy commanding views over Hanbury's grounds and the Hertfordshire countryside beyond. As you would expect after such an intensive refurbishment scheme, each bedroom has been superbly designed in 'aristocratic' style. Some contain alcoves, others have bay windows, and some have four-poster beds. The rooms are spacious and comfortably furnished, and all of them have a colour television (with satellite TV and a video channel), a personal bar, a hairdryer and trouser press. The bathrooms have both a bath and a shower and are well-stocked with toiletries and thick towels. There are fresh flowers and bathrobes, as well as magazines, all of which gives the bedrooms a welcoming feel.

Hanbury Manor sets great store by its cuisine. Apart from a restored chapel which now offers banqueting facilities, there are three elegantly proportioned dining rooms, each established under the guidance of Albert Roux, patron of Le Gavroche, one of only two Michelin three-star restaurants in Britain. From the classical choice of cuisine offered in the Zodiac Room, to the light and healthy food of the Conservatory, to the brasserie fare of the Vardon Grill, Roux's culinary excellence is very much in evidence. For example, one might start dinner in the Zodiac Room with Consommé of Crustaces with small Ravioli of Lobster, followed by Native Oysters warmed in Champagne on a bed of Cucumber and Caviar. For fish course, Lobster braised with Girolles and a lightly creamed Sauce Americaine makes a mouthwatering choice, while Fillet of Scotch Beef with a Glaze of Red Wine, Roasted Salsify and Girolles forms a memorable main course option. The dessert menu includes Assiette of Dark and White Chocolate and various French and English cheeses. An extensive wine list includes classics from Bordeaux and Burgundy together with a selection of wines from Australia, the Americas, and England. In the Conservatory, lighter meals range from classics such as Smoked Salmon to more adventurous dishes like Compote of English Rabbit with Eau de Prune, or Breast of Duck with Braised Endive and Fresh Lime. Refreshing desserts include Mandarin Crêpes with Mandarin Sorbet and Raspberry Crème Brûlée with Almond Tuille. The Vardon Grill offers brasserie food of the highest quality. There is also a special children's menu with favourites like sausages and beefburgers. Afternoon tea is served in the Oak Room, and room service is available twenty-four hours a day. The menus change regularly and vegetarians can easily be catered for, although some advance notice is preferred. There is also a Cocktail Bar. Dress is formal in the Zodiac Room, less so in the Conservatory and the Vardon Grill.

The hotel also boasts a standard-setting portfolio of health, sport and leisure facilities. The original nine-hole golf course designed by Harry Vardon in the 1920s has been expanded into an eighteen-hole championship course by Jack Nicklaus II. This 100-acre project, which cost £2 million, has been designed with both skilled and novice players in mind, and there is a highly experienced golf professional on hand. It is easily accessible from the hotel, and the eighteenth green lies literally at the door of the manor! In addition to golf, there are three all-weather tennis courts, a croquet lawn, billiards room and fitness centre with Polaris equipment. There is an indoor swimming pool measuring a respectable 17 by 8 metres, whirlpool, sauna, steam baths, two squash courts, an aerobic/dance studio and a beauty clinic which offers aromatherapy, massage, sunbeds and facials. There is also a hairdressing salon. Fitness and nature trails have been laid out in the grounds, and clay pigeon shooting, archery, riding, fishing, paragliding, punting, and hot-air ballooning can all be arranged within the vicinity. There is a helipad in the grounds. Specialist lectures can also be arranged on subjects ranging from buying at auction to decorating country houses. Services available include babysitting, car hire, laundry, foreign exchange and secretarial.

Nearby attractions include Cambridge, less than an hour to the north; Hatfield House; St Albans; Whipsnade Zoo; and Oxford to the west. London is just forty minutes away, although within the secluded ambience of Hanbury Manor, the capital city's turmoil will probably be far from your thoughts.

54

HINTLESHAM HALL

Address Hintlesham, Suffolk IP8 3NS
Tel: 047 387 268 Fax: 047 387 463

Nearest town Ipswich.
Directions From Ipswich, Hintlesham Hall is easily
located just five miles west, on the main A1071.
A member of the **Relais et Châteaux** consortium.
Awards AA *** graded; Egon Ronay 82%; 1988 *Good
Hotel Guide* César Award; RAC Blue Ribbon.
Open throughout the year.
Special breaks A number of theme breaks –
shooting, racing and so on – are available.
Price for dinner, with wine, bed and breakfast for
two – £100–£150.
Credit cards Access, Visa, Amex and Diners.
*The hotel is unsuitable for the disabled; children over ten
are allowed, and dogs by special prior arrangement only.*
Overall mark out of ten 9

Set in 170 acres of gardens and parkland, it is not difficult to see why Hintlesham Hall is occasionally referred to as the most beautiful Country House in East Anglia. The original house was built in 1578, during the reign of Elizabeth I, but it was substantially altered during the Georgian era at the end of the eighteenth century by Richard Powys, then serving as a principal clerk of the Treasury.

Today the hotel still has a long, straight drive running to the front door. Well-groomed lawns and white-chain-linked posts line the edge of the substantial gardens, and this rather direct approach to the front of the hotel allows visitors to really appreciate the marvellous Georgian façade. The main building is built in the fashion of a single rectangular E-shaped block, with two extended and symmetrical wings protruding past the entrance lobby. One small feature you cannot miss is the fat Georgian chimneys, with their wide tops, which provide an evocative reminder of the days when wood-burning fires were more fashionable than the more messy, but longer-lasting coal fires.

Your first glimpse of the interior of Hintlesham Hall will be the long, cool entrance hall which acts very much as a 'no man's land' between the warm interior of the hotel and the outside world. Its smooth hexagonal stone tiles are complemented by marble benches and large wandering pot plants. Inside, the public rooms are no less impressive, and the huge drawing room and bar are clad with beautifully painted pine panels and filled with comfortable armchairs. A number of antique oil paintings offer a pleasing alternative for you to admire should you ever tire of the views far across the hotel grounds from the drawing-room windows.

Hintlesham Hall has thirty-three bedrooms, all luxuriously furnished, and a number of the suites are reckoned to be among the most comfortable in East Anglia. The Rosette Room, with its rose-pink decor and fine cloth-draped four-poster, is understandably one of the most popular rooms in the hotel. All bedrooms have private facilities, and a range of little extras, such as a refrigerated mini-bar, towelling robes and Penhaligon or Crabtree and Evelyn toiletries.

The hotel has three restaurants, although the smallest of the three, which can accommodate up to sixteen people at once, is reserved for private functions. The Parlour dining room is lined with honey-coloured pine panels, complementing the main drawing room and bar areas, and the end result is as relaxing as it is pleasing to the eye. Hintlesham Hall has developed a fine reputation for its cuisine, and it is extremely popular with non-residents who are advised to book well in advance for both lunch and dinner. Lunch is available all week except Saturdays.

The style of cooking is modern French and English, with, interestingly, distinct Japanese influences. Local home-produced ingredients are used as far as possible, but the addition of some splendid foreign delicacies works extremely well. A three-course à la carte menu is available from Sunday to Thursday at a price of £25, while on Friday and Saturday evenings a four-course à la carte menu is offered at £35. Highlights from the range of starters include fresh Langoustines and Sole in a Filo Pastry Basket, with Coriander and Almond Sauce, and Escalopes of Foie Gras with Caramelized Orange and an Endive Salad. Four courses for two, including wine, will leave you little change out of £90 – and will cost even more if you go for the top-price dishes – but the quality is indisputable.

Two recommended specialities from the nine or ten main-course options are Breast of Norfolk Guineafowl, served with Smoked Bacon and Green Lentil Ragout, and a Boneless Dover Sole, Gratinée with Herbs, and served in a Noilly Prat Cream Sauce.

One outstanding feature of Hintlesham Hall is its wine list, which is easily one of the best of any hotel featured in this guide. Stretching to over twenty closely typed pages, several hundred vintages are available. Virtually all come from Italy, France or Germany, and prices range from a very respectable house white – a light, dry Quincy – at around £13 a bottle, right up to a number of bottles in excess of £250. There are some classic red Bordeaux included, offering most vintages right back to 1955, at very reasonable prices.

Nearby attractions include a wide range of walks and strolls within the hotel grounds, and facilities for tennis, fishing, horse riding and golf. In addition, you can visit Flatford Mill, best known for its association with the painter Constable, the regional capital Norwich with its ancient cathedral and castle, the town of Colchester with its nearby oyster farms, and the university colleges of Cambridge.

55

MAISON TALBOOTH AND TALBOOTH RESTAURANT

Address Stratford Road, Dedham, Colchester, Essex
CO7 6HN
Tel: 0206 322367 Fax: 0206 322 752

Nearest town Colchester.
Directions From London on the A12, travel towards
Ipswich, seven miles past Colchester take the road
to Dedham and Stratford St Mary. Follow this road
for one mile. Take right turn to Dedham. Continue
for half a mile. Maison Talbooth is on the right hand
side.
Founder member of **Pride of Britain**.
Awards AA *** (red); RAC *** (Blue Ribbon);
Michelin three Red Turrets, (Restaurant) Three Red
Knives and Forks; Egon Ronay recommended 1989.
Open all year round.

Price for dinner with wine, bed and breakfast for
two – over £150.
Credit cards Access, Visa, Amex, Diners.
There are ground-floor rooms suitable for disabled visitors;
children are welcome, but not dogs, although kennelling
can be arranged nearby.
Overall mark out of ten 8½

Maison Talbooth is a charming, spacious Victorian Country
House Hotel with a warm and friendly atmosphere. Its location
provides spectacular views of the Vale of Dedham, frequently
painted by John Constable. Set on the tranquil banks of the
River Stour, Le Talbooth Restaurant was originally a Tudor
weaver's house and later became a toll booth both for horse-
drawn and river traffic.

All of the suites at the hotel have English poets' names and
are distinctively and individually decorated. The principal suites
may include special features such as circular sunken or jacuzzi
baths. Decor is traditional and tastefully executed.

The Maison offers breakfast in bed, and light snacks throughout the day. However, the main restaurant is situated about
half-a-mile away. Transport is available to Le Talbooth Restaurant which is known internationally for its high standards of
cuisine and service.

Gerald Milsom first spotted the Talbooth in 1952 when passing
by on his way to Harwich. He fell in love with the building
which at that time was a simple English tea shop. On assuming
ownership he changed it into a restaurant, and his takings in
the first month were £100. After many years of hard work, he
built up the Talbooth's reputation to the standard for which it
is now justly renowned. His company has expanded to include
three further establishments within East Anglia, all of which Mr
Milsom runs with the help of his two sons, David and Paul.

Favourites from the à la carte menu include as a starter Gamba
Prawns flavoured with Thai herbs and White Port, all bound in
a light curried sauce and topped with Apple; followed by Baby
Fillets of Beef on a nest of Potatoes and Spinach topped with a
duo of sauces; and completed with a dessert Brandy Snap Basket

filled with a trio of sorbets and fresh seasonal fruits on a mirror of Mango Coulis. The traditional wine list is extensive and complements the cuisine perfectly, although prices are high.

Being only one and a half hours from London, Maison Talbooth is a good choice for a restful stay away from the hustle and bustle of the city. You can while away the hours on the croquet lawn or giant garden chess set. Alternatively, a number of sporting activities such as clay pigeon shooting can be arranged. Sight-seeing is a must, with an abundance of beautifully timbered Suffolk villages nearby. Dedham, it has to be said, is one of the most typically English villages in·the country, with its tea room, antique shops, craft centre and charming local church.

56

THE OLD RECTORY

Address Great Snoring, Fakenham, Norfolk NR21
OHP
Tel: 0328 820597 Fax: 0328 820048

Nearest town King's Lynn.
Directions From King's Lynn, it is twenty-two miles
on the A148 to Fakenham. Follow signpost to village
of Great Snoring and The Old Rectory is behind the
church on the Barsham Road.
Awards British Tourist Authority Caesar Award
1990; recommended by Michelin and Egon Ronay.
Open throughout the year except 25 and 26
December.
Special breaks available from November until
March inclusive.
Price for dinner, with wine, bed and breakfast for
two – £100–£150.
Credit cards Amex and Diners.
*Not suitable for disabled guests; children not encouraged
and dogs not allowed.*
Overall mark out of ten 7

The name Great Snoring cannot fail to conjure up in your mind all sorts of romantic images of a secluded little English village. It is a tiny place, and your impressions of the area will be confirmed as you first drive through the village's attractive Norfolk setting; indeed, one of the best features about the Old Rectory hotel is its wonderful location for exploring the beautiful countryside all around you.

Today the hotel is rather more than the average country parsonage you would expect to find in this part of the world. It is a former manor house noted for its fine architecture dating back to Tudor times. The early history of the house is lost, but it is thought to date back to around 1500 when it was the family seat of Sir Ralph Shelton. At that time the building was hexagonal – a rather difficult shape to imagine when you look at the present, rather solid, rectangular block. During the Victorian era the house underwent considerable alterations and over-enthusiastic restoration work which completely altered the design of the building.

You can still see traces of the marvellous Tudor workmanship around the outside of the house. On the south-east façade, for example, the stone mullioned windows are bordered with frieze designs in terracotta tiling. Alternate male and female heads are depicted, and it can only be assumed that these represent the original Shelton family who first lived here. The Shelton crest can also be seen on the large oak front door, facing the village church nearby.

Relaxed informality is assured at the Old Rectory, and the combination of this and the peaceful surroundings makes this hotel an ideal option if you're after a complete 'away-from-it-all' break. There are fresh flowers in all the public rooms, and generally in the bedrooms as well. During the summer, these mostly come from the hotel's grounds. There is a one-and-a-half-acre garden for guests to enjoy.

The pleasingly informal atmosphere is made possible by the size of the hotel: it is small, with just seven bedrooms and only a couple of airy public rooms. All seven bedrooms have their own private bathroom facilities, colour television, direct-dial telephone, and are individually decorated to ensure that one stands out from another. The overall result at the Old Rectory is the feeling that you are staying more as a family visitor than a paying guest.

Probably the nicest feature about the hotel is its dining room. This is a bright, adaptable room with authentic old oak beams and stone mullioned windows. It is not a restaurant as such, and accordingly is not open to non-residents, but it specializes in serving good English-style food to residents.

Dinner is served between 7 p.m. and 8 p.m. with a choice of appetizers: the home-made soup is the most popular. There is also a choice of dessert and a good selection of cheeses. The menu range is quite simple, and although the food is delicious and presentation impressive, the choice is rather unimaginative.

Local game and fish may feature on the selection of main dishes: the Sole served in a White Wine Sauce, garnished with Grapes, is superb, and other specialities include a rich Escalope of Pork, steeped in a Cider and Cream Sauce; also Stroganoff of locally shot Pheasant. A small wine list of around a couple of dozen bins is available.

Nearby attractions include the towns of Norwich, King's Lynn, Ipswich and Colchester, together with the popular summer holiday resort of Great Yarmouth.

57

SALISBURY HOUSE

Address Victoria Road, Diss, Norfolk IP22 3JG
Tel: 0379 644738

Nearest town Diss.
Directions Approaching Diss on the A143 from
Bury St Edmunds, turn left on to the A1066 to
Thetford. Salisbury House is on the left after the
railway bridge.
Awards Listed in the *Good Food Guide*, Michelin and
Egon Ronay guides.
Open every day except Sunday and Monday,
throughout the year. Closed for one week at
Christmas and two weeks in summer. No special
breaks available.
Price for dinner, with wine, bed and breakfast for
two – £100–£150.
Credit cards Visa and Access.
The hotel is not suitable for disabled visitors. Although it

*is not ideal for children, they can be accommodated. Dogs
are not allowed in the house.*
Overall mark out of ten 7

Although Salisbury House certainly manages to create the ambience of a relaxed and friendly country home, it differs from the majority of establishments in this guide in being primarily a restaurant, with just three rooms where a very select number of guests may stay overnight and then have breakfast the next day.

Barry and Sue Davies took over Salisbury House in 1987 after running Francine's Restaurant in Maldon for nine years. Barry Davies is the chef, although he will certainly not be too busy to come out and greet you upon your arrival and help you with your luggage.

The Cane Room and the Blue Room are on the first floor and, although perhaps not quite deserving of their rather grand titles, are generously and thoughtfully furnished. Many extra touches in the rooms such as ice for your pre-dinner drink, fruit, flowers and bath-robes add to guests' pleasure. The Blue Room has a half-tester bed and a private bathroom just across the landing. The larger Cane Room has a wonderfully high Victorian bedstead and an en suite bathroom with that ultimate bathtime toy, a whirlpool bath. The third room is behind the main house by the conservatory.

Downstairs two intimate sitting rooms and two airy dining rooms are freshly decorated to give a period feel in keeping with the house's early Victorian style. Built in 1817 around the core of a much older mill house, Salisbury House combines well-proportioned rooms with the quaintness of the occasional exposed beam.

Delicious cooking is the true *raison d'être* of Salisbury House, and one's expectations are marvellously gratified. The à la carte menu offers an attractive mix of contemporary French and British cuisine, with around eight first courses, a couple of middle courses and eight or so entrées. Non-fish-eating vegetarians and people with special dietary needs would do well to let Mr Davies know of this beforehand, but otherwise the choice is excellent. One might begin, perhaps, with Watercress Pancakes stuffed with Crabmeat, or Pheasant Terrine studded with Pistachio Nuts, followed by an exquisite sorbet or creamy scallops. Main courses are irresistibly set off with perfect sauces and the freshest vegetables. The emphasis throughout is on the very best raw ingredients prepared with an ideal degree of care – elegant but never fussy. Add to this a very good list of over 150 predominantly French wines, spanning a suitably broad price range (house wine is £7) and you have the makings of a memorable meal.

As well as changing their à la carte menu every month, the Davieses also arrange special events and seasonal dinners which are often extremely good value: game in season, wine-tasting suppers, meals where each course is the favourite creation of a renowned chef. In summer breakfast, lunch and even dinner can be served in the pretty conservatory which looks out over the orchard. In all, the gardens cover an acre of land and are pleasantly laid out to give a sense of seclusion and variety. There's a lawn which can be used for boules, and an intriguing red obelisk.

Nearby attractions include Snape Maltings and Aldeburgh, both deservedly famous for their musical events, the charming seaside town of Southwold and, inland, Stowmarket, Bury St Edmunds and Norwich. Diss itself, dating back to Saxon times, is built around a six-acre lake and was described by Betjeman as 'the perfect English market town'.

58

SECKFORD HALL

Address Woodbridge, Suffolk IP13 6NU
Tel: 0394 385678 Fax: 0394 380610

Nearest town Ipswich.
Directions From Ipswich, follow the main A12
north-east – the road is signposted so you can
avoid the centre of town. Seckford Hall is
signposted west of the Woodbridge bypass.
Awards AA *** RAC graded.
Open throughout the year, except Christmas Day.
Special breaks Weekend breaks available all year,
as are half-board mini-holidays for two, three or four
nights.
Price for dinner, with wine, bed and breakfast, for
two – £100–£150.
Credit cards All major cards accepted.
*The hotel is suitable for the disabled; children are welcome,
as are 'well behaved' dogs which must remain on a lead
unless in owner's bedroom.*
Overall mark out of ten 9½

For over five centuries, Seckford Hall was a private home, and for a couple of hundred years the ancestral home of the Seckford family. Its relatively recent transformation into one of the finest Country House Hotels in East Anglia has ensured that very little of its pedigree history, and all that goes with it in terms of fittings and atmosphere, has been lost.

Little documentary evidence has survived about the house's early years, although it is known that it was built for one Thomas Seckford. It is uncertain precisely when the imposing, ivy-covered Tudor house was finished, although it was definitely sometime between 1541 and 1550. Evidence remains of an even older timber-built house which stood on the present site before then, and this marvellous reminder of medieval English architecture has been built into bedroom number seven, with the authentic Tudor Bar beneath it.

The greatest in a long line of Seckfords was the first Thomas Seckford, who served as Master in Ordinary of the Court of Requests to Her Majesty Queen Elizabeth I. In 1574 he was responsible for commissioning the first detailed set of maps of all the English counties. The finished atlas appeared in 1579 and quickly became the definitive English atlas for generations. It was widely believed that Elizabeth I once held Court at Seckford Hall, although, sadly, written evidence has neither proven nor disproven this popular local belief.

Today Seckford Hall retains many contemporary furnishings and has lost very little of the Tudor splendour that Elizabeth I is likely to have known if she ever did visit the house. Virtually all the gracious public rooms and luxuriously furnished bedrooms have oak-beamed ceilings – and one instinctively knows these are part of the original make-up of the house rather than purely decorative. The house was completely refitted after the Second World War, by which time it had been allowed to slowly deteriorate from its original glory.

Then, as now, the focal point of the whole building is the Great Hall, a marvellous old room surrounded by intricately carved and lovingly restored wood panelling. The old fireplace is not elaborate, but its depth and contrasting white surround are obvious reminders of former days when a huge log-burning fire in this room was the principal source of heating for the entire building. Elegant gold and purple suites have taken the place of the more barren Tudor furnishings which the first Seckfords would have known, and make this most attractive room the finest in the house.

Wherever you go in Seckford Hall you are surrounded by a sense of age and history. Suits of armour stand guard at the end of corridors; sweeping Tudor-style drapes hang in public rooms; and the original stonework has been preserved throughout the interior as far as possible. The furnishings are almost entirely period pieces, some inherited from Windsor Castle. The very chair in which King Edward VII died, on 6 May 1910, is here, although it has been re-upholstered since then.

Apart from the Great Hall, this sense of history is nowhere more strong than in the recently extended restaurant which can seat up to seventy. The hotel strives to maintain an atmosphere of quiet dignity, which it does with considerable success, and the very detailed à la carte menu is as absorbing as it is mouthwatering just to read. About sixteen starters are available, including such gems as Smoked Haddock Chowder, and Giant Prawns peeled and tossed in hot garlic butter.

The house speciality is lobster, which can be prepared in Thermidor, Broiled, or Salad style. A large lobster tank is kept stocked throughout the year, with surprisingly few seasonal price variations. Other specialities are Norfolk Duckling, Orford Smoked Salmon, and a good range of local game from estates throughout Suffolk.

Recently, ten 'cottage style' suites have been constructed from the old granary, farmhouse, dairy and coach house, taking the number of bedrooms to thirty-four. All are individually furnished and all have the highest standard of modern comforts: large private bathrooms, remote-control colour Teletext televisions, and tea- and coffee-making facilities. Five rooms have antique four-posters, one of which dates back to 1587, the year when Elizabeth I agreed to the execution of Mary, Queen of Scots, at the not too distant Fotheringay Castle.

A heated swimming pool, with spa bath, gymnasium and solarium were opened in 1989, together with a Buttery restaurant. Golf, horse riding, trout fishing, sailing and yacht charter can all be easily arranged locally. Other nearby attractions include beauty spots at Flatford Mill, Dedham and painter John Constable's familiar countryside around Kersey and Lavenham. Around the Suffolk coast you can visit Aldeburgh, Snape with its large concert hall, and Minsmere bird sanctuary; and the ports of Felixstowe and Lowestoft are gateways to mainland Europe.

59

WHITEHALL

Address Church End, Broxted, Essex CM6 2BZ
Tel: 0279 850603 Fax: 0279 850385

Nearest town Bishop's Stortford.
Directions Leave the M11 at junction 8 and follow
the B1051 towards the village of Broxted. The hotel
is at the 'church end' of the village.
A member of the **Pride of Britain** consortium.
Awards AA rosette; Egon Ronay and Michelin
guide recommended.
Open throughout the year.
Special **winter breaks** are available from November
until March.
Price for dinner, with wine, bed and breakfast for
two – over £150.
Credit cards Access, Visa and Amex.
*The hotel is suitable for the disabled; children under five
and dogs are not allowed.*
Overall mark out of ten 8

Sitting on a hillside overlooking the beautiful countryside of north-west Essex, Whitehall is one of the oldest properties in this part of England which is still occupied. The village of Broxted is recorded in the Domesday Book, and the earliest known reference to the present manor was in 1151 when Alured de Bendaville is known to have given it to the hospital of St John of Jerusalem. The gift was endorsed by King John early in the thirteenth century, confirming that the Order could establish a preceptory in Essex.

By 1541, the manor house was granted by Henry VIII to George Harper, a shadowy historical figure about whom very little is known. Within two years, Harper had conveyed the house to Sir Thomas Audley, then Lord Chancellor of England, and after a number of owners it was eventually occupied by the famous Edwardian hostess the Countess of Warwick around the turn of the century. Current proprietors Gerry and Marie Keane have run Whitehall as a hotel since Spring 1985.

The hotel today has retained an 'old' feel about it. Little has changed structurally in the last few centuries, and it would not be unkind to suggest that parts of the building have been adapted less well than others to the demands of a luxury hotel. The old window frames, for example, have been in place for generations, in some cases for centuries – and do look a little odd with straight new curtain rails concealing their crooked shape. The main public area is the warm reception hall, complete with roaring log fire and delightfully informal atmosphere.

The restaurant is a converted ale house, and has an authentic beamed ceiling (where no two beams are exactly the same shape, size or colour), enormous brick fireplace with exposed chimney and good views across the garden. Like the rest of the hotel, the restaurant is decorated in soft pastel colours. Advance booking is recommended for non-residents, but seldom more than a couple of days is necessary unless you plan to visit on a Saturday evening or public holiday. Food is served in traditional English Country House style, although distinct continental influences can be detected. An impressive three-course table d'hôte menu (plus coffee and *petits fours*) is offered each evening at around £30 per head inclusive of VAT and service. Alternatively, a six-course 'Menu Surprise' is available, and this is made up of light and delicate foods which are sure to create a meal of subtle flavours and imaginative presentation.

There are usually at least half a dozen choices available for each course on the main menu, and you may care to open your meal with a popular starter like Home-Cured Salmon, or else experiment with something a little different such as a Mélange of Calves Liver and Mange Tout, served on a bed of French Leaves in a Raspberry and Walnut Oil Dressing.

Main courses are less adventurous and have two characteristics: good-quality raw ingredients and subtle sauces. Two favourite dishes are Salmon Mille Feuille with Saffron Sauce, and Noisette of Lamb in a Sorrel Sauce. To finish off, you can choose from an extensive cheese board or range of sweets which includes Meringue Cones filled with Honey Ice-Cream on a Chocolate Sauce. Whatever your choice, an extensive wine list is available, with a number of good clarets, to complement your meal.

Whitehall has twenty-six bedrooms, each with a definite character of its own, and decorated in soft pastel shades. On the whole, the rooms are furnished in a modern style, although original fireplaces (not in use) and dark wood panelling have been retained wherever possible. Each one has private bathroom facilities, colour television, direct-dial telephone and additional accessories like a hair dryer and trouser press to make your stay here as trouble-free as possible.

Among the leisure facilities at Whitehall which residents can enjoy are a tennis court, a heated outdoor swimming pool and a large walled garden. Nearby attractions include the natural beauty of Constable country, in Dedham Vale to the east; the historic city of Cambridge; the quaint villages of Thaxted and Finchingfield; and the popular old market town of Saffron Walden.

The Midlands

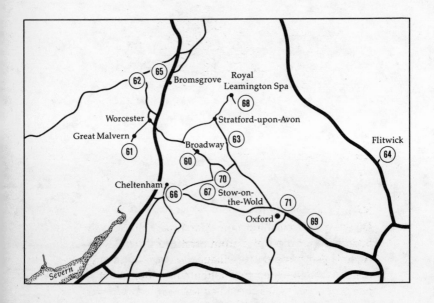

The Midlands

60 Buckland Manor
61 Cottage in the Wood
62 The Elms
63 Ettington Park
64 Flitwick Manor
65 Grafton Manor

66 The Greenway
67 Lords of the Manor
68 Mallory Court
69 Le Manoir aux quat' Saisons
70 The Manor
71 Studley Priory

BUCKLAND MANOR

Address Buckland, near Broadway, Gloucestershire
WR12 7LY
Tel: 0386 852626

Nearest town Broadway
Directions From Moreton-in-Marsh take the A44 to
Broadway, or the B4632 from Stratford-upon-
Avon, head through the village and turn left along
the B4632 signposted to Cheltenham. After about
one and a half miles there is a turn-off to Buckland
signposted on the left-hand side of the road.
Awards AA *** (red) graded and rosette; Best New
Hotel in Britain Award in the 1984 AA Motel and
Restaurant Guide; Michelin red M award; British
Tourist Authority highly commended; highest
rating of any Cotswolds hotel in the 1990 Egon
Ronay guide, a distinction the hotel has had since
1983; 1986 Top English Hotel Award from Andrew
Harper's Hideaway Report.
Open Early February until mid-January.
Price for dinner, with wine, bed and breakfast for
two – over £150.
Credit cards Access and Visa.

*The hotel is suitable for the disabled; children under twelve
are not permitted in the hotel, nor children under eight
in the restaurant; dogs are not allowed.*
Overall mark out of ten 8½

Tucked away in the heart of the Cotswolds, Buckland Manor
assures you a warm and homely welcome. Settled in several
acres of ornamental garden, this small Country House Hotel is
ideally located for touring central England, with Shakespeare's
Stratford-upon-Avon just seventeen miles in one direction and
attractive Regency Cheltenham fourteen miles in the other direction. Its superb setting and de luxe standards make it easy to
understand why the hotel has won a string of major awards
since opening less than a decade ago.

Few Country House Hotels can trace their origins as far back
as Buckland Manor. The first written record of a house on the
site of the present hotel stretches back almost one and a half
millennia to the seventh century AD, further even than the history of England as a united nation. In the Dark Ages the estate
of Buckland was given by Kynred, King of Mercia, to the Abbot
of Gloucester. The very fact that those distant origins are known
today helps explain the name Buckland: the title to the land,
unusually for the Dark Ages, was inscribed in a book and the
Old English 'bookland' was corrupted to form the name of the
village.

The estate remained in the ownership of the church until 1536
when, on the dissolution of the monasteries, the land passed
into the private hands of the Gresham family. Two famous sons
of this family rose to become Lord Mayors of London. Buckland
Estate was sold again in 1802, and has been owned by four
private families since then, prior to its purchase in 1981 by
Adrienne and Barry Berman who converted it into a luxury
Country House Hotel.

A principal aim at Buckland, according to the owners, is 'to
pamper and cosset each guest in the tranquillity of the Cotswolds' and certainly no one could accuse the staff of being
inattentive in the care of their guests. Elegant public rooms
are sumptuously furnished with authentic antiques and deep-

cushioned sofas and armchairs. Throughout the hotel you will be struck by the old panelled walls, thick-beamed ceilings and narrow-paned windows – and nowhere more so than in the superior ground-floor dining room.

The style of cooking at Buckland Manor is an interesting combination of traditional English Country House and the best of French cuisine. An impressive à la carte menu is available each evening and, since few places are generally available for non-residents, advance booking is strongly recommended. Huîtres Tièdes au Gratin de Zérès comprise a favourite starter, while following a sorbet course, a choice of eight main dishes, each equally highly recommended, confronts guests. The Pan-fried Loin of Dutch Veal served sliced with a Lemon and Orange Sauce flavoured with Cointreau is highly regarded.

Buckland Manor has eleven bedrooms, including a large family suite of two adjoining twin-bedded rooms – which is a rather interesting feature considering this hotel takes the Victorian view that children under the age of twelve are not allowed (and how many parents want their secondary school-stage offspring sharing their room?). Two rooms are really four-poster suite-size doubles and all rooms have their own bathroom facilities, with bathwater drawn straight from the manor's own spring water, just as it has been for centuries. Each bathroom has been recently upgraded to a high standard. All bedrooms are individually furnished and it has not been difficult to create a distinct identity for each, considering the hotel is relatively small.

In terms of leisure facilities, Buckland Manor has an outside heated swimming pool, putting green, croquet lawn, tennis court, ornamental gardens, facilities nearby for riding and golf, and acre upon acre of naturally beautiful gardens and paddocks. A thirteenth-century church is next door to the hotel, with a wonderfully ornate ceiling, and other nearby attractions include the towns of Stratford-upon-Avon (with all its numerous places of interest associated with William Shakespeare), Worcester with its famous porcelain works, and countless Cotswold villages with their timeless charm.

61

COTTAGE IN THE WOOD

Address Holywell Road, Malvern Wells,
Worcestershire WR14 4LG
Tel: 0684 573487 Fax: 0684 560662

Nearest town Great Malvern.
Directions Leave the M50 at junction 1 and follow
signs to Malvern. After going through Upton-on-
Severn follow signs to Malvern Wells which will
bring you to a T-junction with the A449. Turn right
and then first (sharp) left, past the Jet (Honda)
petrol station.
A member of the **Consort Consortium** of top hotels.
Awards AA *** graded; English Tourist Board four
Crowns; Egon Ronay recommended.
Open throughout the year except for the first full
week of January.
Special breaks are available throughout the year.
Price for dinner, with wine, bed and breakfast for
two – £100–£150.
Credit cards Access and Visa.

Children are welcome but dogs are only permitted in the Coach House and Beech Cottage.
Overall mark out of ten 7½

The first part of the name 'Cottage in the Wood' is a bit of a misnomer as you'll find a modern-day hotel rather more than a tiny Cotswolds cottage, but it certainly does nestle in acres of secluded forest. The hotel is, in fact, a charming Georgian dower house set in seven acres of private woodland, and guests have the option of accommodation in one of three hotel buildings: the main house has eight bedrooms, the Coach House (about 100 yards from the main hotel building) another eight, and Beech Cottage another four, about seventy-five yards from the hotel proper.

The hotel was first built and owned by a minor Georgian noble, Duke Gondolphi, and converted into a hotel shortly after the end of the Second World War. In the decades which followed, demand to stay at this tranquil haven increased, and Beech Cottage and the Coach House were also converted into comfortable accommodation.

Wherever you choose to stay at the Cottage, in the main house with its lovely views across thirty miles of Severn Valley, the charming Beech Cottage, or the old Coach House with its smaller but no less intimate rooms, you can be assured of very high standards of comfort. All rooms have private bathroom facilities, colour television, clock radio, tea- and coffee-making facilities, telephone, and are furnished in a very individual style which clearly distinguishes one from another. A recent programme of refurbishment and redecoration has transformed the bedrooms. Four-posters are now present in most rooms. Beech Cottage and Coach House guests have the option of taking breakfast in the main hotel dining room or in their room. The Cottage in the Wood has one main public lounge, a simple but comfortably furnished room in Georgian style. There are no beamed ceilings or antique tables, which is a little disappointing, but you can be assured of a very high standard of personal care and attention from resident proprietors John and Sue Pattin.

The dining room can seat up to fifty at any one time; dinner is served from 7 p.m. until 8.30 p.m. (last orders). Lantern-style lights create a gently intimate atmosphere and reflect off the Indian prints all around the dining room walls in a rather intriguing fashion. Chef Kathy Young has developed a good reputation for producing English Country House-style cuisine of a very high quality, and you are unlikely to be disappointed by either her à la carte or table d'hôte selections.

Local produce is used as much as possible to create her speciality dishes, and fresh line-caught salmon is a favourite base for starters and main courses alike. One of the best dishes is Medallions de Bœuf Lyonnais, although Quail with Cherries provides an equally delicious alternative. Soup and fish courses are offered and the chef will be delighted to cater for vegetarian and special diets if requested in advance. Among the mouthwatering range of home-made desserts, Caribbean Ginger Mousse and Kumquat Dessert stand out in particular.

The table d'hôte lunch-only menu is reasonable, and good value. Main course options include Fillet of Rainbow Trout steamed with Mussel Seasoning and Pink Peppercorns, and Lymeswold Stuffed Chicken Breast, dusted with breadcrumbs. Two dishes do stand out from a typical evening's à la carte menu, however, and of the two menus this one can be recommended more enthusiastically: Breast of Guinea Fowl in Dill and Mushroom in a fine pastry and dressed with a rich Watercress Cream is delicious, but still cannot beat the chef's Boned Quail Pot Roast with Chicory and Walnuts, served with a fresh truffle.

The hotel has no leisure facilities of its own available, although the location is a walker's paradise and nearby attractions are numerous. Guests can also make use of corporate membership of the local squash and snooker clubs. The Wye Valley and Wales are accessible by a short drive, as are the three cathedral cities of Worcester, Hereford and Gloucester and the old town of Tewkesbury with its ancient abbey. The obvious scenic attractions of the Cotswolds are all around you, and an interesting day trip can be made to the Worcester porcelain factory about nine miles away to see how this amazing chinaware is made.

62

THE ELMS

Address Abberley, near Worcester, Worcestershire
WR6 6AT
Tel: 0299 896 666 Fax: 0299 896 804

Nearest town Worcester.
Directions From the M5, turn off at junction 5 from
the north, or junction 7 from the south towards
Worcester. Drive through the city and pick up the
A443, signposted to Tenbury Wells. The Elms is
on the right, twelve miles from Worcester and two
miles after passing through Great Witley.
A member of **Queens Moat Houses plc**.
Awards AA ***; RAC *** graded and Blue Ribbon;
British Tourist Authority commended; Egon Ronay
recommended; Michelin 1990.
Open throughout the year.
Special breaks Weekend breaks available all year;
special Christmas programme.
Price for dinner, with wine, bed and breakfast for
two – over £150.
Credit cards Access, Visa, Amex and Diners.

Children are welcome but dogs are not allowed – kennels located nearby and can accommodate dogs by prior arrangement.

Overall mark out of ten 8

The Elms Hotel is undoubtedly one of the architectural treasures of Worcestershire, and for years has had the distinction of being the first hotel listed in the AA handbook. A solid old baronial country seat, the house is one of the few outstanding architectural creations from the reign of Queen Anne. The Elms was completed in 1710 and designed by architect Gilbert White, a pupil of Sir Christopher Wren who built St Paul's Cathedral in London. White was also responsible for the imposing design of the Guildhall in Worcester and many of its features are reflected in those of this hotel: the main pediment and, particularly, the amazing moulded cornices in the rooms of both buildings are alike.

The Elms has always been known by that name. Records show that the sweeping carriageway was lined with elm trees for generations. Presumably they were planted here when the house was built, but they have long since gone and today the driveway from the main road up to the front of the house is flanked with lime trees. In 1840 the Country House became part of Abberley Hall Estate and was, for a while, the home of Admiral Malin. In the late 1920s new owners built two new wings on to the hotel, but on the first night of occupancy, after they were completed, a devastating fire completely gutted the house, leaving only the bare shell standing. The then owner, Sir Richard Brooke, had the house completely rebuilt as before – except that a flat roof was added – and he continued to live at the Elms until 1946, when it was finally turned into a luxury hotel.

All the public rooms are bright, spacious and comfortable, largely furnished with antiques and offering majestic views across the surrounding countryside. The library bar is particularly distinctive and, like most of the large rooms, still retains its original fireplace and the huge mahogany bookcases, despite the fire in 1927. Fresh flowers are a nice touch in all the public rooms and most of the twenty-five bedrooms.

There are nine bedrooms in the adjoining Coach House, and all are furnished to very high standards of comfort with colour television, private bathroom facilities and direct-dial telephone as standard. There is a four-poster bedroom available. All of the Elms's bedrooms have recently been individually decorated by Jenny Harry of Mary Home Interiors of Bath.

The hotel has a particularly attractive dining room, furnished in rich Regency style. Tables are a good distance apart and the sensible limit of sixty persons dining at one time (well below the realistic capacity of this lovely room) means that guests have space to sit back and enjoy a thoroughly relaxing dinner without any feeling of being 'hemmed in' which is so often a complaint even in the best restaurants and hotels. A dark wood antique fireplace, with a mirror hung above, is an effective centrepiece to the whole room.

In keeping with the style throughout the rest of the hotel, the style of food is traditional English. The Elms is fortunate in having a large herb garden, giving an interesting French aspect to many of the main dishes. There is an excellent à la carte menu available and, in common with the table d'hôte, this is changed daily. One highlight is their Whole Young Chicken grilled and served on a bed of Leeks with a Lime and Vermouth Sauce. A good selection of British cheeses is available as an alternative to a choice from the sweet trolley.

A number of leisure facilities are available: croquet, tennis and putting within the hotel grounds, and both riding and golf can be easily arranged nearby. Other nearby attractions include the historic city of Worcester, with its famous cathedral, Royal Porcelain factory and Civil War centre; Elgar's birthplace and museum near Worcester; the Elizabethan moated manor house at Harvington Hall; Hartlebury Castle; and a number of National Trust properties including Croft Castle, Berrington Hall and Hanbury Hall.

63

ETTINGTON PARK

Address Alderminster, near Stratford-upon-Avon,
Warwickshire cv37 8bs
Tel: 0789 740740 Fax: 0789 87472

Nearest town Stratford-upon-Avon.
Directions Follow the A34 Stratford to Oxford road
and the hotel is five miles along this road.
Awards AA *** graded and rosette for food; *Good
Food Guide* Newcomer of the Year 1986.
Open throughout the year.
Special **weekend breaks** are available throughout
the year.
Price for dinner, with wine, bed and breakfast for
two – over £150 (approaching £300).
Credit cards Access, Visa, Amex and Diners.
*Children under seven are not permitted; dogs are not
allowed.*
Overall mark out of ten 10

Everything about Ettington Park Hotel typifies the highest international standards of comfort which the hotel has striven to

achieve since ISIS, the world-wide construction group, bought this outstanding property in 1983. From the quality of the complimentary toiletries right down to the depth of the polish on the intricate hand-carved wooden friezes above the fireplace in the reception lobby, there can be no question that Ettington Park is one of Britain's finest hotels.

Even the history of the Ettington estate has an impeccable pedigree and puts this hotel at the top of the luxury Country House Hotel market. Ettington Park is remarkable in that it is the only property in England still in the same ownership as at the time of the Domesday Book – and it is almost certain that the tenure of the Shirley family was established long before the Norman Conquest of England in 1066. Although the present house dates almost entirely from the nineteenth century, the Gothic-style architecture has clearly been influenced by the legacy of earlier manors on this site. In 1086 the original manor was held by a nobleman known as 'Saswalo' (or Sewallis), and it was his grandson, another Sewallis, who became 'de Shirley' from the village of Derbyshire where he already held lands.

A direct line of descent can be traced from the time of the Conquest to the present Shirley family, who live nearby and take a keen interest in the overall running of the hotel. Fourteen bas-reliefs around the exterior of the hotel record a number of more noteworthy members of the family who all knew the Ettington estate through the ages: Sir Thomas Shirley, a great crusader; Sir Ralph Shirley, who fought bravely alongside Henry V at the Battle of Harfleur; and Sir Robert Shirley, who fought nobly for his king, Charles I, and was imprisoned by Oliver Cromwell during the English Revolution. During the lifetime of William Shakespeare, who lived and worked at nearby Stratford-upon-Avon from 1564 to 1623, Sir Robert Shirley was acquainted with the Underhill family who leased the house for a while at the end of the sixteenth century.

Ettington Park Hotel today stands amid forty acres of grand estate, dominated by an enormous lawn whose rigid stripes are lovingly groomed, and it really is impossible not to be hugely impressed by your first sight of this Gothic house. With its narrow windows and pointed cornices you can understand why the author of at least one guidebook said: 'One could run out of superlatives to describe Ettington Park.'

The various public rooms are furnished in the most sumptuous fashion, and the main public lounge is breathtaking, simply because of its scale. Like in a grand Edwardian ballroom, long blue curtains form the perfect accompaniment to the rich white and gold ornate ceiling. Few other hotels could have a grand piano in their main lounge which looks so distinctly 'settled'. Look out for those finely carved wooden fireplaces, complete with inset family crests. Gently pass your hand over their intricate surface and feel the sense of history beneath your fingers. One of the highlights of the hotel is the beautifully panelled dining room with its 1740 rococo ceiling and glorious views out across the garden.

Executive chef Christopher Hudson has a strong team working with him, and has introduced one of the finest Country House menus in Britain. An à la carte menu is available, but many guests seem more than content with the four-course set table d'hôte menu (changed daily) around £28 per person. House specialities are a blend of the finest English and French cuisine and are really too numerous to mention; suffice to say that a favoured dish requested by a dinner guest will always be prepared by the chef and his brigade. Favourite specialities are the Fillet of Beef topped with a Tomato and Fresh Herb soufflé, and the Rack of Lamb cooked in the classical manner and carved at the table. Advance booking, particularly at weekends, is essential.

The hotel has a total of forty-eight individually furnished bedrooms, including nine suites, whose decor can only be described as luxury of the highest grade. Original antiques and fine oil paintings complement spacious private bathroom facilities, colour television and telephone, and provide the perfect setting for that special break.

An integral part of Ettington Park is the quite superb leisure complex, providing a variety of activities which can be as relaxing or as energetic as you choose. In addition to a large heated indoor swimming pool, you can relax in the sauna, whirlpool spa bath or solarium. Virtually all outdoor sports, from tennis to fresh-water fishing, can be arranged easily through the hotel reception.

Nearby attractions include Stratford-upon-Avon and all that has to offer: Shakespeare's birthplace, Anne Hathaway's cottage, the World of Shakespeare centre, and superb shopping facilities. Warwick Castle and the towns of Oxford and Banbury are within easy reach.

64

FLITWICK MANOR

Address Church Road, Flitwick, Bedfordshire MK45 1AE
Tel: 0525 712242 Fax: 0525 712242

Nearest town Flitwick.
Directions Leave the M1 at junction 12 (travelling from London) and continue along the A5120 for a few miles. The hotel is signposted shortly before you reach Flitwick itself.
Awards AA *** graded and rosette for food; RAC *** graded; British Tourist Authority commended; recommended by Egon Ronay and Michelin guides.
Open throughout the year, except Christmas.
Special breaks Very occasional weekend breaks are available.
Price for dinner, with wine, bed and breakfast for two – over £150.
Credit cards Access, Visa and Amex.
The hotel has a number of ground-floor rooms suitable for the disabled; children are welcome, but dogs are not allowed.

Lying approximately half-way between both Oxford and Cambridge and between the Green Sand Ridge and the Chiltern Hills, Flitwick Manor is a classic old English Country House Hotel. Since Saxon times there has been a settlement on the high ground where the hotel now stands: the Saxons created the village of 'Fleotwic' – which literally means 'dwelling on the river' – after the Romans left their original village near where the manor stands today.

A manor was known in Flitwick even before Norman times, but the present building dates mainly from the late seventeenth and early eighteenth century. Old records show that in 1674, the then owners, the Rhodes family, were required by law to pay Hearth Tax on ten fireplaces, including the one which you can still see in the hall today. Ann Fisher later inherited the house as part of a marriage settlement with George Hesse and, after his death in 1783, married one George Brooks whose family remained squires in this part of Bedfordshire until 1932.

Today the public rooms are decorated in an informal Regency style, outstanding amongst which is the Brooks Room, with its salmon-coloured napiary, mahogany furniture and a number of elegant family portraits. The garden room was adapted by Sir Albert Richardson RA in the 1930s and has a fascinating collection of sporting trophies for residents to admire should they ever tire of the lovely garden views from this room.

The main dining room has a fine reputation with residents and non-residents alike, and advance bookings are generally required by at least a week. An imaginative à la carte and a choice of three table d'hôte menus are available nightly with a strong emphasis on fish on all the menus throughout the year. 'Senders' have been recruited in fish markets throughout the UK to select only the finest ingredients for the Flitwick Manor kitchen.

Led by Head Chef Shaun Cook, a team of seven young chefs is responsible for the creative and original range of dishes available each evening. One of the table d'hôte menus is devoted to shellfish, the centrepiece of which might be a large selection of fresh shellfish including two varieties of Prawn, Venus Clams, Shrimps, Langoustines and one Oyster. Another menu is devoted to vegetarian dishes and includes a choice of starter and main course. Most of the à la carte specialities are asterisked, and the little note at the foot of the menu indicates that these dishes signify a 'new concept in low calorie eating'. Whether you are calorie counting or not, the range of dishes is outstanding, and the thoughtful preparation and presentation a real delight. Starters include native Helford Oysters, Dressed Crabmeat and a Salad of Smoked Duckling Breast served with Watercress and Exotic Fruits.

Main dish specialities include locally farmed Lamb, Breast of Chicken filled with a Mousse of Forest Mushrooms and Fresh Duck Breast which has been panfried with Peppered Pineapple. Fish dishes, though, are cooked to perfection and one of the favourite choices is a superior plate of shellfish which includes everything you could have as a starter, together with half a lobster. Lobster – served hot or cold from the hotel's own seawater tanks – is also available on its own. Whatever your inclination, a wine list with nearly 100 bottles includes most popular French choices, and also features a range of vintage ports sold by the bottle.

Flitwick Manor has fifteen bedrooms, including seven new luxury rooms which opened late in 1987. All fifteen are furnished in a relaxing period style with antique furnishings used wherever possible. In addition to en suite bathrooms with a generous selection of quality toiletries, each room has a veritable plethora of extra comforts, including a remote-control colour television, an 'honesty' tray, iced water, a bowl of fresh fruit, a selection of hardback books and games, and a direct-dial telephone. The two best rooms in the hotel are the Four-Poster Suite, with its antique bed and private sauna, and the Garden Suite which has a spa bath and sitting room.

Nearby attractions are numerous: the charming little Georgian village of Woburn, with its famous abbey, is just five miles away, and stately homes of note within a short drive include Luton Hoo and the two Rothschild bequests of Ascott and Waddesdon. Sulgrave Manor was the home for many years to George

Washington's ancestors, and you can come more up to date historically by visiting Althorp, the family seat of the Princess of Wales's father, Earl Spencer. Towns within easy reach include Oxford, Cambridge, Stratford-upon-Avon and Windsor.

65

GRAFTON MANOR

Address Grafton Lane, Bromsgrove, Worcestershire
B61 7HA
Tel: 0527 579007 Fax: 0527 575221

Nearest town Bromsgrove.
Directions The hotel is situated a mile and a half
from the centre of Bromsgrove, just off the B4091
twelve miles north of Worcester.
A member of the **Pride of Britain** consortium.
Awards AA rosette in *Good Food Guide*; Michelin red
M; Ashley Courtenay recommended.
Open throughout the year.
Price for dinner, with wine, bed and breakfast for
two – over £150.
Credit cards Access, Visa, Amex and Diners.
*The hotel is not suitable for the disabled; children under
the age of seven are not permitted and dogs are not allowed
unless kept in kennels outside the hotel bedrooms and
public areas.*
Overall mark out of ten 7½

Although the distinguished old Grafton Manor Hotel dates from
'just' 1567, it is built on the site of a much older manor house
which was for many years home to a cousin of William the

Conqueror. Today Grafton flourishes in more peaceful times, but remains surrounded by twenty-six acres of Worcestershire parkland and garden which haven't changed all that much over the last few centuries.

Few major events in English history have failed to touch the Grafton estate in some way. Sir Humphrey Stafford was lord of Grafton Manor during the reign of Henry VI, and his loyal friendship to his monarch cost him his life in a violent feud. The estate was inherited by his nephew, another Sir Humphrey, who fought bravely alongside the usurper Richard III at the Battle of Bosworth in 1485. Unlike his sovereign master, Sir Humphrey managed to escape with his life but was brutally executed as a traitor after dismissing a pardon from the new king, Henry VII, and launching a hopeless coup against his government.

The Talbot family inherited the estate after Stafford's disgrace, and probably the best-known member of the family was one John Talbot, who was a reluctant co-conspirator in Guy Fawkes's gunpowder plot to blow up parliament in 1605. He escaped with his life, only to die of natural causes five years later, but several decades earlier he had built a completely new Grafton Manor which forms the basic shell of the present hotel.

The manor was all but destroyed by fire in 1710, a very common fate for the great houses which have now become Country House Hotels throughout Great Britain, but the entrance hall and adjoining gable in the hotel give you an idea of the proportions of John Talbot's new home. Over the next forty years the manor was rebuilt to its original form, and some of the rooms were made even grander than those which were lost in the great fire. The main public room, for instance, is still known today as the Great Parlour and had an ornate ceiling and large family coat of arms added when it was rebuilt.

Grafton Manor remained the family seat of the Earls of Shrewsbury until 1934, when it was finally sold. The present proprietors have owned the estate since 1970, but it was a further decade before Grafton Manor opened its doors as a luxury hotel.

The dining room seats forty-five and has been furnished in traditional decor, complete with oil paintings and open log fire, which creates a warm atmosphere. The style of food is distinctly modern British, but has been carefully developed by the Morris family who own the hotel.

A four-course table d'hôte menu is offered each evening, although residents must make a specific point of reserving a dinner place as this is not done automatically. The menu opens with a soup and is followed by a choice from at least four or five starters – most restaurants open with a starter and follow with the lighter soup course before the main dish, but this slightly unconventional presentation makes little difference to the overall enjoyment of dinner at Grafton.

Squid Provençal is a commendable option to open with, and two in-house specialities from a typical menu are Supreme of Chicken poached in White Wine and served with a Ginger and Cardamom sauce, or the equally delicious Loin of Pork sautéed in butter and served with a Herb Ratatouille and a Madeira Sauce. A very positive plus is the option of a full vegetarian table d'hôte alternative menu, at the same price (around £27) as the standard menu, instead of the rather token vegetarian main course offered by so many restaurants.

Grafton Manor is one of the smallest Country House Hotels included in this guide. It has just nine bedrooms, all individually furnished to the highest standards of comfort, featuring an excellent combination of period furniture and the attractive option of an open fire, and private bathroom facilities, colour television and direct-dial telephone. A number of rooms have four-posters with a rather unusual velvet drape hanging from a central point above the bed. Pleasing little extras are the bowl of fruit and bottle of Malvern mineral water left in each bedroom.

Grafton Manor is close to the main motorway network, so nearby attractions are plentiful. Worcester and Birmingham can be reached within thirty minutes by car, and Stratford-upon-Avon, with its theatre and Shakespearean associations, is just under an hour's drive away. Additional attractions include the Avoncroft Museum of Buildings and the Brierly Crystal factory.

66

THE GREENWAY

Address Shurdington, Cheltenham,
Gloucestershire GL51 5UG
Tel: 0242 862352 Fax: 0424 862780

Nearest town Cheltenham.
Directions Leave Cheltenham on the A46 Stroud
road, pass through the small village of Shurdington,
and on leaving the village you will see the entrance
Lodge and gates on your left.
A member of the **Pride of Britain** consortium.
Awards AA *** (red) graded and rosette for food;
British Tourist Authority commended; Michelin
three red Turrets; Egon Ronay 79%; one of
Wedgwood's Top Fifty Hotels of the World;
English Tourist Board highly commended.
Open throughout the year, except for two weeks in
January.
Special **winter breaks** are available from 1
November until mid-March.
Price for dinner, with wine, bed and breakfast for
two – £100–£150.
Credit cards All major cards.

The hotel is suitable for the disabled; dogs and children under seven are not allowed.

Overall mark out of ten 8

Surrounded by three acres of ornamental garden, the Greenway enjoys the luxury of being hidden from the hustle and bustle of daily life and within view of the sweeping Cotswold hills. In darker centuries, the translation 'green way' meant drove or sheep road and the hotel takes its name from a pre-Roman path which led from the hotel to the hills. The path makes an interesting afternoon's stroll as it eventually leads to Long Barrow, an ancient burial site and the remains of a pre-Iron Age fort dating back 5000 years.

The land upon which the hotel now stands was originally known as the Little Shurdington Estate, and early records reveal that it belonged to the Lawrence family as early as 1521. The family itself can trace its roots back to the twelfth century, and the records show that one William Lawrence commenced construction work on his new manor house in 1584. The family originated in Lancashire, and it can be reasonably assumed that they were involved with the wool trade, using Gloucester docks, and hence their interest in the Cheltenham area.

By 1616 the Greenway was complete, and in that year it first appears in the Court Manorial Rolls for England. The Lawrence family sold the hotel in 1854, and it went through a succession of different owners before finally being opened as a Country House Hotel in 1947. Ever since then, the emphasis has been on personal, friendly and attentive care for all guests – without being obtrusive. (When the hotel is full, a maximum of thirty-four guests are looked after by a total staff of fifty-three.) This approach, combined with the Greenway's other considerable standards, has justly earned it an English Tourist Board rating as one of the top nineteen hotels in England.

All the Greenway's public rooms, including the bright reception area with its proud old grandmother clock, are airy and informal. The main drawing room has a charming period decor, matching the deep floral-patterned armchairs and fine antique

228

furniture in the room. The warmth and comfort of this room, and indeed the hotel as a whole, are unforgettably relaxing.

The hotel's dining room is actually an elegantly restored conservatory, seating up to fifty guests at once and offering fine views of the gardens and parkland all around. The restaurant is very popular with non-residents, and on average the proportion of residents and non-residents is about half and half. Advance booking, by at least a week and particularly at weekends, is essential.

The cooking is in the modern Country House style and a fixed-price table d'hôte menu is presented each evening by Head Chef Edward Stephens. First courses can be a choice of homemade soup – beetroot, or something similar – or a more substantial starter like Sausage of Smoked Salmon with Saffron and Fennel Farce with Salmon Caviar, or Salad of home-smoked Goose Breast with a Hazelnut and Leek Dressing.

Main dish options are reasonably varied and include venison, veal, beef, chicken and at least two fish dishes. Particularly to be recommended is the Roast Quail with Forest Mushrooms on a Brioche Croûte and a rich Port jus; or the Roast Fillet of Cotswold Lamb with Noodles and a piquant jus infused with black olives. The sweet menu is extensive, and not for those even beginning to contemplate a diet! A popular speciality of the Greenway is their Hot Walnut Soufflé.

The Greenway has eighteen bedrooms, of which sixteen are either double or twin-bedded and all with private bathroom facilities, remote-control colour television, direct-dial telephone and, above all, outstanding views of the surrounding garden and countryside. Each one is individually furnished and styled, and a number still have an authentic supporting beam under the ceiling as a gentle reminder of the age of the hotel.

A number of special leisure facilities are available to residents at the Greenway; in addition to three acres of lovely garden, there is a croquet lawn and no fewer than four eighteen-hole golf courses within a four-mile radius of the hotel. In addition, tennis, squash and horse riding can all be easily arranged. For something really special, you will have difficulty resisting the appeal of a tour of the Cotswolds in an eight-seater 1934 Rolls

Royce. Picnic lunches are served from a traditional hamper strapped to the back of the car and, honestly, if the weather is kind then there are few more idyllic ways of getting a real glimpse of life as it was a couple of generations ago for those fortunate enough to live in a house like the Greenway throughout the year.

67

LORDS OF THE MANOR

Address Upper Slaughter, Bourton-on-the-Water,
Cheltenham, Gloucestershire GL54 2JD
Tel: 0451 20243 Fax: 0451 20696

Nearest town Cheltenham
Direction The hotel is in the village of Upper
Slaughter, some fifteen miles east of Cheltenham;
it is two miles west of the Fosse Way (A429)
between Stow-on-the-Wold and Bourton-on-the
Water.
Awards AA *** RAC graded; British Tourist
Authority commended; Egon Ronay recommended.
Open throughout the year.
Special breaks are available from the start of
October until the end of April.
Price for dinner, with wine, bed and breakfast for
two – over £150.
Credit cards Access, Visa, Amex and Diners
The hotel is suitable for the disabled; children are welcome,
and dogs are permitted in the bedrooms only.
Overall mark out of ten 8½

A couple of miles on from Bourton-on-the-Water, unquestionably one of rural England's most attractive villages, the colourfully named Lords of the Manor hotel is a converted country rectory that has lost little of its rustic appeal. The building dates from the seventeenth century, although major structural additions were made in the eighteenth and nineteenth centuries. It is a yellowing, elongated stone house and lies below a small hill invariably planted with wheat during the main arable season.

For two centuries the house was home to the Witts family who were parish rectors for four generations between 1763 and 1913, and were designated Lords of the Manor (hence the hotel's name) from 1852. Business entrepreneur James Gulliver purchased the hotel in 1985. Years of work and £2.5 million later, Lords of the Manor was established in the top league of British Country House Hotels.

When you first approach the Manor – as it is more usually called – you are likely to be pleasantly surprised by its setting. It quite dominates the little village of Upper Slaughter and is surrounded by creaking old boughs, leafy country lanes and long meadows – real Laurie Lee stuff! Well-tended gardens enhance the exterior of the Manor and make a delightful splash of colour throughout the busy summer season. A small lake has formed within the hotel grounds, through which the River Eye runs, and trout fishing on this particular stretch is a popular attraction.

Upper Slaughter itself makes an interesting stroll, though the rather sinister name is derived from nothing more harmful than the old Anglo-Saxon word 'sloh' meaning 'a marshy place'. It has a church dating from Norman times, and half a mile upstream on the River Eye (a tributary of the River Thames) Milton is reputed to have written his great classic *Paradise Lost*. Virtually no new building has taken place anywhere near the Manor since the turn of the century, and with no through traffic allowed, the area is a very peaceful haven from the bustle of everyday city life.

The various public rooms are large and comfortably furnished, with a welcoming period 'feel', as a result of the recent major alterations. The old dining room, created from the merger of a number of smaller rooms, has been converted into a small intimate lounge, a new library and a ground-floor bedroom for disabled guests. The old barn and granary have been sympathetically converted to provide extra bedrooms, while a conservatory-style meeting room caters for business and social functions.

An extensive à la carte menu is available each evening, and Head Chef Richard Mundy offers a style of food best described as modern English with more than a hint of continental influence. The atmosphere in the dining room is informal and unhurried, and the menu contains a number of interesting surprises. A very rich hors d'oeuvre is the chef's crisp French Salad dressed in a Honey Vinaigrette and accompanied with Oak Smoked Salmon and Venison. From a typical main course selection, two house specialities stand out: Breast of Cornvale Duck, gently cooked and enhanced with quite a strong Game Sauce – and a hint of Beaumes de Venise – and a less exotic Cornish Sea Bass, lightly cooked with Vermouth, Basil and finely sliced vegetables. The Lords boasts an outstanding selection of wines in its cellar.

Each of the twenty-nine bedrooms has its own character and is named after the numerous families with whom the Witts family have been connected through marriage over the last couple of centuries. In addition to private bathroom facilities, all have one or two pieces of antique furniture and more up-to-date luxuries like colour television and telephone.

Nearby attractions include the Duke of Marlborough's Blenheim Palace (birthplace of Sir Winston Churchill), the magnificent Warwick Castle, Sudeley Castle (once home of Katherine Parr, one of Henry VIII's six wives), Chastleton House, Broughton Castle and Berkeley Castle, where Edward II was murdered in 1327.

233

68

MALLORY COURT

Address Harbury Lane, Tachbrook Mallory,
Leamington Spa, Warwickshire CV33 9QB
Tel: 0926 330214 Fax: 0296 451714

Nearest town Leamington Spa.
Directions Drive two miles south out of Leamington
Spa, on the B4087. Take the left turning signposted
to Harbury and the hotel is about half a mile away
on the right-hand side.
A member of the **Relais et Châteaux** consortium.
Awards AA *** (red) graded and rosette for food;
Egon Ronay recommended; Michelin
recommended – and the only restaurant in the area
with a coveted rosette as well.
Open throughout the year.
Special **winter breaks** are available; rates on
application.
Price for dinner, with wine, bed and breakfast for
two – over £200.
Credit cards Access, Visa, Amex and Diners.

The hotel is unsuitable for disabled visitors; children under twelve and dogs are not allowed.
Overall mark out of ten 9½

Mallory Court is an outstanding example of early twentieth-century architecture and, despite being one of the youngest Country House Hotels featured in this guide, it nevertheless promises as warm and luxurious a welcome as any which has been standing for centuries. It embraces many features from earlier periods of building, such as its mellow stonework and leaded windows, and this combines with the space and comfort which are associated with properties belonging to this century.

The house was actually built between 1913 and 1915, and was for many years the family home of Sir John Black, who founded Standard Motors. It remained a family home up until 1977 when the present owners, Jeremy Mort and Allan Holland, bought it. Within a short space of time, the delicate task of upgrading it from a comfortable, but private, family home into a luxury hotel was completed.

Of all the outstanding rooms in the hotel, most agree the huge Pink Lounge is the *pièce de résistance*. The decor speaks for itself, and there really can be few public rooms in any hotel more attractive than this grand lounge. It makes no pretences to echo a particular period in history, but, like the rest of the house, offers a combination of the best of several periods, and the overall effect is most pleasing.

The front of the house was the first part to be refurbished and opened as a smart restaurant before the remainder of the hotel was ready to be opened to the public. Even today, the dining room holds pride of place at Mallory Court. It is a magnificent oak-panelled room, with seating for up to fifty people, and the sensibly arranged tables are not too close together, so offering a level of intimacy and informality which should be the envy of many larger establishments.

Shining silver and crystal glasses rest on pale lemon table-cloths, and the overall impression is one of great elegance. Demand by non-residents to dine here is considerable, so advance booking by at least a week really is essential.

Food is light and innovative, and served in a classical French style. Co-owner Allan Holland is a trained chef and personally supervises the kitchen most evenings. The influence of French-style *nouvelle cuisine* is considerable; sauces made from cream and stock rather than the usual butter and flour mix are only one example. The extensive table d'hôte menu is one of the most expensive featured in this guide (about £39 for three courses), but be in no doubt that the quality and presentation are outstanding, and after one meal at Mallory Court you will understand why the restaurant deserves the generous accolades it has received over the past fourteen years.

Just to give you an idea of the type of choice you can expect at Mallory Court, two of Allan Holland's exquisite starters are: a delicate Warm Mousseline of Lobster filled with White Crab Meat and surrounded with a light Lobster and Dill Sauce; and a Mould of Smoked Salmon enclosing a Smoked Trout Mousse served on a bed of Leeks with a Dill Sauce and garnished with Asparagus.

Main course choices are no less sumptuous. Two easily recommended delights are Breast of Guinea Fowl, roasted with Honey and served with a light Garlic and Cream Sauce flavoured with Brandy and Red Wine, and Thin Fillet of Veal, grilled and garnished with a Julienne of Fresh Ginger, Grapes and Lime Segments served with a Port Wine and Lime Sauce. If you still have room for a dessert, you are likely to have difficulty resisting one such as Hot Coconut Soufflé, flavoured with Malibu and accompanied with a Pineapple Sorbet.

Mallory Court has ten bedrooms, all double or twin rooms, and one luxury suite. The standard of furnishings and comfort in all the individually decorated rooms is extremely high, and all enjoy fine views across the surrounding Warwickshire countryside. As you would expect, all have good-sized private bathroom facilities, colour television, telephone and a complimentary range of toiletries. The Blenheim Room has to have the edge over the others, though, with its king-sized double bed, huge bay windows, balcony and south-facing view across a flourishing rose garden.

Leisure facilities at Mallory Court include ten acres of landscaped gardens to explore, an outdoor swimming pool, squash court, all-weather tennis court and a croquet lawn. Golf, riding and fishing are all available nearby. Other features of the surrounding area include Warwick Castle, historic Stratford-upon-Avon, Farnborough Hall, Packwood House, and the numerous attractions of easily reached nearby towns such as Tewkesbury, Gloucester, Worcester and Cheltenham.

69

LE MANOIR AUX QUAT' SAISONS

Address Great Milton, near Oxford, Oxfordshire
OX9 7PD
Tel: 0844 278881 Fax: 0844 278847

Nearest town Oxford.

Directions From London leave the M40 at junction
7, a few miles to the south-east of Oxford. Follow
the A329 Stadhampton road for about two miles,
taking the second right-hand turn indicating Great
Milton. After a short distance, Le Manoir appears
on the right adjacent to the church.

Awards Michelin ** since 1984; Certificat du Club
des Cent 1985; Egon Ronay Restaurant of the Year
1986 (87%); AA ***; Best Restaurant in Great Britain
18/20 1986 (*Good Food Guide*) to date; Best
Restaurant in Great Britain 19/20 1986 (Gault et
Millau) to date; Relais et Châteaux Yellow and Red
Shield and Relais Gourmand since 1987; *Times*
Restaurant of the Year 1990.

Open throughout the year.

Price for dinner, with wine, bed and breakfast for two – over £150.

Credit cards All major cards are accepted.

The hotel welcomes children of all ages but is not suitable for the disabled. Dogs are not permitted in the bedrooms or public rooms, although kennel facilities are available within the grounds free of charge.

Overall mark out of ten 9

Nestling in a beautifully landscaped setting, Le Manoir aux Quat' Saisons skilfully combines renowned gastronomic excellence with delightful rural Oxfordshire surroundings, yet is only forty-five minutes from London. This traditional English country manor has a history dating back to the fifteenth century. Located in the village of Great Milton, the grounds of Le Manoir aux Quat' Saisons include a swimming pool, tennis court and attractive water garden.

The history of the manor at Great Milton can be traced back some 750 years. It belonged originally to a Norman nobleman, fragments of whose effigy can be seen in the adjacent village church. Part of the attraction of Le Manoir aux Quat' Saisons is the fact that while the estate itself has remained substantially unchanged for over 500 years, it is totally up to date in its standards of luxury and technology (there is even the facility to land helicopters in the grounds).

From the moment you enter its gravelled drive, Le Manoir presents a distinctly English appearance: within, its soft furnishings, inviting sofas, oil paintings and open log fires combine to create a relaxing ambience. There are currently nineteen luxuriously appointed bedrooms, all decorated to a high standard. By a clever use of varied fabrics and colours, each room has a character all of its own. Private bathroom (some with a whirlpool bath or steam shower), direct-dial telephone, colour television and twenty-four-hour room service are standard, while attention to hospitality (each room has a decanter of Madeira and fruit awaiting guests, for instance) is exemplary.

It is principally for its cuisine that Le Manoir aux Quat' Saisons is justifiably well known. When Raymond Blanc opened his first restaurant – Les Quat' Saisons – in Oxford in 1977, he was generally regarded with some suspicion. After all, this young Frenchman was self taught and lacked any proven track record. However, despite these doubts, the restaurant soon rose to become one of the most prominent in the country, and the name of chef Raymond Blanc one of the best known in the world. Le Manoir aux Quat' Saisons opened in 1984 and is currently one of the very few Country House Hotels in Great Britain to boast a Chef Patron.

The high standard of Le Manoir aux Quat' Saisons's cuisine is reflected in the several accolades gained during its short but glorious existence to date. It is the only restaurant in Britain to have been awarded the distinction of the Certificat du Club des Cent, and the only restaurant in England to receive both Yellow and Red Shield from Relais & Châteaux and Relais Gourmand (to put this into perspective, France has just eight such establishments). Essentially French in style and character – though individually and delightfully 'à la Blanc' – the menu varies according to season, changing frequently. Guaranteed freshness of vegetables in season is assured from Le Manoir's extensive vegetable and herb gardens. Especially recommended are the Caille des Dombes Farcie, Jus au Vin de Pamplemousse et Pineau des Charentes, and the Cuisse et Râble de Lapin Braisés au Vin de Banyuls et Jus aux Graines de Moutarde. An extensive wine list complements the menu superbly while a separate part of the restaurant is designated a non-smoking area. Alain Desenclos – the restaurant director – is attentive yet unobtrusive.

In July 1990 a further nine bedrooms were opened in a converted stable block – each with their own private terrace overlooking the gardens. Even the sixteenth-century dovecote has been transformed into a *pièce de résistance* – a sumptuous and unique bedroom suite for an unusual and unforgettable stay. The new kitchen and conservatory (which adjoins the building somewhat uneasily) opened officially in February 1990, doubling kitchen space and providing additional room in the restaurant.

Not just 'a restaurant with rooms', however, Le Manoir aux

Quat' Saisons is an ideal base from which to explore southern central England, or to relax after a trip into London. Some fifteen minutes' drive takes you to the 'dreaming spires' of Oxford's colleges, while Blenheim Palace in nearby Woodstock is home to the Duke of Marlborough and ancestral seat of the Churchill family. All in all, Le Manoir combines restful surroundings with a very convenient location, and luxurious accommodation with exquisite cuisine. Raymond Blanc's intention is to make his premises one of the top five country hotel-restaurants in Europe. He is well on the way to achieving his goal.

70

THE MANOR

Address Lower Slaughter, Gloucestershire GL54 2HP
Tel: 0451 20456 Fax: 0451 22150

Nearest town Stow-on-the-Wold.
Directions From Evesham follow the A44 (which changes to the A424) to Stow-on-the-Wold. Then follow the A429 turning for the villages of Upper and Lower Slaughter. As you reach Bourton-on-the-Water, the Manor is the big house in front of the stream.

A member of the **Prestige** hotel group.
Awards AA *** (red) graded; English Tourist Board five Crowns.
Open all year.
Special breaks available.
Price for dinner, with wine, bed and breakfast, for two – over £150.
Credit cards Access, Visa, Amex and Diners.

The hotel is unsuitable for the disabled; children under ten, and dogs, are not allowed.
Overall mark out of ten 8½

Most of the Country House Hotels featured in this guide offer a combination of supreme peace and tranquillity in a rural setting with high standards of comfort. The Manor more than fits that description, standing, as it does, in many acres of private ground and surrounded by mature shady trees and colourful narrow flowerbeds.

A manor house was known on the site of the present hotel as long ago as 1004 AD, and in 1443 it became a convent housing nuns from the order of Syon. The medieval two-storey dovecote that you can still see within the grounds is said to have supplied the nuns with a source of food for decades. The Manor returned to the Crown shortly after 1534 when the order was dissolved as a result of Henry VIII's break with Rome.

In the year James VI of Scotland ascended the British throne as James I, The Manor was granted to Sir George Whitmore, High Sheriff of Gloucestershire, and it remained in the possession of his family for over three centuries, until 1964. Most of the present hotel dates from 1655 when Sir George's son, Richard, had the old house almost completely rebuilt. One Valentine Strong was contracted for the task, as old records show, 'For the sum of £200-0s-0d in lawful English money'. Valentine Strong's son was destined to outstrip even his father's achievements as an architect when he was employed by Sir Christopher Wren in the building of St Paul's Cathedral in London.

Like most Country Houses in Great Britain, The Manor has been altered considerably by successive generations; fashions change, but thankfully few of the main interior fittings have been altered. As you enter the hotel for the first time, you cannot fail to be struck by the attractive old stone fireplace in the main reception area. This dates from 1658, around the time when the entire West Wing was constructed. The ornate ceiling in the drawing room, the hotel's most appealing public room, is decorated in a pattern incorporating medallions of fruit, flowers, birds and angels, and is contemporary with the seventeenth-century additions to the building.

A further small addition was made to the west of The Manor in 1864, and the present East Wing dates back no further than 1891. A rather fetching feature of the staircase in the hotel is the attractive gazebo window located on the main landing. The view overlooking the gardens to the north is a treat, and this is one of the best vantage points from which to admire the grounds in all their glory.

The restaurant seats up to thirty people and is luxuriously decorated. Traditional English country-style cooking is preferred, and locally grown produce and herbs from the hotel's own gardens are used throughout. A table d'hôte menu is available each evening with a choice of at least five dishes for every course. If you enjoy unusual dishes then you will adore The Manor's own creation of Calves' Sweetbreads and Kidneys lightly sautéed with Wild Mushrooms and bathed in a rich Champagne Sauce. It is a truly magnificent dish of subtle flavours, and even those not normally keen on these ingredients will be impressed.

Main course dishes are strong on local fish and game: Breast of Chicken (which, they point out, was maize-fed) is served with an imaginative parcel of Puff Pastry containing Livers and Shallots; Fan of Salmon and Brill is a favourite fish dish, and comes steamed and served with Baby Leeks in a Vermouth Sauce, already seasoned with Fresh Basil and Julienne of Vegetables. An excellent wine list, bound like a little twenty-page booklet and enriched with a few well-chosen quotes from Walter Scott to Thackeray about wine drinking, will accompany your menu. A separate aperitif list is available should you decide on a modest tipple in the library before dining.

The hotel has a total of nineteen quite luxurious bedrooms, all with private bathroom facilities and the additional trimmings you would expect in an upper-class Country House Hotel. Guests have the added advantage of a range of good leisure facilities at The Manor, and can enjoy a heated indoor swimming pool, sauna and solarium, outdoor hard tennis court and a croquet lawn.

Nearby attractions include day trips to historic Stratford-upon-Avon, Gloucester, Oxford and Tewkesbury. One of the joys of this part of England is the choice visitors have to explore all the history and culture of large towns like Stratford and Oxford, or else enjoy the scenic beauty of the surrounding countryside – and all the quaint little villages like Upper and Lower Slaughter, and Bourton-on-the Water.

71

STUDLEY PRIORY

Address Horton-cum-Studley, Oxford OX9 1AZ
Tel: 086 735 203 Fax: 086 735 613

Nearest town Oxford.
Directions From Oxford, travel to end of the
Banbury road, taking the third exit (towards
London) along dual carriageway for about three and
a half miles. Follow signs to Horton-cum-Studley,
and stay on the same road until you reach a
staggered junction. Hotel at the top of a hill in the
village.
A member of the **Consort Hotels** group of
independent hotels.
Awards AA *** RAC graded; British Tourist Authority
commended; English Tourist Board four Crowns;
Egon Ronay (65%) and Michelin recommended.
Open throughout the year, except for the first week
in January.
Special breaks Available for any two consecutive
nights; special Christmas programme available;

Chocoholic Weekends (for chocolate addicts) available.
Price for dinner, with wine, bed and breakfast for two – £100–£150.
Credit cards Amex, Mastercard, Visa, Access, Diners.
The hotel is suitable for the partially disabled as it has ground-floor rooms; children welcome.
Overall mark out of ten 8

Situated amid thirteen acres of wooded grounds, Studley Priory is just seven miles from the historic city of Oxford and an hour's drive from the outskirts of London. As its rather unusual name suggests, the hotel was originally a nunnery, founded under the Benedictine order in the twelfth century. On the dissolution of the monasteries during the reign of Henry VIII, the estate was purchased by the Croke family, in whose hands it remained for nearly three and a half centuries.

A private chapel was consecrated in 1639, and the present North Wing added in 1666. Only the most minor structural improvements have taken place since the late seventeenth century and the present owners, the Parke family, purchased the house in 1961 in order to turn it into a Country House Hotel.

Studley Priory's most striking public room is its beautifully proportioned bar. Originally part of the main Elizabethan Withdrawing Room, most of the smooth wood panelling you can see today dates from the later Jacobean period. It is not a large room and is furnished with a rather odd assortment of simple dining-room-style chairs and bar stools which match the colouring of the walls. A large open fire blazes on cooler evenings, and the crackle of the logs is the perfect finishing touch to an utterly convivial atmosphere.

The hotel is a very popular conference venue, and for private dinner parties a fine Tudor Parlour can take up to thirty-six people. The low-ceilinged oak-panelled room was formerly the library of the original manor house, and this is an understandably more intimate setting than the main dining room – the Croke Restaurant.

The restaurant, which offers both English and French cooking in a modern style, has recently undergone extensive refurbishment. Rather fresh-looking beams seem strangely out of place in this part of the hotel, though the overall effect is still pleasing, and the high standard of cuisine ensures all eyes are table-bound not heavenward-raised. A two-, three- or four-course table d'hôte menu is available each evening, with about three or four choices available for each course.

The evening Gourmet menu comprises six courses for around £35. Greatly tempting is the Pithiviens of Scallop Mousseline on a light Spring Onion Butter and for the main course, Medallions of Beef Accompanied by a mild Garlic and Thyme Choux Bun filled with Duck Livers in a Smoked Mushroom Sauce.

A detailed wine list has over 150 bottles available, and many great wines from the 1950s and '60s have been included. Six vintage ports are also available.

Studley Priory has nineteen bedrooms, including five master doubles and one superb suite known as the Elizabethan Suite. All nineteen have private facilities, including colour television, tea- and coffee-making facilities, and direct-dial telephone, but the very popular Elizabethan Suite is easily the most sumptuous bedroom available. A huge, solid half-tester bed dominates the completely oak-panelled room. The stone mullioned doorway and windows, and the view far across the surrounding countryside, have altered little since Elizabethan times, and advance booking for this superb bedroom is essential. It costs roughly double that of an average twin/double room (around £150 per night for bread and breakfast) but this particular room really does represent a first-class opportunity to sample comfort in an Elizabethan style.

Leisure facilities at Studley Priory, and in the immediate area, are reasonable. There is a croquet lawn and a grass tennis court, and clay pigeon shooting (by prior arrangement), golf, horse riding, and indoor swimming are all accessible. Other nearby attractions include the historic city of Oxford just seven miles away, the beauty of the surrounding Cotswolds, Blenheim Palace (birthplace of Sir Winston Churchill) and Waddesdon Manor. Even the city of London, with its countless attractions for visitors, is just fifty-five miles away by fast train or car.

London

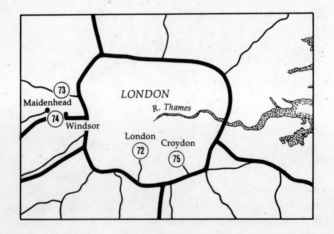

London

72 Cannizaro House
73 Cliveden
74 Oakley Court
75 Selsdon Park

CANNIZARO HOUSE

Address West Side, Wimbledon Common, London
SW19 4UF
Tel: 081 879 1464 Fax: 081 879 7338

Nearest town London.
Directions From the south-west, take the M25, then
the A3 to Tibbets Corner. Coming from Central
London, cross the Thames at Putney Bridge, head
for Putney Hill and Tibbets Corner. From Tibbets
Corner take the Wimbledon exit and travel along
Parkside until you reach Cannizaro Road. West
Side is a quarter of a mile on the right.
Awards AA and RAC **** graded; English Tourist
Board five Crowns; Ashley Courtenay and Egon
Ronay recommended 1989.
Open throughout the year.
Price for dinner, with wine, bed and breakfast for
two – over £150.
Credit cards All major credit cards accepted.
Children and dogs are welcome by prior arrangement.
The hotel is suitable for the disabled.
Overall mark out of ten 8

Cannizaro House has been operating as London's premier luxury Country House Hotel only since September 1987, yet within that time has become well known and respected both domestically and internationally. Conveniently situated at the edge of Wimbledon Common, Cannizaro House overlooks the majestic lawns, gardens and woodlands of Cannizaro Park.

The first recorded owner of Cannizaro House – Thomas Walker – appears in the Court Rolls of 1727. Later that century, Lyde Brown, the then Governor of the Bank of England, took over its lease. He was followed by Viscount Melville, who made many improvements to the house and park, including the planting of considerable numbers of trees, many fine examples of which remain today. In 1817 the property was taken over by an impoverished Sicilian – one Francis Platemore – who bore the title Count St Antonio. Following his marriage to the daughter of the wealthy Governor of West Florida Commodore George Johnstone, the Count became the Duke of Cannizaro, from which title the house derives its present name. Now restored to its former Georgian glory, Cannizaro House is a favoured retreat both for business guests seeking a secluded boardroom setting, and travellers wishing to enjoy a visit to London without having to stay in its metropolitan bustle.

On entering the main salon, you are immediately greeted with a beautiful display of flowers, renewed daily by the resident florist. In summer the French windows are opened on to the terrace, allowing warm breezes to waft within, while in winter a log fire blazes in the open hearth. Whatever the season, this room provides an atmospheric setting for evening recitals given by the resident harpist or pianist.

Cannizaro House has forty-eight luxurious bedrooms, which include individually designed suites and four-poster-bedded rooms. Each bedroom is furnished in the English Country House style, with pretty chintzes, soft colours and antiques, while the en suite bathrooms have marble fittings.

The restaurant offers an array of dishes best described as 'cuisine moderne-light', combining the best of British and French styles. The à la carte and table d'hôte menus are changed on a weekly and daily basis respectively. One of the most popular choices as a first course is a Foie Gras Terrine marinated in Sauternes, garnished with Truffles and served with a warm home-made Brioche. Main courses include Breast of Chicken wrapped around Dublin Bay Prawns and served with Mussel 'Fument'; and Boned Quail stuffed with Foie Gras, cooked in a Brandy Sauce and surrounded by Grapes and Button Onions. Fish – fresh from the market – is always available in a wide selection of dishes.

With vintages variously from France, Spain, Germany and Italy, the cellar offers a diverse choice of some 250 wines, including all the major Champagne houses. At around £15 a bottle, the French house wine – Sauvignon St Foy – is particularly good value, while for those wishing to celebrate in style, the Château Petruse 1980 is definitely recommended. One speciality of the hotel is a selection of Leopold Gourmel early bottled Cognacs with their distinctively light and delicately perfumed bouquet.

Cannizaro's gardens are superb whatever the season, but especially so during spring. Its broad sweep of well-tended lawn beckons you down to the ornamental lake, while amongst the trees and ornamental shrubs lie unexpected delights: here a statue, there an aviary. Other local diversions include walks on nearby Wimbledon Common; golf on one of the nearby courses, and horse riding. Proximity to some of the finest riding countryside in England is exemplified by nearby race courses – Epsom, Ascot and Sandown Park. Wimbledon itself is synonymous with the world-famous tennis courts. Here, tennis fans can visit the museum and Centre Court at the All England Lawn Tennis and Croquet Club. Of historical interest are Hampton Court Palace, Windsor Castle and Eton, all short drives away, while closer at hand lie the internationally renowned Kew Gardens.

With its convenient yet secluded setting for guests – close enough to the city for shopping and sightseeing, yet far enough away from the madding crowd – Cannizaro House combines the best of both worlds: a quiet Country House within a bustling capital city.

73

CLIVEDEN

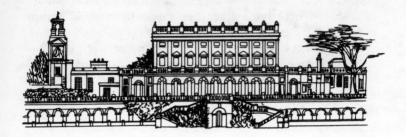

Address Taplow, Berkshire SL6 0JF
Tel: 0628 668561 Fax: 0628 661837

Nearest town Slough or Maidenhead (both six miles away).

Directions Leave the M4 at junction 7, turn left on to the A4 towards Maidenhead and at the next roundabout turn right where you see the signpost for Burnham. Follow this road for about four miles until you reach a T-junction. The main gates of Cliveden will be in front of you.

A member of the **Prestige Hotels** consortium and the **Leading Hotels of the World**.

Awards AA ***** graded, Egon Ronay (89%) and Michelin recommended.

Open throughout the year.

Price for dinner, with wine, bed and breakfast for two – over £200 (likely to be at least double that).

Credit cards Access, Visa, Diners and Masthercharge.

The hotel is suitable only for partially disabled guests; children and dogs are welcome.

Overall mark out of ten 10

Few can deny that Cliveden is one of the finest hotels in Europe. It certainly qualifies as the finest Country House Hotel in the United Kingdom, and the only stately home in England which has the distinction of being a hotel. Everything about Cliveden is magnificent: the 375 acres of gardens and parkland in which the house is set, the house's long and distinguished history ever since the original building of 1666, the sumptuous bedrooms and public rooms, and, of course, the highest standard of international cuisine.

Cliveden was built by the second Duke of Buckingham, a wealthy courtier, from whose family the Earl of Orkney inherited the house. The Duke of Buckingham was created England's first Field Marshal after the Duke of Marlborough's death, and altered the house and grounds considerably. From 1739 until his death in 1751, George III's father, Frederick, Prince of Wales, lived here before the house passed through a number of hands until the first Duke of Westminster acquired it in 1869. It was he who sold Cliveden to William Waldorf Astor, father-in-law of Cliveden's most famous resident, Nancy Astor, whose husband Waldorf received the house as a wedding present in 1906.

Nancy became Britain's first woman Member of Parliament to take her seat and made numerous improvements to Cliveden (it was she, for example, who called every bedroom after people closely associated with the house): Churchill, Balfour, Rudyard Kipling, Lawrence of Arabia and Bernard Shaw were all regular guests during her stay. Cliveden was eventually given to the National Trust during the Second World War, and in 1984 was entrusted to Blakeney Hotels who completely refurbished the house to its former grandeur and opened it as a de luxe hotel in March 1986.

It is easy to run out of superlatives to describe the public rooms at Cliveden. The Great Hall is an enormous room, with ornate wall panelling all around, huge sculpted fireplace and Flemish tapestry wall hangings. Priceless Astor family antiques add immeasurably to the charm of the hotel. The famous Sargent portrait of Nancy Astor, for example, hangs here and is reckoned to be worth at least a million pounds. The library is a much more intimate, panelled room, with plush period-style armchairs and one or two more family portraits. Arguably the most perfect room in any British hotel in which to relax with the Sundays and just soak up the sense of history all around you.

Nancy Astor's writing room is now the Boudoir, a marvellous Adam-style morning room, which is ideal for small private parties. An even more outstanding location is the small French dining room, where you will dine, with its rich gold panelling taken from Madame de Pompadour's dining room in the Château d'Asinières near Paris. The intricate gold leaf in the ceiling pattern is equally magnificent, and a perfect contrast to the reflection of the chandeliers in the huge polished mirrors.

The main dining room has undoubtedly the finest views of any room at Cliveden, stretching out across the parterre and down towards the River Thames. It can seat sixty in the grandest of Edwardian surroundings, gentle pastel shades making the perfect decor to relax the eye while you are dining. Head chef Ron Maxfield prepares a modern-style à la carte menu and fixed-price menus for lunch and dinner, based on classical cuisine, but never losing a strong British influence.

In 1990 a second restaurant, Waldo's, opened downstairs. A four-course set dinner for £46, five-course for £50, or chef's proposal for £60 is on offer here. The food is fabulous. A typical starter would be Cornish Crab with Lime and Pimentoes, grilled Scallops and a warm Potato and Chive Salad on a Red Pepper Coulis. To follow Lobster Lasagne, then Noisettes of Lamb with a gâteau of Provençal vegetables flavoured with olive oil and herbs. Then you might end with Dark Chocolate Box filled with a Banana and White Chocolate Parfait in a Honey Anglaise Sauce. Waldo's opens every evening except Monday.

Cliveden has thirty-one bedrooms, each one as enormous and luxurious as the next, with twin or double beds made up with pure linen sheets manufactured to the highest standards. (These are on sale opposite the Footman's Desk at £300 a pair if you fall in love with the luxury.) All of the bedrooms have their own fireplaces, and all have grand private bathrooms with huge bathtubs and specially designed Cliveden bath robes and toiletries as standard, together with a welcoming tray of drinks, in lead crystal decanters. Room rates begin around £185 and go up to £500 for the Royal Suite per night, but the quality of furnishings is simply breathtaking. The Lady Astor Suite, for example, has two enormous family portraits and elegant drapes all around the room's numerous grand windows; the Lord Mountbatten, on the other hand, has a much more 'masculine' feel, with a raised writing table, ornate ceiling and rich wood panelling.

There is an extensive range of leisure facilities available for residents at Cliveden, the most obvious being the sheer enjoyment of 375 acres of magnificent gardens and woodland. This is one of the finest private gardens in Britain and many guests travel up from London by boat on the River Thames, which literally runs through the estate. A handy booklet, prepared by the National Trust, has a number of suggested walks clearly marked on a map of the grounds.

Squash, tennis and fishing are among the most popular facilities, and equipment is available for guests who do not have their own with them. A heated outdoor swimming pool, in the walled garden, is available between 7.30 a.m. and 8 p.m. when weather permits, and riding, boating and golf can all be arranged locally. The new Pavilion, with its sixty-foot heated indoor swimming pool, Turkish and spa baths, also contains a gym and a wide variety of massage and health treatments. There is a wealth of nearby attractions including Windsor Castle, and surrounding safari and parkland, racing at Ascot, Windsor and Newbury, Henley regatta, and the beautiful university city of Oxford.

74

OAKLEY COURT

Address Windsor Road, near Windsor, Berkshire
SL4 5UR
Tel: 0628 74171 Fax: 0628 37011

Nearest town Windsor.
Directions From the M4, leave at junction 6 and
follow the A332 towards Windsor. Turn on to the
A308 towards Maidenhead and the hotel is located
on the right-hand side.
Owned by **Queens Moat House** and a member of
the **Prestige Hotels** consortium.
Awards AA **** graded and rosette for food; RAC
**** graded; British Tourist Authority commended;
Egon Ronay's highest recommended hotel in
Berkshire.
Open throughout the year.
Special breaks Weekend rates, winter breaks and
Easter breaks are available.
Price for dinner, with wine, bed and breakfast for
two – over £150.
Credit cards All major cards accepted.

The hotel is unsuitable for disabled visitors; children are not discouraged but dogs are not allowed.
Overall mark out of ten 9

It is likely that you will feel a certain familiarity with Oakley Court the first time you set eyes on its semi-Gothic, semi-château stonework. Between 1955 and 1969 it was one of the principal locations for Southern Pictures and about 200 feature films were made in and around the property including most of the classic *St Trinian's* series. Tommy Steele's famous *Half a Sixpence* was filmed here, as were many of the Hammer Horror Dracula productions. In 1981 the old house was opened as a luxury hotel after a major programme of refurbishment.

Rather surprisingly, very little is known about the early history of Oakley Court, despite its fame through so many films. It was originally built in 1859 for Sir Richard Hall Saye, and legend has it that it was built in the style of a French château to comfort his homesick French wife. The building passed through a number of hands, and it is believed that the English headquarters for the French resistance were based here during the Second World War. If this is the case, it is pretty certain that President De Gaulle stayed in one of the Mansion bedrooms.

Oakley Court is another of the largest Country House Hotels featured in this guide, with a total of ninety-two bedrooms. It is inevitable that hotels of this size have a reputation for impersonality, but the staff and management at Oakley Court are friendly and informal, and they work hard to provide as personal a service as possible to all guests.

Wherever feasible, the public rooms were restored to their original Victorian splendour during the £5 million renovation programme. Most of the hotel's furnishings are highly ornate and had to be hand finished. The dark wood staircase leading off from the reception, and the carved fireplace in the drawing room, have been painstakingly polished back to the authentic shine. A further major refurbishment programme took place in 1988 resulting in redesign of the major public rooms. Luxury bathrooms have been installed in all the Mansion suites. Take a moment to admire the rich plastering in the drawing room, all of which is original.

The Oakleaf restaurant is one of the most delightful rooms in the hotel, and very popular with non-residents. Up to 120 can be seated but, even so, advance booking by at least a week is advisable. The food is prepared by one of England's leading chefs, Murdo MacSween, who holds the rare qualification of Master Chef of Great Britain. To describe his cuisine as a combination of English and French styles would be something of an understatement, but it will give you some idea of the type of dishes to expect.

A set-price six-course Gourmet Menu (around £35–£40 per person at the time of publication), together with a table d'hôte and an à la carte menu, are available each evening. Specialities change from season to season, but a typical selection of starters would include a unique Paupiette of Sole Stuffed with Seaweed and a Mousse of Saffron, served with Spinach and a White Wine Sauce, or a Terrine of Pheasant, Partridge and Foie Gras served with Redcurrants in Port Jelly.

Main dishes include Parcel of Turbot, Salmon and Dill in Filo Pastry served with a Spinach Butter Sauce. A more original favourite of Murdo MacSween is an exquisite dish made up of a pair of Quails stuffed with a Mousse of Tarragon, wrapped in Greek pastry and baked, served with a light Orange Sauce. The desserts are equally delicious, and in fact Oakley Court's cuisine is reason enough to pay a visit to this gastronome's delight.

The total of ninety-two bedrooms includes seven lovingly restored rooms in the main house, four of which have antique four-poster beds. Most of the rooms, though, are housed in the Riverside and Garden Wings which were added to the main building between 1979 and 1981. All rooms are comfortably furnished with private bathrooms, colour television, direct-dial telephone and period furniture wherever possible.

The hotel stands in thirty-five acres of beautifully maintained gardens on the banks of the River Thames, surrounded by woodland and green fields. Leisure facilities include a nine-hole pitch and putt course, a croquet lawn and the opportunity for private fishing. Inside the hotel there is a full-sized billiards table which dates back over 300 years.

Major sporting centres, including Sunningdale and Wentworth for golf, Windsor and Ascot for horse racing, Marlow and Henley for boating and Twickenham for rugby are within a short drive. Other nearby attractions include Windsor Castle, Eton College, the towns of Windsor and Maidenhead, Medmenham Abbey, and Marlow, where you can visit Albion House, the former home of the poet Shelley and the place where his wife Mary wrote her classic horror story *Frankenstein*.

75

SELSDON PARK

Address Sanderstead, South Croydon, Surrey CR2
8YA
Tel: 081 657 8811 Fax: 081 651 6171

Nearest town Croydon.
Directions Leave the M25 (London ring road) at
junction 6. Follow A22 until junction with B270.
Take first left after joining B270 to Sanderstead up
Tithepit Shaw Lane. Turn left at the end, on to
B269 Limpsfield road to the first roundabout. Take
the third exit right towards Selsdon on A2022 and
you will see the hotel entrance on the right after
half a mile or so.
Awards AA and RAC **** graded; English Tourist
Board five Crowns; Egon Ronay and Ashley
Courtenay recommended.
Open throughout the year.
Special breaks Weekend and winter breaks are
available, together with Christmas breaks.
Price for dinner, with wine, bed and breakfast for
two – over £150.

Credit cards Access, Visa, Amex, Diners and En
Route.
The hotel is not suitable for the disabled; children and
dogs are welcome.
Overall mark out of ten 9½

With 170 bedrooms and one of the finest leisure complexes of
any hotel in Britain, Selsdon Park is the largest hotel featured
in this guide. It can also claim the honour of being the biggest
proprietor-owned hotel in the country. With the added advantage of being situated just thirteen miles out of Central London,
it is extremely popular with businessmen and holiday-makers
alike who want to stay within easy reach of the capital.

The hotel is an enormous stately old building, and everything
about Selsdon Park is organized on a grand scale. Your first
sight of it, after you sweep up the long drive, will be its magnificent ivy-clad exterior which has watched over the Selsdon Park
estate in one form or another for the best part of twelve centuries. A manor house was recorded on the site of the present
hotel as far back as AD 891 which was owned by a Saxon nobleman, Earl Aelfred, who had received an earldom after the Battle
of Thanet. When Aelfred and his family lived here, the mansion
probably covered no more than the area the indoor swimming
pool covers today!

Over the centuries, of course, Selsdon Park passed through
many hands and changed size and form many times. The Domesday Book, completed in 1086, records a substantially larger
estate than that which Aelfred would have known. Many cru-
sading lords stayed at Selsdon during the Middle Ages and by
1540 the manor was granted to Sir John Gresham, a close friend
and adviser to Henry VIII. He became a great servant to Elizabeth I, and the Virgin Queen is known to have visited Selsdon,
and hunted in its grounds, on a number of occasions. In 1924
the estate was bought by Allan Sanderson, father of the present
owner, who turned it into a hotel soon afterwards.

Although most of the present building dates from no earlier
than the seventeenth century, and it has taken many major
alterations since that period to turn it into the present luxury

hotel, the public areas retain a marvellous sense of informality and unpretentious quality. Solid old beams still line many of the corridors and rich wood panelling adorns many of the walls. Everyone from the reception staff to the ebullient proprietor, Basil Sanderson, makes an effort to be genuinely courteous to all guests, whether they are non-residents making a first visit for dinner, or millionaires staying a month in the best suite.

The main restaurant is an enormous room, well lit by natural sunlight during the summer evenings and decorated with modern furnishings which blend well with the restful blue, grey and cream decor. Up to 250 can be seated at once, but advance booking is still essential for non-residents. An à la carte and table d'hôte menu is available each evening: both are extensive and the style of cuisine is broadly based and international.

The standard of service is exemplary; a small desk-style buffet area in the centre of the restaurant provides an extensive array of impressive hors d'oeuvres to open your meal. A typical four-course table d'hôte menu would start with a choice of three or four starters which might include Saumon Fumé or a delicious Terrine de Légumes Cressonaire. A speciality soup or light fish course precedes the main course which is likely to include a fish dish like Paupiette de Plie Bonne Femme (a fillet of plaice filled with prawn mousse and coated with a white wine and mush-room sauce), or one of the chef's more adventurous favourites like Jardinière de Boeuf et Veau Orientale (strips of beef and veal, sautéed with beanshoots, peppers, onion, pineapple, spring onion and almonds, and served up with a sweet and sour sauce).

All Selsdon Park's 170 bedrooms were extensively refurbished in 1990 and come complete with remote-control colour tele-vision, direct-dial telephone, spacious private bathroom facilities and a range of complimentary toiletries. The management has successfully created a blend of 'homely' fabrics and colours, and most rooms have the additional advantage of good views (particularly to the front of the hotel) across the surrounding gardens and golf course.

Selsdon Park has a magnificent tropical leisure complex which residents can enjoy completely free of charge (with a few minor exceptions such as sun beds). Most indoor sports can be enjoyed, and the complex forms part of the main hotel building which means there is no need for a chilly dash in the open air to reach it as is the case with so many hotels. Facilities include a heated swimming pool, jacuzzi, sauna, steam room, squash courts, gymnasium and even a dry beach where you can relax with a drink after your swim. Outdoors, there are an eighteen-hole championship golf course, a second heated swimming pool during the summer, floodlit tennis courts, croquet, riding, putting and a children's play area.

Nearby attractions include Hever and Leeds Castle, Chartwell (formerly home to Sir Winston and Lady Churchill), Penshurst and Polesden Lacey. The scenic and historical attractions of Kent, Surrey and Sussex are within easy reach, and Brighton is under an hour's drive away. For golf enthusiasts, Sunningdale and Wentworth are just two of the many great golf courses nearby.

South-east England

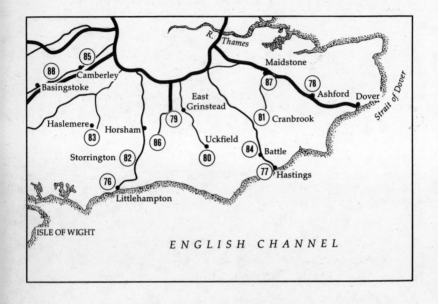

South-east England

76 Bailiffscourt
77 Beauport Park
78 Eastwell Manor
79 Gravetye Manor
80 Horsted Place
81 Kennel Holt
82 Little Thakeham

83 Lythe Hill
84 Netherfield Place
85 Pennyhill Park
86 South Lodge
87 Tanyard
88 Tylney Hall

BAILIFFSCOURT

Address Climping, Littlehampton, West Sussex
BN17 5RW
Tel: 0903 723511 Fax: 0903 723107

Nearest town Littlehampton.
Directions Leave the M25 at junction 9 and follow
the A29 as far as the junction with the A284. Follow
the A284 to the roundabout below Arundel linking
Chichester and Brighton by the A27. Take the
route marked Ford and Climping and turn right at
the T-junction up the A259 Littlehampton to
Bognor road. The hotel is a few hundred yards
down the first left turning.
Awards AA **** graded.
Open throughout the year.
Special rates are offered mid-week all year round.
Price for dinner, with wine, bed and breakfast for
two – over £150.

Credit cards All major cards accepted.
The hotel is not suitable for the disabled; children under eight are discouraged but dogs are 'encouraged to bring their owners'. Baskets and food can be provided.
Overall mark out of ten 9

Few visitors to Bailiffscourt can argue that it is not one of the most fascinating and intriguing properties in southern England. It is built to resemble a sprawling medieval manor house whose Gothic-style windows you can just see glinting through the trees from the nearby main road. Its solid stonework epitomizes the sombre dignity of the Middle Ages.

Ironically, though, Bailiffscourt is the youngest hotel featured in this guide, since it was completed in 1933 – at a fabulous cost – to satisfy a caprice of the late Lord Moyne. The final bill was never revealed, but even in the 1930s it must have cost around £1 million to create this unique house. Architecturally correct down to the smallest detail, both inside and out, the management freely admits that Bailiffscourt would have been an utterly shameless fake were it not for the fact that the house had been built almost entirely from genuine bits and pieces taken from old houses the length and breadth of Britain. The full story of Bailiffscourt, which has been a hotel since 1948, is fascinating, and it is not hard to understand why one leading architect, quoted in *Harper's Bazaar* in 1969, said: 'One fake like this is all right because, as the only one of its kind, it is a unique piece of art. But heaven help us if we have any more.'

Inside the house the attention to detail is amazing. In the Music Room there is an outstanding moulded oak ceiling which came from a fifteenth-century rectory in Somerset. In this room alone there are also two sixteenth-century fireplaces. Throughout the public rooms there are examples of intricate needlework, and tapestry wall hangings, dating back several centuries. There are at present plans for the expansion of the hotel.

The main restaurant is a delightfully grand room, with a slightly arched oak ceiling and a seating capacity of sixty-five. Medieval drapes, high-backed Jacobean-style chairs and flickering candles quite complete the romantic atmosphere. The chef described his style of cuisine as 'modern classical' – a description as typically paradoxical as the rest of this wonderful hotel. A most impressive table d'hôte and an à la carte menu are available each evening.

Opening specialities include a rich Game Terrine studded with Fresh Truffle and Pistachio Nuts, placed on a rosette of salad leaves and served with Cumberland Sauce, and a Pastry Pillow filled with Creamed Spinach and Fresh Asparagus Tips, accompanied by a Raspberry Butter Sauce. Main course options include a strong selection of local meat and game. For two persons, an interesting suggestion is best end of English Lamb Baked in a Salt Crust, presented and accompanied by a golden Mint Hollandaise Sauce with a light Rosemary Jus. Another option might be a selection of fresh market Fish, poached in Dry White Wine and Shallots and placed on a Scallop and Noilly Prat Sauce. All main dishes are served with a selection of fresh market vegetables and potatoes.

As you might expect, all eighteen bedrooms (plus two separate cottages nearby) are superbly furnished in the same mock-medieval style as the rest of the hotel. Each bedroom is completely different from the one before it: most have solid oak beams running across the ceiling, and a delightfully spacious feel to them. Eight have four-poster beds, nine have open log fires, and you will be struggling to find a more romantic setting anywhere in this part of England in which to enjoy these particular 'extras'. All bedrooms have their own bathroom facilities, colour television and direct-dial telephone.

One or two leisure facilities, including an (unheated) outdoor swimming pool, are available for residents to enjoy. In addition, there is a 'tee to green' golf practice area on the rear lawns, a croquet lawn (with the necessary equipment available) and a hard tennis court. Clay target shooting can be arranged if guests wish. Nearby attractions include the magnificent Arundel Castle (stately home of the Duke of Norfolk); Chichester, with its famous theatre; Portsmouth, with its many naval attractions including the Mary Rose museum; and the coastal towns of Southampton, Brighton and Eastbourne.

77

BEAUPORT PARK

Address Battle Road, Hastings, Sussex TN38 8EA
Tel: 0424 851222

Nearest town Hastings.
Directions The hotel is situated just off the A2100,
approximately half-way between (and three miles
from both) Hastings and Battle.
Awards AA and RAC *** graded; English Tourist
Board four Crowns.
Open throughout the year.
Special **bargain breaks** are available all year round
for a minimum of two nights half-board.
Price for dinner, with wine, bed and breakfast for
two – £100–£150.
Credit cards Access, Visa, Amex and Diners.
*The house is not suitable for disabled visitors; children
are welcome, and dogs are allowed.*
Overall mark out of ten 8

Situated at the western end of a ridge of hills which shelter Hastings from the north and east, the Beauport Park hotel enjoys a commanding position with magnificent views in all directions. This site appealed to General Sir James Murray (1721–94), who built Beauport Park between 1763 and 1766, and eventually built up his estate to almost 2000 acres of prime Sussex countryside. General Murray was one of England's most distinguished soldiers during the latter half of the eighteenth century, having first achieved distinction as a Brigadier General under General Wolfe at Quebec: indeed, Beauport Park is named after the village of Beauport near Quebec. He served for some time as Governor of Minorca at the end of a long spell during which the island was under British rule.

Among the many distinguished visitors to Beauport Park while it was a private residence in the two centuries which followed was Queen Victoria's eldest daughter, Princess Victoria. She was staying at nearby St Leonards-on-Sea in 1868, and came to take afternoon tea with the then owners, the Brassey family. She subsequently wrote to Queen Victoria that she 'liked being here immensely at the house of the Brasseys with the wonderful gardens and especially the trees'.

Although the original mansion was accidentally burnt down in 1923, the main structure survived and it was rebuilt soon after (with the exception of one wing). Inside the public rooms have been decorated and furnished in comfortable Georgian style. The main public lounge has full-length drapes, a polished marble fireplace and soft armchairs.

Both the cocktail bar and the large restaurant overlook the Italian sunken gardens, and the chef has an excellent reputation for traditional English Country House-style cuisine. Both a daily table d'hôte and a regular à la carte menu are available, and the hotel specializes in flambé dishes cooked at your table. A la carte starters include popular openers like Avocado with Prawns, and Smoked Salmon with Cucumber and Dill Salad, together with more continental favourites like Marinated Mussels and Burgundy Style Snails cooked in Garlic Butter.

Delicious fish dishes range from Coquille St Jacques Singapore to Rolled Fillets of Sole, poached and served with a Lobster

Sauce and Truffles. Two of the more popular house specialities are Brochette Royale, a dish for two persons comprising choice pieces of veal, beef and lamb, cooked on a sword with mushrooms and peppers. This is flamed in front of you and served with rice pilaff. Alternatively, you may prefer Salmon en Croûte: medallions of salmon with spinach and egg, cooked in a pastry case and served with lobster sauce.

The hotel has twenty-three bedrooms, all decorated in a modern style with quality reproduction furnishings and en suite bathrooms. Additional comforts like remote-control colour television, direct-dial telephones and tea- and coffee-making facilities come as standard. The Honeymoon Suite has a four-poster bed, and both the large suites have private jacuzzis for that extra luxury.

The hotel is situated in thirty-three acres of private wood and parkland, which includes some of Britain's rarest trees, with well-kept informal gardens at the rear of the hotel. Other leisure facilities available for residents include a heated outdoor swimming pool, a croquet lawn, putting green and an all-weather tennis court. There is an eighteen-hole golf course adjacent to the hotel, and both squash and riding can be enjoyed locally.

Other nearby attractions include the Cinque Ports of Hastings and Rye; many famous castles including Bodiam and Pevensey; the former home of Rudyard Kipling, Batemans; Sir Winston Churchill's country residence at Chartwell; and, of course, the site of probably the most famous battle in history, the Battle of Hastings, which took place three miles from the present hotel in October 1066.

78

EASTWELL MANOR

Address Eastwell Park, Boughton Aluph, near
Ashford, Kent TN25 4HR
Tel: 0233 635751 Fax: 0233 635530

Nearest town Ashford.
Directions From London, leave the M2 at junction
6. Continue along the A251 and Eastwell Manor is
twelve miles along this road.
Owned by **Queens Moat Hotels** and a member of
the **Prestige Hotels** consortium.
Awards AA **** graded and rosette for food; English
Tourist Board five Crowns; British Tourist Authority
commended; Egon Ronay and Michelin
recommended.
Open throughout the year.
Special breaks Mid-week breaks all year round;
special Christmas programme.
Price for dinner, with wine, bed and breakfast for
two – £100–£150.

Credit cards Access, Visa, Amex, Diners and Mastercharge.

Children are welcome but dogs are not permitted in the hotel.

Overall mark out of ten 9½

Surrounded by sixty-five acres of undulating parkland in the heart of the north downs of Kent, the present Eastwell Manor dates from no earlier than 1926, although the original manor on this site has a far longer history, dating back to the eleventh century. Eastwell takes its name from the spring known to the Saxon herdsmen of the downs and forests, and prior to the Norman Conquest of 1066 a Saxon nobleman by the name of Frederic held the lordship of the manor from Edward the Confessor.

The manor has had a long and colourful history down the centuries, and this makes fascinating reading in the back of one of the hotel's publicity booklets. In the early sixteenth century, a previous owner of the estate, Sir Thomas Moyle, discovered one of his bricklayers reading Latin and subsequently identified him as Richard Plantagenet, illegitimate son of King Richard III. Sir Thomas took kindly to the disgraced king's son and had a small cottage built for him on the estate where the younger Richard lived peacefully until his death in 1550.

Sir Thomas Finch, who inherited the house in the seventeenth century, distinguished himself by fathering twenty-seven children by his four wives. A couple of centuries later, in 1875, Her Royal Highness Princess Marie Alexandra Victoria (later to become Queen of Romania) was born in the manor. It was demolished after lying untended for a number of years after the First World War, and rebuilt in 1926 by Sir John de Fonblanqua Pennefather, using the original stonework as far as possible, combined with imported architectural accessories to make the 'new' manor even more striking than before.

All the public rooms are designed in a style which is typical of a period much earlier than the 1920s. All have elaborately patterned ceilings and wood panelling, but the main lounge is the *pièce de résistance*. With its soft leather armchairs, enormous carved fireplace and diamond-crossed windows this is a grand room in every sense.

Up to eighty can be seated in two magnificent dark wood-panelled dining rooms which both offer excellent views across the gardens and surrounding estate. Guests sit back and relax in comfortable leather 'Captain's' chairs as they enjoy a blend of modern cuisine which is influenced considerably by classical French, traditional English and, as the management term it, chef Mark Clayton's 'own interpretation of his culinary art'.

Table d'hôte and à la carte menus are available each evening, and the end result of the combination of styles is an adventurous range of first-class dishes. Speciality starters include a delicious Mediterranean Red Mullet Soup served with Croûtons, and Breast of English Woodpigeon, set on a bed of salad leaves with crisp strips of Bacon and Leeks. Main dishes include a delicious selection of traditional items such as Scotch beef, veal and English lamb, together with some more unusual choices such as Artichoke Heart filled with Wild Mushrooms, Garlic and Leeks on a bed of spicy Red Cabbage, served with a Girolle Butter Sauce. Whatever your choice, the Manor has an extensive wine list with a particularly good range of French wines, together with a few more popular bottles from other countries.

Eastwell Manor has twenty-three grand bedrooms including three master suites, one de luxe suite, and two standard suites. All rooms are individually styled with period furnishings or quality modern reproductions. Each one has its own private bathroom and the style of some of these 'additional' rooms is extremely attractive. The Edwardian bathroom, for instance, attached to the Countess of Midleton suite has changed little since the turn of the century and comes complete with an enormous mirror, deep bath and marble surround.

A number of sports and leisure facilities are available at Eastwell Manor, or nearby, for residents to enjoy. There is a panelled billiard room adjacent to reception and during the summer months a croquet lawn is set up within the grounds. The hotel has a hard tennis court, but you may prefer to indulge in more relaxing trout fishing which can be arranged locally; both Ashford and Faversham golf courses are within easy reach and both horse riding and squash can be arranged at local centres.

Nearby attractions include the ancient town of Canterbury with its famous cathedral, Dover Castle, Hever Castle, Leeds Castle, Sissinghurst Gardens and the ports of Dover and Folkestone. An added attraction of staying in this part of the UK is the relative ease with which it is possible to make day trips across to Calais or Boulogne on the French coast.

79

GRAVETYE MANOR

Address Near East Grinstead, West Sussex RH19 4LJ
Tel: 0342 810567 Fax: 0342 810080

Nearest town East Grinstead.

Directions From London, take the A22 (the
Eastbourne road). About seven miles past Godstone,
you will reach a crossroads where you turn right on
to the B2028 for Turner's Hill.

A member of the **Relais et Châteaux** consortium.

Awards AA *** (red) and rosette for food; RAC Blue
Ribbon; British Tourist Authority commended;
Egon Ronay (80%) and Michelin recommended;
Egon Ronay Hotel of the Year 1978; Hideaway of
the Year 1981.

Open throughout the year.

No **special breaks** available other than a Christmas
programme, which is always popular.

Price for dinner, with wine, bed and breakfast for
two – over £150.

Credit cards None accepted.

*The hotel is unsuitable for disabled visitors; the hotel
welcomes 'babes in arms' and children aged seven or over;
dogs are not allowed.*
Overall mark out of ten 9½

An internationally famous hotel which has a deserved reputation as one of Britain's finest Country House Hotels, Gravetye
Manor offers exceptionally high standards of comfort and cuisine. In 1978 it won the prestigious Hotel of the Year Award
from Egon Ronay, who described it then as 'an outstanding
exemplification of Country House hospitality in a beautiful setting, combined with dedicated, professional hotel keeping'. Few
could argue that its standards have moved in any direction but
upwards since then.

Gravetye Manor was originally built in 1598 by Richard Infield
for his new bride Katharine Compton. You can still see their
initials carved in stone above the main entrance from the Formal
Garden and their wood-carved portraits hang in the master bedroom. The manor's most distinguished owner was William Robinson, one of the greatest gardeners of all time, who bought the
manor and the one thousand acres in which it still stands in
1884. He realized many great ambitions for the gardens around
the house before his death in 1935, and today the gardens are
among the most famous of the English Natural Gardens of which
Robinson was the pioneer.

The style of all the public rooms is distinctly late Victorian, and
much of the wood panelling throughout the hotel was added by
William Robinson at the end of the last century from wood on
the estate. The sitting room has wood panelling all around and
a sumptuous ornate plaster ceiling which you cannot help but
gaze at in amazement as you wonder precisely how it was
constructed.

The restaurant, particularly, is a magnificent old room, with
a capacity for fifty guests. The combination of solid wood panelling and candlelight creates just the right level of informality
which a hotel of this class deserves. Chef de Cuisine Mark
Raffin's style is influenced by French *haute cuisine* and the best
of traditional English cooking. A la carte and table d'hôte menus

are available each evening, both of which are presented to diners in an attractive glossy card menu folder decorated with tasteful sketches of house and grounds. A number of starters are also suitable as light main courses. These include Salmon, fresh from the hotel's own smoke-house, Creamed Eggs served with Mussels and Saffron, and an intriguing Middle Eastern speciality – Steamed Lamb's Brains, served in a Light Puff Pastry Slice with a Sorrel Sauce.

Main dishes are all accompanied by a bouquet of vegetables to complement the type of meat or fish chosen. There is a strong selection of fish dishes available, including Roulade of Salmon and Savoy Cabbage, Roast Monkfish Tail and an interesting dish made up of Boneless Fillets of Mullet and Bream poached in a Fish Bouillon, all served perfumed with herbs. Meat dishes include Grilled Fillet of Beef and Pot Roasted Breast of Duck. Gravetye Manor has a superb wine list, one of the finest in England, with over 350 wines on offer.

The hotel has fourteen bedrooms, including two singles; each one is named after an English tree. All are furnished in a mood of quiet comfort with antique furniture and high-quality soft furnishings throughout. All are bright and spacious, and doubles are available in a choice of three sizes. Each bedroom comes complete with private bathroom facilities, colour television, direct-dial telephone, bathrobes, and a range of hardback books and quality complimentary toiletries, in keeping with the overall luxury standards of the hotel.

Leisure facilities at Gravetye are deliberately limited so that guests may have the opportunity to relax and enjoy the peace and quiet without too many distractions. Horse riding and golf can be arranged locally, though, as can fly-fishing for brown and rainbow trout on the hotel's three-acre lake between May and September. Clock golf and croquet are available on the hotel's long lawn. Nearby attractions include Hever Castle, Chartwell (the former country home of Sir Winston Churchill) and the Glyndebourne Festival Opera.

80

HORSTED PLACE

Address Little Horsted, Uckfield, East Sussex TN22 5TS
Tel: 0825 75581 Fax: 0825 75459

Nearest town Uckfield.
Directions Horsted Place lies forty-two miles from London and sixteen miles from Brighton. It sits just off the A26 Uckfield to Lewes road, about a mile from Uckfield.
A member of the **Prestige** consortium.
Awards AA *** (red) graded; Michelin four Red Turrets; Egon Ronay 80%; British Tourist Authority commended.
Open throughout the year.
A special **winter rate** is available from November until mid-March.
Price for dinner, with wine, bed and breakfast for two – over £200.
Credit cards All major cards accepted.

The hotel is suitable for disabled visitors; dogs, and children under seven, are not allowed.
Overall mark out of ten 9

Opened in June 1986 as a luxury hotel, Horsted Place has the distinction of being one of the most recently transformed Country Houses which is already one of the country's best. It has only been a few years since the old Victorian house was one of the principal private residences in this part of southern England, regularly playing host to Her Majesty the Queen and many other senior members of the Royal Family.

Horsted was built in 1850 by George Myers for a wealthy London dyer called Francis Barchard. The main influence in the design of the house came from Augustus Pugin, who is probably best known for his work on the House of Lords. The house was eventually bought by Lord Rupert Nevill in 1965. Lord Rupert was for many years Private Secretary to Prince Philip, and became a good friend of the Queen, hence both Her Majesty and Prince Philip, and a number of other senior members of the Royal Family, visited Horsted Place as guests of Lord and Lady Nevill.

One of the most striking features of the hotel is the main staircase, hand-carved in solid English oak, to Pugin's design. A section of the staircase was exhibited in the Medieval Court of the Great Exhibition of 1851 – and the original Victorian packing slip for the delivery of the staircase to Lewes station is still on display in the hotel.

All the public rooms at Horsted are very comfortably furnished and have been carefully designed in a style typical of the Victorian era, when the house reached its zenith as a private residence. The main lounge is a bright room, with its colourful armchairs, two solid stone fireplaces and illuminated oil paintings all around. The little friezes above the doors are a nice touch, typical of the flamboyance of early Victorian craftsmanship.

The centrepiece of Pugin's interior design, however, is the main dining room with its original ceiling. The style of decor is traditional, but this is complemented by modern porcelain tableware, crisp linen tablecloths and silver cutlery. Cuisine is in the modern British Country House style expertly presided over by Chef de Cuisine Allan Garth.

An extended, six-choice table d'hôte menu is offered each evening, with at least three options for each course. A typical dinner could open with a Warm Terrine of Smoked Salmon and Spinach, or Parfait of Chicken Livers, before a main course of Prime Scottish Beef or Dover Sole. The pudding menu is rather limited although the speciality, a light Sponge Roulade filled with Cinnamon Buttercream and served with a Lemon and Saffron Sauce, is delightful.

Horsted Place has a total of seventeen bedrooms, all of them suites, with the exception of three extremely comfortable double rooms. Each one has a private bathroom, with bath and shower, and is furnished to 'North American luxury' standards. In addition to remote-control colour television, direct-dial telephone and magnificent views across the gardens or Sussex Downs, each suite is individually decorated and comes with its own separate sitting area.

The hotel has a good range of leisure facilities available for residents, including a heated indoor swimming pool, an all-weather tennis court, a croquet lawn and twenty-three acres of private garden. In addition, other activities such as shooting and fishing can be easily arranged. The recent addition of two back-to-back eighteen-hole golf courses ranks Horsted Place as a mecca for golf enthusiasts.

Other nearby attractions include the coastal towns of Brighton and Eastbourne, Royal Tunbridge Wells, countless places of historical interest along the coast, and the possibility of day trips to France.

81

KENNEL HOLT

Address Cranbrook, Kent TN17 2PT
Tel: 0580 712032 Fax: 0580 712931

Nearest town Cranbrook.
Directions The hotel is situated one and a half miles
north-west of Cranbrook, on the main A262
Cranbrook to Goudhurst road. It is signposted a
mile past the A229/A262 junction.
Awards AA ** (red) graded; RAC ** graded and
Blue Ribbon; British Tourist Authority
commended; recommended by Michelin and Egon
Ronay guides.
Open all year.
Special winter breaks available.
Price for dinner, with wine, bed and breakfast for
two – £100–£150.
Credit cards Access and Visa.
The hotel is not suitable for disabled visitors; children are

welcome, but at the proprietor's discretion if under six
years of age; dogs allowed by prior arrangement.
Overall mark out of ten 7½

An outstanding example of a pedigree Elizabethan Country House, Kennel Holt was built in 1560 and positively exudes period charm. A well-kept gravel driveway leads up to the house with its five magnificent brick chimneys which dominate the roofline of the hotel. These wide stacks, with their even wider tops, built in the days when wood-burning fires were much more common than coal or any of the modern options, are typically Tudor.

Kennel Holt has been considerably renovated since Elizabethan times, and modern comforts have been added to existing period fittings to create a pleasingly informal atmosphere. There are two large sitting-rooms, both with thick-beamed ceilings and open fires. The Oak Room and Library is the more appealing of the two, with its soft furnishings and good range of reading material for guests to enjoy.

The front drawing room has a larger fireplace and leads off the main entrance and hall. It is rather more open than the Oak Room, but is, nevertheless, a delightfully relaxing room and the perfect place to sit back with an after-dinner coffee or liqueur and watch the sunset during the long summer evenings.

The alcove restaurant is a relatively small room, with a capacity for only twenty-five diners of whom a maximum of eight are non-residents. The room is charmingly intimate and boasts an original fireplace. Probably the best feature about Kennel Holt, however, is its wonderful menu which the proprietor's wife Ruth Cliff has developed to near perfection over the years. Ruth has impeccable qualifications to take charge of the kitchen, having been a teacher at a resident Cordon Bleu cookery school for a number of years.

A different five-course table d'hôte menu is offered each evening. Typical starters include Avocado with Tomato Ice, Smoked Haddock Gratin, or Danish Tartlets. A soup or sorbet course precedes the main dish, and four selections are usually highlighted as the dishes of the day. Favourite specialities include

New Forest Pork with Nuts, Poached Sole stuffed with Scampi or Supreme of Duck Montmorency. In season, fresh vegetables are provided straight from the hotel garden, and there is a very respectable wine list available for such a relatively small hotel.

There are ten bedrooms furnished in a modern style, including eight doubles with a private bathroom or shower, plus a further small double and one single, which also have their own facilities. A number of the doubles are on the small side, but all are comfortably furnished with a colour television (usually portable), hair dryers and radio alarm clocks. Two of the doubles have a four-poster bed and most of the rooms have excellent views across the duck pond and surrounding five-acre garden.

Within easy driving distance of Kennel Holt are at least fifty distinguished historic houses, castles and gardens. Sissinghurst is a famous Tudor estate literally just down the road, and Scotney Castle is a fourteenth-century moated castle about five miles away. Other attractions include the gardens at Great Comp and Great Dexter, Hever Castle (once the home of Anne Boleyn), Chartwell, Batemans (where Rudyard Kipling used to live) and Leeds Castle. In addition, there are the ports of Dover, Folkestone, Ramsgate and Sheerness with their day-trip ferry excursion possibilities, and the historic towns of Canterbury, Hastings and Royal Tunbridge Wells.

82

LITTLE THAKEHAM

Address Merrywood Lane, Storrington, West
Sussex RH20 3HE
Tel: 0903 744416 Fax: 0903 745022

Nearest town Storrington.
Directions From Storrington (forty-eight miles from
London) follow the B2139 towards Thakeham. After
just over a mile turn right into Merrywood Lane
and the hotel is 400 yards on left.
A member of the **Pride of Britain** consortium.
Awards British Tourist Authority commended;
Egon Ronay and Michelin recommended.
Open throughout the year (except Christmas
period).
Special breaks Mid-week breaks are available.
Price for dinner, with wine, bed and breakfast for
two – over £150.
Credit cards All major cards accepted.
*There is one ground-floor bedroom suitable for the
disabled; children are allowed, but no dogs.*
Overall mark out of ten 7½

The *Book of Modern Homes* described Little Thakeham thus:
'Amongst the less frequented roadways [and] views of the

countryside, which are unsurpassably charming . . . we may meet with this charm of the "back-water" country, free from busy traffic and the mad rush of motor-cars.' That description was first written in 1909 and it holds true today. Little Thakeham has a superb setting on the South Downs, with commanding views across six acres of orchard and private gardens, and yet remains within an hour's drive of London.

Little Thakeham is reckoned to be one of the finest examples of a Country House built by the renowned Edwardian architect Sir Edwin Lutyens. It dates from around the turn of the century, and although it is by no means one of the largest Country House Hotels in England, its public rooms have been designed and furnished to give a definite impression of space.

All the bedrooms and public rooms include at least one or two pieces of antique furniture, and the medieval-style Minstrel's Gallery is particularly attractive. One of the most striking features about the symmetrically designed rear of the house is the enormous five-sided bay window which protrudes from the centre of the building. A writing table sits behind these huge windows offering commanding views across the gardens.

The restaurant seats thirty and is decorated in a charmingly period 'arts and crafts' style. The chairs are contemporary with the house as a whole, having been fashioned by Ambrose Heal in 1901. Guests eat with antique silver cutlery, and pink linen napkins and tablecloths set off the decor of the room nicely. Food is prepared in a blend of traditional English and modern French styles and presented as a five-course à la carte menu.

Starters range from Warm Duck and Citrus Salad, to Mushrooms stuffed with Crabmeat, and include more unusual dishes like Avocado with Stilton and Walnut Dressing, and Potted Chicken Livers with Green Peppercorns. Main courses include Fresh Salmon, grilled and served with Lime Butter, Roast Rack of Southdown Lamb with garden Mint Sauce, and Fillet of Hare with Beetroot and Orange. The wine list is extensive, with the emphasis on French wines and including many rarer French châteaux wines and some fine vintage ports.

Little Thakeham has ten bedrooms, all double- or twin-bedded, and a number have been carefully converted from old attics and nurseries. Each one comes with a private bathroom (all of which are bright and modern in design), remote-control colour television and direct-dial telephone. Rooms are of a good size, and are better described as 'small suites' as they all have a reasonable amount of space to let you stretch out and relax in front of the television, enjoy a drink, or just sit and read if you so choose.

Among the leisure facilities available for guests are a heated outdoor swimming pool, a grass tennis court, and a croquet lawn. In addition, Little Thakeham sits in six acres of magnificent gardens which were created by Gertrude Jekyll, one of the foremost garden planners of the nineteenth century. The hotel is within an hour's drive of the outskirts of London and all that the capital has to offer visitors to southern England. Other nearby attractions include Arundel Castle, ancestral home of the Duke of Norfolk, and the country houses of Petworth, Parham Park and Goodwood. For businessmen or visitors to Britain, Gatwick Airport is just twenty-two miles away.

83

LYTHE HILL

Address Petworth Road, Haslemere, Surrey GU27
3BQ
Tel: 0428 51251 Fax: 0428 4131

Nearest town Haslemere.
Directions From Guildford, follow the A286
towards Haslemere. Head left along the B2131
when you see the road signposted and you will
soon reach the hotel (on your right).
Awards RAC Merit Award for Main Hotel
Restaurant.
Open throughout the year.
Weekend breaks are available all year round.
Price for dinner, with wine, bed and breakfast for
two – £100–£150
Credit cards Access, Visa and Amex
*The hotel is not suitable for the disabled; children and
dogs are both welcome.*
Overall mark out of ten 7½

Situated in one of the most naturally attractive and unspoilt
parts of southern England, the Lythe Hill hotel sits amid four-

teen acres of beautiful parkland and even has its own private lake for guests to admire. The oldest part of the hotel was originally built as a farmhouse in the late fourteenth century. Early histories of buildings this age are always sketchy, but the estate was known to be in the possession of one Peter Quenell, a yeoman, in 1511 and it stayed in his family for several generations. Peter's son, Thomas, leased some of the land in 1570 to the first Viscount Montague of Cowdray, and the Imbham Ironworks were subsequently built on that ground. No traces remain of what must have been one of the busiest local industries in the late sixteenth century, other than the hammer-pond close by the hotel. Interestingly, Montague failed to produce his quota of arms for Queen Elizabeth I and was summoned before the Privy Council to explain himself. The Viscount's land soon reverted to the family when Thomas Quenell's brother, Robert, took over the furnace in 1574.

The public rooms retain much of their Tudor charm. A 'new' wing, today's East Wing, was added in 1580 and its square-and-circle-patterned timbering presents a fascinating contrast to the late fourteenth-century part of the house. Seldom will you have the opportunity to see so finely preserved contrasts in English architectural style. Antique furniture has been used throughout the house, although modern comforts have not been forgotten. The main lounge has an assortment of large armchairs, and is dominated by a big open fire. The owner has a large collection of copper and pewter which is displayed in various public rooms.

Lythe Hill has a popular main restaurant, although there is a smaller but more atmospheric restaurant in the oldest part of the hotel – Auberge de France – which is open from Tuesday until Sunday. Advance booking is strongly advised for both restaurants. The oak-panelled Auberge offers classic French cuisine and terrific views overlooking the gardens and lake. The recently refurbished Main Restaurant, on the other hand, offers more traditional English dishes, although subtle continental influences can be detected in the choice of herbs and sauces.

Starters in the main restaurant, in which most residents will dine, are on the whole tasty and original and, in one or two cases, unique to Chef de Cuisine Roger Clarke. They include a cocktail of Mango, Dates and Grapefruit set in a pool of Orange and Darjeeling Tea with roasted Pine Kernels; and a warmed Salad of Scottish Smoked Salmon and Fresh Scallops dressed on a bed of French Leaves.

For your main course, the style of cooking is no less imaginative. Typical specialities range from Fillet of Veal dressed on a bed of Straw Potatoes surrounded by a light Crab and Brandy Sauce, to Duo of King Scallops and Avocado simmered with a Shallot and Lime Butter Sauce.

As a result of the refurbishment and renovating programme which was completed by the start of 1988, Lythe Hill now has forty comfortable bedrooms. Five rooms are in the oldest part of the hotel, the Auberge de France. The standard of decor and furnishings in all rooms is high. All are individually furnished to a high standard, some with Italian marble tiled floors and Italian mirrors. Trouser presses and hairdryers are among the range of bedroom facilities designed to offer an extra welcoming touch. One of the older rooms has a magnificent wood-carved four-poster bed which dates from 1614. This is one of the oldest beds in regular use in any hotel in Britain, and the bedroom in which it is located is furnished in first-class Tudor style, complete with wooden beams and wall-mounted candle-style lights similar to those which adorned the walls in the days before electric lighting. All of the rooms, regardless of their age or history, have private bathroom facilities, colour television, and direct-dial telephone.

Within the hotel grounds, leisure facilities available for guests include a hard tennis court, a croquet lawn, and a French *boules* pitch. Golf, horse riding and squash can easily be arranged nearby. Local tourist attractions include Clandon Park near Guildford, Hatchlands (an eighteenth-century red-brick house, with sizeable park, that was decorated by Robert Adam in 1759 as his first commission), Petworth House, Parnham House near Pulborough, and the remains of a Norman fortress at Bramber, near Steyning in Sussex.

84

NETHERFIELD PLACE

Address Battle, East Sussex TN33 9PP
Tel: 04246 4455 Fax: 04246 4024

Nearest town Battle.
Directions The hotel is two miles north-west of
Battle. From Battle, continue along the A2100
towards Netherfield and you will soon see the hotel
signposted on the left-hand side.
Awards AA *** (red) graded.
Open all year except for three weeks over Christmas
and New Year.
No **special breaks** are available.
Price for dinner, with wine, bed and breakfast for
two – £100–£150.
Credit cards Access, Visa, Amex and Diners.
*The hotel is not really suitable for disabled guests unless
they can manage shallow stairs to the first-floor
bedrooms; children are welcome, but dogs are not
accepted.*
Overall mark out of ten 8

In the heart of historic Sussex, Netherfield Place stands amid thirty acres of delightful gardens and parkland. It is just a few miles from the site of the Battle of Hastings, probably the most famous battle in world history, and certainly the most significant of English history. Netherfield Place is a relatively young building, having been built, in Georgian style, only in 1924. The house was originally owned by Sir Peter Reid, founder and owner of Reid Paper Mills.

Inside, the public rooms are bright and comfortable. The standard of decor and furnishing is high, and proprietors Michael and Helen Collier aim constantly to up-grade the hotel. A log fire usually burns in the main lounge (off which the cocktail bar can be found) and there really can be few more relaxing places in this part of southern England in which to sit back and enjoy an aperitif, or after-dinner liqueur.

The restaurant at Netherfield Place is an attractive wood-panelled room, popular with residents and non-residents alike, and has a seating capacity of forty. Comfortable elbow chairs match the light-coloured panelling. The style of cooking is modern French, and Michael Collier takes charge personally in the kitchen to ensure his guests are served with the highest standards of cuisine possible.

Fresh fruit and vegetables are selected daily for the kitchens from the one-acre walled garden, and a number of more unusual herbs are included among this impressive display. Menu specialities, naturally, vary from season to season, but a typical selection of hors d'oeuvres is likely to include a smooth Chicken Liver Pâté, wrapped in Brioche pastry and accompanied by a Warm Butter and Herb Sauce, Mediterranean Prawns which can be served either hot or cold with Garlic Butter or Marie Rose Sauce depending on your preference, and a delicious 'surprise' House Salad composed of strips of Mango, Pineapple, Grapes, Apple and Toasted Almonds presented on a bed of wild lettuce accompanied with a fresh Yoghurt and Cherry Dressing.

The range of entrées is highly commendable and includes one or two more unusual choices such as fresh Quails, boned and filled with a light Chicken Mousse and served with a Port Wine and Grape Sauce, and a most original veal dish made up of thin

295

slices of Veal rolled with Spinach on a bed of Tomato coated with Calvados and Pistachio Sauce. One fish dish which stands out as an alternative main course is Steamed Turbot filled with Crab and coated with a fresh Herb and Butter Sauce. Whatever your preference, the hotel has an excellent wine list which includes nearly 300 bins.

There is a total of fourteen bedrooms including one particularly comfortable room, the Pomeroy, which features a large four-poster. The best room in the hotel is the Mandeville Suite, a bright, warm room decorated with a blend of soft colours. All rooms have private bathroom facilities, colour television (with Teletext), telephone and radio, and come complete with an assortment of welcoming little extras such as a bowl of fruit, fresh flowers and complimentary mineral water.

Netherfield Place has its own tennis courts, in addition to which there is a good range of popular sports, including squash, tennis and golf, available nearby. For the fishing enthusiast, trout fishing can be arranged at the Bewl Bridge Reservoir, and horse riding is possible along a wide selection of country lanes and National Trust footpaths.

Nearby tourist attractions include the town of Battle, where William the Conqueror defeated Harold at the Battle of Hastings in 1066; the castles of Bodiam, Hastings, Pevensey, Leeds, Chiddingstone and Rye; the former homes of Sir Winston Churchill at Chartwell and Rudyard Kipling at Batemans, and the magnificent gardens at Sissinghurst.

85

PENNYHILL PARK

Address Bagshot, Surrey GU19 5ET
Tel: 0276 71774 Fax: 0276 73217

Nearest town Camberley.
Directions Leave the M3 at junction 3 (signposted
Bracknell, Camberley, Guildford) and follow signs
for Bagshot. Continue until you reach a T-junction
at the end of the village and turn left on to the
A30 and then right into Church Road (with the Hero
public house on the corner). The hotel is up on
the left at the end of this road.
A member of the **Prestige Hotels** consortium.
Awards AA and RAC **** graded; English Tourist
Board four Crowns.
Open throughout the year.
Special breaks Good value weekend rates available,
inclusive of half-board accommodation,
complimentary chocolates, champagne and flowers
in your room on arrival. Sporting interest weekend
breaks.

Price for dinner, with wine, bed and breakfast for
two – over £200.
Credit cards Access, Visa, Amex, Diners,
Mastercharge and Carte Blanche.
Children and dogs are welcome by prior arrangement.
Overall mark out of ten 8

Pennyhill Park is a magnificent early Victorian country mansion
which was built in an area of prime parkland once owned by
King James VI and I, and his ill-fated son, Charles I. Both monarchs used to enjoy hunting around this part of southern England a couple of centuries before the present house was built.
The house was originally designed by a distinguished Canadian
who was best known, prior to then, for building the first bridges
across the St Lawrence River in 1849. Today the stonework
has matured into stately elegance with dense shrubbery slowly
covering it from top to bottom.

Pennyhill Park remained a private residence until relatively
recently. Today a large staff works hard to retain much of the
attentive charm of a bygone era, and all the public rooms are
spacious and comfortably furnished. Authentic period furniture
has been retained where possible and numerous oil paintings
adorn the walls in all the public rooms.

The hotel has a very popular restaurant, the Latymer Room,
which is Tudor-styled with authentic Victorian beams. All the
chairs are high-backed cane and tapestry-styled and the tables
and chairs are arranged in a banquet fashion around the peri-
meter of the room. Traditional English and French cuisine is the
speciality of the chef, although there is always an emphasis on
fresh seasonal produce whenever it is available. The à la carte
menus change periodically. Local products are almost always
used, and there are usually at least one or two dishes available
for vegetarians.

There is a more informal restaurant available in the beautifully
restored Orangery. Built in 1891, this delightful building now
houses the hotel's country club, containing most of the leisure
facilities available for residents. The restaurant offers a more
relaxing alternative to the main dining room overlooking the

swimming pool and tennis courts. The Orangery decor is altogether brighter, although very modern, and most food is served buffet style. A recently constructed residents' lounge provides a relaxed setting in which to enjoy a drink beside the open fire.

Pennyhill Park has seventy-six bedrooms, of which a dozen are ideal for families as they have two double beds. A number of the rooms are a little on the small side, but all have private bathroom facilities, colour television, radio and telephone. Most have good views across the surrounding parkland which gives the hotel its name, and all have retained many of the original antique furnishings. Recently, the two separate buildings comprising the hotel have been joined by a sympathetic extension, its style blending with both buildings.

The hotel has a range of leisure facilities for residents to enjoy, including an outdoor heated swimming pool, sauna, three hard tennis courts, a nine-hole golf course, a private trout lake covering just over three acres, horse riding stables, clay pigeon shooting and 120 acres of private parkland and immaculate gardens. Nearby attractions include Royal Ascot, Windsor Castle, Saville Gardens, the ancient city of Winchester, Eton College, Sandhurst Military Academy, Sutton Place, Berkshire Vinery and Henry VIII's magnificent palace Hampton Court.

86

SOUTH LODGE

Address Brighton Road, Lower Beeding, Horsham,
West Sussex RH13 6PS
Tel: 0403 891711 Fax: 0403 891766

Nearest town Horsham.
Directions From London, follow the M23 Brighton
road which leads on to the A23. Take Handcross
turn-off and follow signs to Horsham on the A279.
At Lower Beeding, turn left on to the A281
Cowfold road and the hotel is about 125 yards on
the right-hand side.
A member of the **Prestige Hotels** consortium.
Awards AA *** (red) graded and rosette; RAC ****;
Egon Ronay recommended (78%).
Open throughout the year.
Weekend breaks are available.
Price for dinner, with wine, bed and breakfast for
two – over £150.
Credit cards Access, Visa, Amex and Diners.

The hotel has one ground-floor suite suitable for disabled visitors; children and dogs are welcome.
Overall mark out of ten 8½

Since opening at the beginning of the summer season of 1985, South Lodge has quickly established itself as one of southern England's most popular three-star Country House Hotels. It sits in ninety acres of spectacular gardens containing many dozens of rare plants and shrubs, and these really are a delightful enhancement to this stately Victorian Country House, particularly if you have the opportunity to visit in late spring or early summer.

South Lodge was originally built by the distinguished Victorian explorer and botanist Frederick Ducane Godmain in 1883. Most of the magnificent gardens which you still see today were designed and planned by him over a century ago. The house remained a private residence until the early 1980s when it was extensively renovated and refurbished to its present standards.

The public rooms are well proportioned and have lost little of their late Victorian beauty, despite considerable renovations shortly before South Lodge opened as a hotel. All the public areas have ornate plaster ceilings, and the lounge is a particularly fine room. It is completely wood panelled, and large Chinese carpets cover the polished wooden floor. Crystal chandeliers and antique chinaware adorn the shelves beside and above the carved fireplace and complete the wonderful period feel of this impressive room.

The dining room is no exception to the spaciousness which is typical of all the public rooms at South Lodge, and it also enjoys good views across the South Downs. With rich oak panelling all around, crystal chandeliers, and a seating capacity of forty, this generously proportioned room is never too crowded, and residents and non-residents alike can enjoy a first-class meal in comfortable surroundings. Chef Timothy Franklin prepares an imaginative combination of English- and French-style cuisine, and meals are served on wide wooden trays.

An à la carte and a set table d'hôte menu, which changes daily, are available each evening and, although selections vary considerably from season to season, many of the fruits, vegetables and finer herbs are grown in the large garden within the hotel grounds. Among the interesting specialities normally on offer are dishes created from South Lodge's own home-smoked salmon and home-cured beef.

South Lodge has twenty-six bedrooms, although a further fourteen are likely to be in use by the time of publication. The majority of rooms are large doubles enjoying magnificent views across the gardens and South Downs. All the rooms are individually styled and decorated in a fashion which manages to combine an ageless appeal with the best in modern furnishings. Each room has a private bathroom, many with polished marble fittings, and all rooms have colour television and direct-dial telephones.

Leisure facilities for residents include a hard tennis court, croquet lawns, clay pigeon shooting, and ninety acres of woodland, azalea, camellia and rhododendron gardens. Other sporting activities, including golf, squash and horse riding, can be enjoyed locally by prior arrangement. Nearby attractions include Arundel Castle (stately home of the Duke of Norfolk), Chartwell (former home of Sir Winston Churchill), Glyndebourne, Hever Castle, Parnham Park Gardens, Leonardslee Gardens and racing at Goodwood.

87

TANYARD

Address Wierton Hill, Boughton Monchelsea, near
Maidstone, Kent ME17 4JT
Tel: 0622 744705

Nearest town Maidstone.
Directions From Maidstone, follow the A274 for a
mile or so towards Tenterden. Turn right at
junction with B2163 (at the Plough Pub) and then
left towards Wierton Place Country Club just
before the Cock public house.
Awards AA National Winners Trophy 1987
(awarded to small hotels, inns and guest houses).
Open from March until December.
No **special breaks** are available.
Price for dinner, with wine, bed and breakfast for
two – £100–£150.
Credit cards Access and Visa.
*The hotel is not suitable for the disabled; children under
six, and dogs, are not allowed.*
Overall mark out of ten 7½

Tanyard is one of the most interesting hotels in the London area, and probably the one which, from the outside, looks least like a hotel of any in this section. Its early history is uncertain, but it is known to have started life as a Yeoman's house, was then a medieval farmhouse, and ultimately a tannery for many generations.

The hotel is thought to date from around the mid-fourteenth century, and has been lovingly restored to as near its original splendour as possible. The public rooms have been renovated considerably: the kitchen and dining room are the oldest parts of the house, having been built around 1350, and the lounge and hall area were a later extension, thought to have been added around 1470.

Magnificent old beams are everywhere, both inside and out; indeed, the ancient beams which have been built into the exterior stonework are one of the first features which strike visitors to Tanyard. The public lounge, leading in off the main hall area, is small and comfortable, its dark leather suite the perfect match for the beamed ceiling and antique furnishings which are typical of all the rooms in the hotel.

The dining room has a massive open fire – its size evocative of the days when small tree trunks were thrown on the central fire which had to heat the whole house. Fourteen can be seated at any one time, and unfortunately this number precludes non-residents from dining. Only residents, and their guests, can enjoy the delicious home cooking which proprietor Jan Davies offers throughout the season. Even then, advance booking by at least two months is desirable for those wishing to stay at Tanyard.

Dinner is served promptly at eight each evening, and can be as formal or informal as you wish. The style of cuisine is as typically English as you are likely to find in the London area – undoubtedly Jan Davies is influenced by the very age and history of her surroundings and, above all, by the number of repeat bookings she receives from visitors who have been impressed by her homely style and wise choice of menu from evening to evening.

A set menu is offered each evening, although variations are

available if required. A typical evening's dinner would open with something like Avocado, Crab Claw and Grapefruit Salad served in a Ginger Mayonnaise, followed by a main course of fresh Scottish Salmon with a Hollandaise Sauce and a selection of vegetables. The only alternative for any course is the option of one of a number of home-made ice-creams instead of the set sweet. A selection of English cheeses follows before coffee in the lounge, or at your table, as you wish.

The hotel has five delightful and quite individual bedrooms, all of which have private bathroom facilities, telephones, tea- and coffee-making facilities and colour television. Each one has been furnished in elegant period style, although there is an interesting combination of brightly coloured bed coverings and easy chairs in a number of bedrooms. For that special break, the entire second floor of the old house has been turned into a single large suite. With two bedrooms, a sitting room and a bathroom, this enchanting suite is ideal for up to four people looking for the perfect 'away-from-it-all' holiday in this part of England.

Tanyard has nothing to offer in the way of leisure facilities other than simple peace and quiet. Some popular activities, such as golf, fishing and a range of indoor sports, are available in the Maidstone area. The hotel is ideally placed for exploring Kent and East Sussex, and nearby attractions include Leeds Castle, Sissinghurst Castle, Bodiam Castle and the historic town of Canterbury with its ancient cathedral. The Channel ports of Dover and Folkestone are only a short drive away, offering plenty of opportunity for day trips to the French coast.

88

TYLNEY HALL

Address Rotherwick, near Basingstoke, Hampshire
RG27 9AJ
Tel: 0256 764881 Fax: 0256 768141

Nearest town Basingstoke.
Directions Leave the M3 at junction 5, taking the
A287 towards Basingstoke. Go straight ahead at the
junction with the A30, turn left at the next T-
junction, then right at crossroads signposted
Rotherwick. The hotel is about half a mile on the
left from here.
A member of the **Prestige Hotels** consortium.
Awards AA B.L. and RAC **** and Merit Awards
H.C.R. graded; Egon Ronay 81%; English Tourist
Board five Crowns.
Open throughout the year.
Special **weekend breaks** are available throughout
the year.
Price for dinner, with wine, bed and breakfast for
two – £100–£150.
Credit cards All major cards accepted.
*The hotel can cater for disabled visitors; children are
welcome but dogs are not allowed.*
Overall mark out of ten 9

The magnificent Georgian-style façade of Tylney Hall dominates the sixty-six acres of private park and woodland in which the house is set, and without a doubt this is one of the most impressive buildings anywhere in Hampshire. Although it has only been open as a hotel since autumn 1985, Tylney Hall has quickly established itself as one of the best hotels in this part of England, offering a class of comfort and service so typical of an earlier era when the house was in its prime as a private residence.

A mansion has been known on the Tylney estate since 1561, although it was not until the start of the eighteenth century that the first Tylney Hall was built by one Frederick Tylney. The family line died with him in 1725 as he failed to produce a male heir, and the original Hall passed into the hands of the fifth Earl of Mornington. He subsequently demolished the house because, it is believed, he was not allowed to fell timber from the surrounding rich woodland so long as the house stood! Lionel Phillips purchased the estate in 1898 and rebuilt the house in the present style.

The interior of the house boasts English oak panelling throughout, and your first sight of this will be the elegant entrance hall, with its sweeping staircase and solid oak pillars. The other public rooms are no less impressive, and the panelled library bar is the perfect place to relax with a pre-dinner drink. There are two public lounges: the Grey Lounge, which is not wood panelled, but has an equally traditional grey decor and an ornate white and gold plaster frieze all round the edges of the ceiling; the Italianate Lounge which has a more spectacular ceiling of intricately carved oak, inlaid with gold leaf, which originally came from the Grimation Palace in Florence.

The restaurant seats eighty, about half of whom are generally non-residents, and the room has views of the Dutch garden and outdoor swimming pool. It is dominated by a large glass-domed ceiling which in summer allows the natural daylight to flood in. The remainder of the ceiling is styled with ornate plasterwork and the walls are adorned with hand-tooled Spanish leather panelling.

Chef Stephen Hine trained at the Dorchester in London and offers a table d'hôte and an à la carte menu each evening, based heavily on traditional English styles, although influenced by *cuisine moderne*. There is an excellent range of dishes available each evening; usually at least three choices for each course on the table d'hôte menu and substantially more on the à la carte. Starters include a delicious Salad of Lobster and Mango bound together in a Sherry Dressing and garnished with Asparagus, and a Cocktail of Assorted Seasonal Melon, sprinkled with a Mint Liqueur and served in a coconut shell.

Main dish specialities range from three small Fillets of Panfried Lamb, Beef and Veal served with three different accompanying sauces, to Fillet of Turbot filled with a Scallop Mousse and steamed before being served with a Brandy and Lobster Sauce. One other fish dish worth looking out for is an intriguing portion of Scampi, sealed in butter, which has been flamed with Pernod and casseroled in a Vegetable Butter Sauce.

Tylney Hall has a total of ninety-one bedrooms, including seven large suites. All are individually styled and furnished to the highest standards of comfort, complete with private bathroom facilities and colour television. All the rooms are a good size, but the suites are particularly large, and each room has at least one or two pieces of antique furniture (a dressing table, wardrobe, fireplace, etc) as a reminder of the days when Tylney Hall was a private residence. A number of the suites also have antique four-posters and private jacuzzis to add that little extra comfort to your stay.

The hotel has a number of leisure facilities available for residents including a heated outdoor swimming pool, two hard tennis courts and a croquet lawn and there is an eighteen-hole golf course adjacent to the estate. A heated indoor swimming pool with whirlpool, multigym, sauna and snooker room are recent additions to Tylney Hall's leisure portfolio. Nearby attractions include Stratfield House (former home of the Duke of Wellington), Windsor Castle, Winchester Cathedral, Stonehenge, and the cities of Southampton and Oxford within an hour's drive, in opposite directions, from Tylney Hall.

South-west England

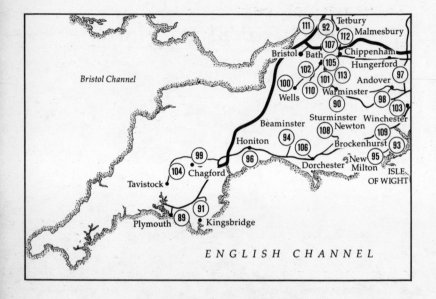

South-west England

89 Alston Hall
90 Bishopstrow House
91 Buckland-Tout-Saints
92 Calcot Manor
93 Careys Manor
94 Chedington Court
95 Chewton Glen
96 Combe House
97 Elcot Park
98 Fifehead Manor
99 Gidleigh Park
100 Glencot House
101 Homewood Park

102 Hunstrete House
103 Lainston House
104 Lewtrenchard Manor
105 Lucknam Park
106 Maiden Newton House
107 The Manor House
108 Plumber Manor
109 Rhinefield House
110 Ston Easton Park
111 Thornbury Castle
112 Whatley Manor
113 Woolley Grange

89

ALSTON HALL

Address Battisborough Cross, Holbeton, near
Plymouth, Devon PL8 1HN
Tel: 075530 259 Fax: 075530 494

Nearest town Plymouth.
Directions The hotel is situated off the main A379
Plymouth to Kingsbridge road. Proceeding
towards Kingsbridge, take the Holbeton road for
about three miles and the hotel is signposted on
your right.
Awards Egon Ronay, Ashley Courtenay and
Michelin recommended.
Open throughout the year.
Special breaks Limited weekend and winter breaks
are available.
Price for dinner, with wine, bed and breakfast for
two – £100–£150.
Credit cards Access, Visa, Amex and Diners.
*The hotel is unsuitable for the disabled; no children or
dogs are allowed.*
Overall mark out of ten 7½

Set in an area of outstanding natural beauty, Alston Hall is surrounded by four and a half acres of private park and woodland. It is a typically grand Edwardian Country House, having been built in 1906 by the vicar of Holbeton as his private residence, and remaining so until the 1960s when it was converted into a small luxury hotel. A considerable amount of work has gone into the house since the 1960s in order to up-grade the building to the demanding standards of a quality Country Hotel and, if the popularity of Alston Hall is anything to judge by, these efforts have more than paid off.

The exterior of the hotel is as solid as it is impressive. Constructed from brick and dressed granite, the steeply sloping red clay tile roof contrasts well with the stone mullions and dense Virginia creeper which is slowly covering the walls. You could be forgiven for thinking the exterior of the building is older than it looks because of its semi-Tudor style roof and wide stone chimneys.

A rich oak theme prevails throughout the public area of Alston Hall, and nowhere is this more striking than in the Great Hall which greets you as you first enter the building. This high-ceilinged room is completely panelled and has a distinctive Minstrel Gallery all around the first-floor level. The Great Hall, with its red leather chairs and wide fireplace, doubles as an additional lounge when the hotel is busy.

The oak theme is continued in the bar, although only the bar area itself is totally panelled. Here you can relax with a pre-dinner drink and appreciate some fine views across Dartmoor. The main lounge is purpose-built and serves as a ballroom for weddings, private parties and other functions.

Up to forty can normally be seated in the comfortable dining room which is open to non-residents. The atmosphere is quiet and informal, and Head Chef Malcolm Morrison blends traditional English and modern French styles of cuisine. A varied table d'hôte menu is offered each evening, together with a reasonable wine list with a good range of younger European bottles to complement your meal.

Starters include rather unusual combinations like Scrambled Egg and Smoked Salmon, and Grilled Avocado and Stilton

Cheese. For your main dish, specialities include Chicken Cagliari (a delicious combination of strips of chicken with prawns in a white wine sauce), Saltimbocca à la Romana (veal wrapped in ham and served in a white wine sauce), or grilled Lemon Sole Meunière. Alston Hall has recently added a new restaurant – the Peony Room – which seats thirty guests. Here the cuisine is international in style, utilizing local seafood and farm produce, and the menu is changed daily.

The hotel has twenty bedrooms, all double or twin rooms and all with private bathrooms and showers en suite. All have been individually decorated and furnished in a bright modern style with remote-control Teletext colour television, radio and direct-dial telephone. Most of the rooms have large windows offering good views across the gardens and Dartmoor.

Alston Hall has a number of leisure facilities available for residents, including heated indoor and outdoor swimming pools, two all-weather tennis courts, sauna, solarium, multigym and a croquet lawn. Other sports like golf and fishing can be arranged locally. There are a considerable number of local castles and abbeys in the area around Alston Hall, and the port towns of Plymouth, Dartmouth and Salcombe are popular with visitors to the area. When the weather permits, Dartmoor and numerous beaches along the southern coast can be visited.

90

BISHOPSTROW HOUSE

Address Bishopstrow, Warminster, Wiltshire BA12 9HH
Tel: 0985 212312 Fax: 0985 216769

Nearest town Warminster.
Directions Bishopstrow House is located a mile and a half south-east of Warminster on the B3414 – off the A36, the main road between Bath and Salisbury. A member of the **Prestige** consortium.
Awards AA **** graded, Egon Ronay 84%; Michelin recommended.
Open throughout the year.
Winter breaks are available for any two days, half-board, between October and March.
Price for dinner, with wine, bed and breakfast for two – over £150.
Credit cards Access, Visa, Amex and Diners.
The hotel has nine ground-floor rooms so is suitable for

disabled visitors; children under three years of age are not
allowed; dogs only by prior arrangement.
Overall mark out of ten 9½

Bishopstrow House is an extremely attractive Regency mansion, deceptively larger inside than its ivy-clad façade leads you to think. It is set in twenty-five acres of private woodland and garden which includes its own river frontage down to the River Wylye. The house has a fairly undistinguished history, having been built by John Pinch of Bath in 1817 and converted into a luxury Country House Hotel this century.

All the public rooms have been furnished in lavish style. The grand entrance hall, with its wide staircase and antique chairs, leads into the drawing room. This bright lounge has enormous curved bay windows offering good views across the garden, and beautiful arrangements of fresh flowers silhouetted against the sunlight.

The hotel has two dining rooms, including one which overlooks the indoor swimming pool. The main restaurant seats sixty and has a very traditional decor which verges on the formal. Original oil paintings and quality ornamental chinaware merely add to this atmosphere which enhances the very high standards of cuisine, which you can expect from Head Chef Chris Suter, voted Young Chef of the Year 1990.

The style of cooking is light and imaginative, using local produce wherever possible. Starters include Fresh Cornish Crab set on a light Tomato Mousse with a Cucumber and Dill Salad, and Ballotine of local Duck served with a homemade Apple and Sage Jelly. Main dishes range from Calves' Liver gently cooked with Avocado and Madeira to a delicious Rosette of Veal cooked in Pink Peppercorns and a Cream Sauce. The separate dessert menu is more adventurous than the choice of main dishes and generally includes a selection of treats such as Meringue Crown filled with a light Raspberry Mousse and Champagne Marquise, or perhaps Caramelized Puff Pastry filled with Oranges and coated in a Cream Vanilla Sauce.

The wine list is as long as it is comprehensive – and is definitely one for the connoisseur. Quality vintages include an outstanding selection of classic French wines, although the very drinkable house white or red at around £10 a bottle may be to more people's liking than the Château Petrus Pomerol 1947 at over £500 a bottle.

There are twenty-six bedrooms available, including eight luxurious suites and one single. Each room is decorated in a lavish blend of soft colours and rich cloth – golds, pinks, yellows and so on – with the occasional piece of antique furniture. A number of newer rooms are situated in a recently converted stable block. All rooms are extremely well appointed and spacious, and come complete with colour television, private bathrooms (and a selection of complimentary toiletries), and direct-dial telephone. One has a round bed, and the addition of a bowl of fruit and fresh flowers adds a personal touch to each bedroom. A number of rooms are fitted with their own safes, and several of the suites have private jacuzzis.

Bishopstrow House has a range of leisure facilities to offer residents including both a very attractive heated indoor swimming pool, complete with white marble surround, and a heated outdoor pool. Both indoor and outdoor tennis courts, together with a sauna and solarium, and the opportunity to enjoy private fishing rights on the River Wylye are available. In addition, there is a golf course two miles away and facilities for horse riding about four miles away.

Other nearby attractions include the stately home of the Marquis of Bath, Longleat House, complete with its famous safari park; Stourhead House and gardens; Wilton House; Stonehenge; Avebury; and the historic cities of Bath and Salisbury.

91

BUCKLAND-TOUT-SAINTS

Address Goveton, Kingsbridge, Devon TQ7 2DS
Tel: 0548 853055 Fax: 0548 856261

Nearest town Kingsbridge.
Directions Bypassing Exeter, head for the A381
signposted Kingsbridge. Pass through villages of
Herbertonford, Halwell and the Mounts. After one
and a half miles turn left opposite sign for hotel
and continue along single-track road for a mile into
Goveton village. Turn right up a steep hill, with a
church on your right, and the second drive on the
right is for the hotel.
A member of the **Prestige Hotels** consortium.
Awards AA and RAC *** graded and RAC Blue
Ribbon Award 1989, 1990; British Tourist Authority
commended; Egon Ronay recommended.
Open throughout the year, apart from two weeks
after New Year.
Special breaks Interlude and Romantic breaks
between 1 November and 31 March; special

Christmas programme available; Lazy Summer breaks in July and August; November Clay Pigeon Shooting Weekends.

Price for dinner, with wine, bed and breakfast for two – over £150.

Credit cards Access, Visa, Amex, Diners, Carte Blanche and Connect.

The hotel is not suitable for the disabled or children under eight; dogs are not allowed.

Overall mark out of ten 8½

The estate on which the Buckland-Tout-Saints hotel has been built has a history which can be charted back to the era before the Norman Conquest of 1066. It was known then simply as 'Bochland' – literally meaning 'by the book' – which meant the land was free of any feudal service to a lord. The Tout-Saints family, after whom the hotel is named, are reckoned to have taken over the estate sometime during the reign of Richard I at the end of the twelfth century. They built the first manor on this site, although the only trace of it now is the stone-flagged floor which is still visible in the basement storerooms of the present hotel.

The building as it now stands was conceived and built by Sir John Southcote at the end of the seventeenth century after he, as a prominent English Catholic, returned from a spell of religious exile in France once the Catholic James II was on the British throne. The architectural style was relatively uncommon in this part of England, but such features as ovolo mouldings for the lower ground-floor windows, and casement rather than sash windows, were already common in eastern England and France where Sir John had already lived.

Many of the public areas of the hotel reflect the grandeur of the late seventeenth and early eighteenth centuries. The wood panelling and ceiling plasterwork in the writing room are among the best examples of the style adapted by Sir John between 1685 and 1693. The main lounge has been altered considerably since then, although the twentieth-century panelling and plasterwork resembles what the original room was said to look like. Look out for the small writing room with its very attractive late eighteenth-century Adam-style mahogany door.

The dining room dates from the Queen Anne era, with the original Russian pine panelling still intact. An ornate plaster ceiling has not survived but this does not detract from the intimate period feel which the rich panelling creates. The style of cuisine is distinctly modern British, using best-quality food, carefully reduced sauces and imaginative presentation.

An impressive three- or four-course fixed price menu is available each evening, presented in a large folder with a detailed explanation of the type of food served, the style of presentation and the variety of raw foodstuffs used in the preparation of your meal. Typical starters include Sautéed Scallops in a Mild Curry Sauce; a Terrine of Brill, Crab and Watercress with Avocado Sauce; and a Puff Pastry of Calves' Liver, Grapes and Mushrooms.

Main dishes change with the seasons, but generally include most traditional British dishes from Scotch Sirloin Steak, with a Red Wine Sauce and Peperonata, to Best End of English Lamb with Herb Sauce and Courgette Rimbale. One or two more original fish dishes are normally available as well as main courses, and those featured might include Turbot à la Duglère served with Cream, Herbs and Tomatoes, or perhaps Steamed Fillet of Brill with a Hazelnut Mousseline.

Buckland-Tout-Saints has twelve bedrooms, including two large first-floor suites. The Buckland Room has a magnificent hand-carved four-poster which has been made from solid mahogany to match the other antique furnishings in the room. The larger, superior rooms – two doubles and two twins – are also on the first floor while the remainder, with their Provençe-style shuttered windows, are on the second floor of the hotel. All have private bathrooms, colour television, direct-dial telephones, hairdryer, trouser press and good views across the hotel's grounds and surrounding countryside.

The hotel does not actively market any special activities or facilities for residents because, the owners say, they prefer to specialize in offering peace and tranquillity combined with informal but attentive service. Golf, sea and fresh-water fishing, tennis and squash can all be arranged locally, and during the summer months there is a croquet pitch laid out on the lawn. Nearby attractions include the natural beauty of the surrounding Devon countryside, a number of National Trust properties, the towns of Exeter and Plymouth, and the coastal resort of Torquay.

92

CALCOT MANOR

Address Near Tetbury, Gloucestershire GL8 8YJ
Tel: 066 689 391 Fax: 066 689 394

Nearest town Tetbury.
Directions From the M5, leave at junction 13
(signposted Stroud) and follow signs for the A46,
turning towards Bath. Turn left at the crossroads
off the A4135 and Calcot Manor is on the left-hand
side after this turning.
A member of the **Pride of Britain** consortium.
Awards AA *** (red) graded and rosette; Michelin
recommended and star for restaurant; Egon Ronay
75%; 1986 *Hotel and Caterer* Newcomer of the Year
Award.
Open throughout the year.
Special breaks Mid-week breaks and weekend
breaks available.
Price for dinner, with wine, bed and breakfast for
two – over £150.
Credit cards Access, Visa, Amex and Diners.

*The hotel has one ground-floor suite suitable for disabled
visitors; children under twelve and dogs are not allowed.*
Overall mark out of ten 8

Best described as a fifteenth-century manor house, Calcot Manor
was originally a large Cotswold manor, complete with a working
farm for centuries, before current owners Brian and Barbara Ball,
together with their son Richard, bought it in October 1983. The
farm was sold separately, but four acres of garden and woodland
have been retained with the house, along with a courtyard of
old stables and an attractive tithe barn which is reckoned to date
back as far as the fourteenth century. Calcot was once part of
the estate of Kingswood Abbey, which was founded by the
Cistercians in 1158.

All the public rooms have been completely renovated and
restored back to the style typical of the splendour of an earlier
era. The house is lavishly furnished with antique family furniture, and the 'peaches and cream' decor of the drawing room is
particularly appealing. The Ball family take pride in running the
hotel in as informal and professional a manner as possible; staff
are never obtrusive but always available to attend to the requirements of residents.

The main restaurant seats up to forty and has attractive French
windows which lead out on to a garden terrace where you can
enjoy a relaxing pre-dinner drink during the milder summer
evenings. A combination of square and circular tables complements the green, apricot and grey decor.

Chef Ramon Farthing offers a most impressive three- (or four-
including cheese) course table d'hôte menu which embraces
the best of modern British cooking. The menu displays a keen
speciality in fish dishes, although if fish is not your main preference you are unlikely to be disappointed by the other choices
available. A recommended first course is Boned Quail
accompanied by Fresh Noodles flavoured with Oregano, Spinach Leaves and a warm Red Wine and Shallot Dressing. For a
main dish, Fresh Salmon panfried on Lyonnaise Potatoes flavoured with Basil complemented by a Clarified Wine Infusion
cannot fail to delight. All dishes are accompanied by a selection

of locally grown vegetables. Calcot's dessert speciality is an Apple Dessert showing Four Classical Presentations.

The hotel has thirteen bedrooms, including three new ones opened in August 1987. Each has a private bathroom and a unique character in keeping with the style of this marvellous old house. All the bedrooms reflect a particular part of the surrounding region: the Chiltern Room, for example, has hedge-row-patterned wallpaper with matching fabrics and the bathroom tiles have an intricate bramble design on them. All bedrooms have colour television and direct-dial telephone, and the master bedroom has a magnificent canopied and draped four-poster, and is one of three rooms with a private jacuzzi.

The hotel is situated in the south Cotswolds and is surrounded by beautiful countryside. The main leisure facility, other than walking in the natural beauty all around you, is a heated outdoor swimming pool which is open from May until September. There is a croquet lawn in the grounds, and tennis, fishing, ballooning and clay pigeon shooting are all available on site, while horse riding can be arranged nearby. Other local attractions include Sir Peter Scott's Wildfowl Trust at Slimbridge, Westonbirt Arboretum ten minutes away by car, Blenheim Palace, Stonehenge, Berkeley Castle, Sudeley Castle and the towns of Oxford and Bath within thirty minutes' drive.

93

CAREYS MANOR

Address Brockenhurst, New Forest, Hampshire
SO42 7RH
Tel: 0590 23551

Nearest town Brockenhurst.
Directions Leave the M27 at junction 1 and follow
the signs to Brockenhurst. The hotel is eight miles
from the motorway exit.
A member of the **New Forest Hotels and
Restaurants Association**.
Awards AA and RAC *** graded; English Tourist
Board four Crowns; Ashley Courtenay and Egon
Ronay recommended; also recommended by a
number of European organizations.
Open throughout the year.
Mid-week breaks available all year round.
Price for dinner, with wine, bed and breakfast for
two – £100–£150.
Credit cards Access, Visa, Amex and Diners.
*The hotel is suitable for the disabled; children and dogs
are welcome.*
Overall mark out of ten 7

Careys Manor was originally built as a hunting lodge in the seventeenth century and frequently used by King Charles II. The hotel is named after a local forester, John Carey, to whom the original lodge was given by Charles II for services rendered. In 1888 the building was considerably extended, and it has operated as a Country House Hotel since the 1930s.

Careys Manor is a particularly popular conference venue, and most of the spacious public rooms are large enough to easily accommodate business meetings, or major social functions, such as wedding and anniversary parties. A new conference suite was completed in 1987 and adjoins the main restaurant. The style of furnishing in the public areas varies from the traditional (such as the wood-panelled reception area) to the modern.

The restaurant has recently been refurbished and is decorated in a rich, soft pink and green colour-scheme. It can seat up to eighty. The style of food is a combination of modern British and French cuisine. A three- or a four-course table d'hôte, or an à la carte menu, is available each evening and popular appetizers include Melon and Pineapple Platter served with a refreshing home-made sorbet, or Smoked Seafood Platter with a Tomato, Basil, Cottage Cheese and Brandy Dressing.

From the selection of main dishes we would recommend Grilled Entrecôte Steak served with Tomato, Mushrooms and Parsley Butter, or for health-conscious guests, Poached Fillet of Brill presented in a Mustard and Cheese Sauce. There is an extensive selection of over 150 wines and ports available, but many diners prefer to look no further than the (French) house wines at around £7 a bottle to accompany their meal. A recent and original development at Careys Manor is the opening of a new French Restaurant, Le Blaireau (the badger) – the most authentic French cafe/bar restaurant in the south of England. It is managed and run entirely by French staff.

Careys Manor has eighty bedrooms, nearly a third of which were added as part of a major refurbishment programme in 1987. All are comfortably furnished, with private bathrooms, colour television, telephone and facilities for tea- and coffee-making, although there is little sense of individuality between many of the rooms. Half of the bedrooms have been refurbished to a high standard, and include personal safes and minibars. The Garden Wing, linked to the main building by a covered walkway, has the most modern-style rooms in the hotel, in terms of decor and furnishings, but these bedrooms have the pleasant advantage of opening directly on to the lawns, or possessing a private balcony which overlooks the five acres of landscaped gardens.

The hotel has an excellent health and leisure complex, the Carat Club, which guests can enjoy on payment of a small daily charge. The centrepiece is an indoor heated ozone swimming pool and jacuzzi (for which there is no charge) which has a 'jetstream' underwater current system installed for the benefit of serious swimmers. In addition, there is a supervised gymnasium, sauna, Turkish Room, impulse shower and treatment room for massage and beauty treatment. There are no fewer than eight golf courses within a fifteen-mile radius of the hotel, and numerous local riding stables have facilities available for residents to enjoy should they so desire.

Nearby attractions include the National Motor Museum at Beaulieu, Broadlands (former home of Earl Mountbatten of Burma), Exbury Gardens, Marwell Zoological Park near Winchester, the New Forest Butterfly Farm, the Royal Naval Museum at Southsea and two of England's most famous historical ships, HMS *Victory* and the *Mary Rose*, which are on display at Portsmouth.

94

CHEDINGTON COURT

Address Chedington, Beaminster, Dorset DT8 3HY
Tel: 093589 265 Fax: 093589 442

Nearest town Beaminster.

Directions Follow the A30 (or from London, the
M3, M303 and A356) to Crewkerne. From there,
continue down the A356 and the hotel is four and
a half miles in the Dorchester direction, just off
the A356 at Winyard's Gap.

A member of the **Historic and Romantic Hotel
Group**.

Awards British Tourist Authority commended;
Egon Ronay and Michelin recommended.

Open throughout the year except for a few days
over Christmas and a month from mid-January.

Special rates available for stays of two nights half-
board or longer.

Price for dinner, with wine, bed and breakfast for
two – £100–£150.

Credit cards Not encouraged, but Visa, Mastercard,
Eurocard and Amex are accepted.

The hotel is not suitable for disabled visitors; children are allowed; dogs are not allowed in the hotel, but can be accommodated in the boiler room if necessary.
Overall mark out of ten 7½

Chedington Court must be one of the most peaceful hotels featured in this guide. It is located in ten acres of mature private park and woodland in the heart of Dorset, and would be the ideal choice for a complete 'away-from-it-all' break, or even a honeymoon.

The house itself is a beautifully romantic old building, although on a stormy winter's night it would be the perfect venue for a horror movie with all its turrets, towers and leaded windows. Chedington Court was built by William Trevelyan Cox in 1840 on the site of a much older house which is known to date back many centuries. By the end of the nineteenth century, the estate comprised over 1500 acres of surrounding countryside but this was destined to be broken up in 1949. The present owners bought the house in 1981, and are constantly making improvements in order to maintain the high standards of hospitality which have been a feature of Chedington Court ever since they first opened it as a hotel.

Inside, Chedington Court has a heavily traditional atmosphere, though perhaps the peacefulness is taken a little too seriously as the place is sometimes so quiet one feels the noise of eating dinner is excessive! That said, it is a perfect place for a truly peaceful weekend. There is no public or cocktail bar but drinks can be served in either the drawing room or the library. Furnishings tend to be solid and antique and, interestingly, some of them came from the state rooms of perhaps the greatest of all ocean-going liners, the *Queen Mary*. One of the bedrooms is named after the old ship as it contains a suite which was obtained after she was decommissioned as a seagoing vessel in the early 1970s.

Chedington Court's dining room is as small as it is intimate. Only twenty-six can be seated at any one time, which makes dinner for non-residents a rare privilege when the hotel has its capacity twenty residents dining at once. It is a lovely old room, with its thick curtains, traditional Country House furniture and a daily four-course menu with a two-option choice of starter and a set fish and main course. Guests dine off fine Wedgwood crockery with silver-plated cutlery, and candle-burning table lamps specially imported from Denmark complete the atmosphere, that is only occasionally broken by softly playing classical music in the background.

Hilary specializes in traditional English cuisine, although the influence of French cooking is unmistakable. The food is beautifully cooked and presented and the standards very high. A typical evening's dinner will open with a starter like Celeriac, Cucumber, Radish and Watercress Salad with herbs, or Carrot Soup with Coriander. A light fish course such as Gratin of Scallops with a Saffron Sauce, or Steamed Salmon Trout with Caper Sauce precedes your main dish.

Main courses rely heavily on traditional English meats, although vegetarian preferences and special dietary requirements can be catered for on request, provided that the kitchen is given some advance warning. Favourite meals include Fillet of Beef in Pastry, Roast Dorset Duckling with Limes, and Rack of English Spring Lamb cooked in an assortment of locally grown herbs.

The hotel has ten large bedrooms, all doubles or twins, which can also be used for single occupancy on payment of a £10 supplement per night. All have private bath or shower rooms (some with gold-plated taps, no less, and a range of complimentary toiletries), and are mostly named after plants or local regions – Rhododendron, Hollyhock, Dorset, Devon and so forth. The 'Four Poster' room speaks for itself, with a magnificent old antique bed, a lovely bathroom with double jacuzzi and shower, and good views across the garden. Other rooms recently refurbished include the Hardy, the Wessex, the Queen Mary, the Somerset and Hollyhock.

Among its most distinctive features are the ten acres of magnificent grounds which surround the house. These are exceptionally well looked after, and within their walls include a number of tombstones in the original churchyard. The fine specimen trees and plants are labelled and cared for by the gardeners.

A walk before dinner in the grounds here is an experience worth driving a long way for. Other leisure facilities are croquet or putting on the sizeable lawns.

Nearby attractions include a wealth of famous sites and historic buildings. Among the better known are Pilsdon Pen, Forde Abbey, Clapton Court, East Lambrook Manor, Barrington Court, Montacute House and Sherborne Castle (and Sherborne's 'old' castle as well). Other attractions include Thomas Hardy's cottage, Abbotsbury Gardens and Swannery, and the towns of Dorchester, Yeovil, Taunton and Shaftesbury.

95

CHEWTON GLEN

Address New Milton, Hampshire BH25 6QS
Tel: 0425 275341

Nearest town New Milton.
Directions Follow the A337 through Highcliffe and
fork left shortly after the 30 mph speed limit sign at
the Walkford junction. Take the first right turning
into Chewton Farm Road, and you will see the
entrance to the hotel drive on your right.
A member of the **Relais et Châteaux Group**.
Awards AA **** (red) graded and rosette; Egon
Ronay 88%; Michelin five (red) turrets and rosette for
food; English Tourist Board five Gold Crowns (the
only hotel outside London with the maximum
award); British Tourist Authority commended; 1985
Executive Travel magazine Best Time Off Hotel
award 1985; Executive Travel Best Small Hotel 1989;
Hotel Restaurant of the Year Award 1989.
Open throughout the year.
Winter breaks are available between 1 November
and 31 March.
Price for dinner, with wine, bed and breakfast for
two – approximately £250.

Credit cards Access, Visa, Amex, Diners and Carte
Blanche.
*The hotel is unsuitable for the disabled; children under
seven and dogs are not allowed.*
Overall mark out of ten 10

If it could not claim the honour outright, Chewton Glen would
certainly come very close to being named as southern England's
finest hotel. With an outstanding reputation for first-class personal service, an enviable country setting which is within a few
minutes' drive of major road and rail links to the rest of the UK,
and some of the highest standards of comfort and cuisine in the
country, Chewton Glen epitomizes everything a good Country
House Hotel should be.

The hamlet of Chewton can trace its origins back to at least
the days of the Normans, but the present Chewton Glen manor
dates back to the 1730s. This was the heyday of the new classical
Palladian architectural style, and a watercolour completed about
a century later (one of the earliest contemporary illustrations of
the house) shows a stuccoed Georgian building with a symmetrical west façade and high proportions typical of the short-lived
Palladian style.

Many changes have taken place since the eighteenth century:
rainwater pipes on the west side of the house bear the date
1904, a new curved central section was added to the front of the
house in the 1830s, and in the last thirty years a new east wing
has been added. The most famous former resident at Chewton
Glen is Captain Frederick Marryat, who built up a popular reputation as a writer and illustrator after his *Code of Signals for
the Merchant Service* was published in 1817. He made a famous
drawing of Napoleon on his deathbed in 1821 (two versions of
which are on display at the National Maritime Museum in
London) and later wrote a series of novels which quickly became
classics of their type. His last book, *The Children of the New Forest*
(written here in 1846), remains in print today.

The public rooms at Chewton Glen have been lavishly furnished with a stately grace that enhances the elegant exterior
and well-tended seventy acres of private gardens and parkland.

The Oak Room has polished wood panelling all round and, like the Sun Lounge, offers magnificent views across the estate. The carefully thought-out blend of deeply upholstered chairs, fine antiques and gentle floral patterns on the curtains and armchairs enhances the feeling of space and timelessness which few luxury hotels manage to achieve with such perfection.

Head chef Pierre Chevillard joined Chewton Glen in 1979 from the world-famous Troisgros restaurant in Roanne. Each evening he and his kitchen staff create a splendid selection of à la carte specialities, in a modern French style, which are served in the relaxing surroundings of the coral pink and green Marryat Restaurant. Seating capacity is 120, and non-residents are encouraged to book at least a week in advance, although it is worth pointing out that a full four-course dinner for two, with a moderate wine, will leave little change from £100.

Speciality openers include Burgundy Snails served in a thin tart case with Tomato, Garlic and Herbs, or Clear Mushroom Soup garnished with Quail Rissoles. Main dishes range from local Dover Sole grilled or sautéed in butter, to Fillet of New Season Lamb served simply with a light 'jus'. The hotel offers an excellent wine list, with a sensible range of moderate wines under £10 a bottle right up to classic vintages such as a 1952 Lafite Rothschild at nearly £200.

All forty-five bedrooms, including a number in the carefully restored Coach House, are large doubles or twins, and there are a further thirteen extremely well-appointed suites. Each one is named after characters in the works of Captain Marryat – Lady Baker, Mr Midshipman Easy *et al*. A personalized welcome note and complimentary sherry greet you on arrival, and it is these little touches (along with the carafe of iced water, fresh flowers and quality Crabtree & Evelyn bathroom toiletries) that help make Chewton Glen that bit extra special. All rooms have private bathrooms, deep pile carpets and the occasional piece of antique furnishing to create a comfortable combination of modern luxury and the timeless charm of an earlier age.

Among the range of leisure facilities available at Chewton Glen are a nine-hole golf course during the summer months, an outdoor heated swimming pool, an all-weather tennis court, a croquet lawn and a snooker room. Within a short drive, you can also enjoy clay pigeon shooting, fishing, sailing, squash and horse riding. At the time of writing, an extensive leisure complex is due to be constructed at Chewton Green. Its proposed facilities are to include swimming pool, hairdressing salon, gymnasium, health treatment rooms and two indoor tennis courts.

A handy booklet is given to all guests on arrival detailing many of the sites and places to visit in the surrounding area. Among the better-known attractions are Beaulieu Abbey and Palace House; Broadlands (former home of the late Earl Mountbatten of Burma); the birthplace of Thomas Hardy; Longleat House and Safari Park; Wilton House; Exbury Gardens; Kingston Lacy House and Gardens; Winchester and Salisbury Cathedrals; HMS *Victory* and the *Mary Rose* Museum at Portsmouth; Stonehenge; and the towns of Portsmouth, Southampton, Salisbury and Bournemouth.

96

COMBE HOUSE

Address Gittisham, near Honiton, Devon EX14 0AD
Tel: 0404 42756 Fax: 0404 46004

Nearest town Honiton.
Directions Combe House is situated off the A30
about a mile south-west of Honiton. The hotel
drive is in the village of Gittisham.
A founder member of the **Pride of Britain**
consortium.
Awards AA ***; British Tourist Authority
commended; Egon Ronay, *Good Hotel Guide* and
Michelin recommended.
Open from the last Friday in February until around
the middle of January.
Winter breaks are available from 1 November until
the end of March.
Price for dinner, with wine, bed and breakfast for
two – over £150.
Credit cards Access, Visa, Amex and Diners.

The hotel is not suitable for the disabled; children and dogs are welcome.
Overall mark out of ten 8½

Dating back to Elizabethan times, Combe House is an attractive old mansion house in the heart of rural Devon. The Putt family held the estate for 232 years, doing much to create the structure of the house and the splendid gardens as they now appear. One family member, Nicholas Putt, was an active Royalist during the period of the English Revolution, and died on his way to London after being carried off by Cromwell's soldiers.

Although the house was ransacked and partly destroyed by fire during Cromwell's time, it has gradually been rebuilt to its former glory and, since 1970, it has been owned and run by John and Thérèse Boswell. Many of the antique furnishings and rare prints which adorn the interior of the house came from Auchinleck House in Ayrshire, the ancestral home of biographer James Boswell. These have undoubtedly added to the period charm of the hotel, and there are few more attractive main halls in any Country House in southern England than that which awaits you at Combe. With its dark wood fireplace, ornate plaster ceiling and family oil portraits adorning the walls all around, you can almost imagine one of the house's fiery old Royalist ancestors sweeping through to join you. All the public rooms have ornate ceilings, but the main lounge area is known as the panelled drawing room and, as its name implies, has plush wood panelling all round. The walls of this charming room are hung with portraits of eighteenth-century ancestors, and the sun streams through the large windows from early morning. The room is finished off by a magnificent rococo marbled fireplace, with a roaring fire when the winter weather so demands.

There are two dining rooms, each with fine carved pine doorcases; one has been completely muralled by Thérèse Boswell; the other has a magnificent Chippendale-carved overmantel and ceiling ornamentation decorated with the fable of the fox and the crow. Both dining rooms can seat approximately twenty-five to thirty guests, depending on the seating plan, and reservations, although recommended at least a couple of days in advance, are not always necessary for non-residents.

Mark Boswell supervises the kitchen where Chef de Cuisine Rosy Higgott prepares a detailed and varied à la carte menu each evening which has a strong emphasis on the best of British traditional Country House-style cooking. Openers range from an unusual 'Covent Garden' Terrine composed of layers of tiny vegetables and a Chicken Mousse, sliced cold and served on a Tomato Vinaigrette, to a light dish of pieces of Fresh Salmon Marinated in a variety of Herbs and Cream before being served in a round and presented with a finely sliced Cucumber Salad.

For those having difficulty choosing from the eight or nine fish and meat dishes offered as main courses, one particular speciality usually available, and which is worth considering, is made up from a Medallion of Scottish Fillet Steak, a Medallion of Veal and a Chicken Breast. The whole dish is served with a colourful trio of red, yellow and green pepper sauces. Other favourites include a Brace of Quail, cooked in an exquisite Sauce of Red Wine and Cognac, and served with Mushrooms and Button Onions.

Combe House has fifteen bedrooms, including one large suite, and all have private bathrooms. All rooms are a good size, with very distinctive individual decor and good views across the estate. Each one is named after a Combe House ancestor (although the favourite is probably the stately Tommy Wax Room) and has a colour television set, direct-dial telephone and a host of antique furnishings which have been personally collected by proprietors John and Thérèse Boswell over the last couple of decades. All bedrooms have one or two little extras, such as a heated towel rail in the bathroom and a vase of cut flowers to bring that extra freshness to your bedroom.

The main leisure facility offered at Combe House is a delightful one-and-a-half-mile stretch of the River Otter, which is ideal for relaxing walks or indulging in a spot of brown or rainbow trout fishing. There is an eighteen-hole golf course at nearby Honiton (three miles away) and riding can be arranged at a local riding school. Nearby attractions include Dartmoor, Exmoor, Dartmouth, the city of Exeter with its cathedral and famous maritime museum, Bicton Park and Gardens, Lyme Regis and the other coastal towns of Sidmouth, Budleigh Salterton and Exmouth.

97

ELCOT PARK

Address Near Newbury, Berkshire RG16 8NJ
Tel: 0488 58100 Fax: 0488 58288

Nearest town Hungerford.
Directions The Elcot Park Hotel is situated just off
the main A4 between Newbury (five miles west)
and Hungerford (four miles east).
A member of **Resort Hotels** consortium.
Awards AA *** graded.
Open throughout the year.
Special breaks Weekend breaks available
throughout the year; also special theme weekends
including Bridge, Theatre and even Hot Air
Ballooning.
Price for dinner, with wine, bed and breakfast for
two – over £150.
Credit cards Access, Visa, Amex and Diners.
The hotel is most suitable for disabled visitors; children
and dogs are welcome.
Overall mark out of ten 7½

One of the primary attractions of Elcot Park has got to be the acres of peaceful woodland in which this former seventeenth-century manor house is set. Although literally a minute's drive off the busy A4, and only a few more from the Berkshire towns of Newbury and Hungerford, Elcot Park occupies a prime location in the magnificent green Kennet Valley.

The hotel was built in 1678 and was formerly the country seat of Lord and Lady Thomas. Today it is still surrounded by a large landscape garden, originally designed by Sir William Paxton (the Royal gardener) in 1848, which, even then, made it an idyllic location for house guests to enjoy that perfect 'away-from-it-all' break without the necessity for city-dwellers to stray more than seventy miles from the capital.

Elcot's main public room, other than the restaurant, is the drawing room, which has now been laid out in the style of an informal lounge. The decor is bright, although there is little in the way of antique furniture, with the outstanding exception of a large art nouveau fireplace which was originally made for the 1900 Paris Exhibition. The Elcot Park is a popular conference hotel, and it has three well-equipped function rooms with all the necessary facilities for just about any kind of business seminar or conference.

The dining room offers probably the best views of any room in the hotel, stretching far across the green Kennet Valley. Up to 100 can be seated in this impressive high-ceilinged room, with its soft blue and yellow decor and sensibly spaced table arrangement. The style of cuisine is distinctly modern British Country House, although continental influences can be clearly detected.

A la carte and table d'hôte menus are available each evening, offering a range of traditional and more original dishes. Two of the more unusual starters include Cornish Scallops and Woodland Mushrooms presented in a puff pastry shell with a Herb Infused Cream Sauce, and Casserole of Berkshire Rabbit braised with Button Mushrooms, Onion and scented with Marjoram.

The à la carte includes a choice of around seven main dishes, including exotics like Fillet of Spring Lamb glazed with a crust of Minted Brioche Crumbs and served with a Compote of Wild

Mushrooms, and Fillet of Red Mullet with Baby Squid and Selona Bouillabaisse Sauce.

The hotel has a total of thirty-four bedrooms, all highly individually designed. Soft pastel shades are predominant and blend well with antique furnishings and modern conveniences such as colour television, direct-dial telephone, hairdryer and a trouser press in each room. A number of larger doubles have particularly soft and luxurious bed coverings: combined with a four-poster, which features in several bedrooms, the setting is perfect for that special romantic break.

Leisure facilities include golf, croquet, horse riding and, for the more adventurous, the opportunity to try hot-air ballooning under the supervision of a qualified instructor and pilot. This facility is an attraction unique to Elcot Park and is available throughout the year, although obviously it depends heavily on the weather. Your fee (around £120 at the time of publication) includes full tuition and is payable only if you get the chance to fly. The recent completion of a health and leisure club and complex makes Elcot Park an outstanding venue for keep-fit fanatics. Other local attractions include Stonehenge, Blenheim Palace, Avebury, Littlecote House, and the cities of Oxford, Winchester and Salisbury.

98

FIFEHEAD MANOR

Address Middle Wallop, Stockbridge, Hampshire
SO20 8EG
Tel: 0264 781565 Fax: 0264 781400

Nearest town Andover.
Directions Take the A303 to Andover and the hotel
is seven miles from here. From the town, you should
follow the A343 and the hotel is just after the village
of Middle Wallop.
Awards AA ** and RAC *** graded; British Tourist
Authority commended; Egon Ronay
recommended.
Open throughout the year, apart from two weeks
over Christmas and the New Year.
Weekend breaks available from November until
around Easter.
Price for dinner, with wine, bed and breakfast for
two – £150.
Credit cards Access, Visa, Amex and Diners.

The hotel is suitable for the disabled; children and dogs are allowed.
Overall mark out of ten 7

The origins of Fifehead Manor date back as far as the eleventh century, making it one of the oldest buildings in this part of Hampshire, although only the foundations remain of the original Norman house. One of the earliest residents is reputed to have been the Saxon Earl Godwin, whose beautiful wife, Lady Godiva, has now passed into legend because of her famous naked ride through Coventry on horseback.

For a while the house served as a nunnery, and America's first president, George Washington, is known to have been a direct descendant of a fifteenth-century 'Lord of the Manor of Wallop Fifehead', as the holder of the estate was then known. During the era of Catholic persecution in the early years of the reign of Queen Elizabeth I, many a fleeing priest is believed to have hidden on a narrow ledge inside the huge chimney stack.

By 1982 only the manor house itself, and just over three acres of garden and woodland, remained from the original eleventh-century estate of 600 acres, although the current owner still retains the right to be called Lord of the Manor. Despite its long history, much of the interior of the hotel is surprisingly modern. The main lounge area is comfortably furnished, and the overall impression of the public areas is relaxing.

The most interesting room in the hotel is the main dining-room. Judging by its size and scale in proportion to the rest of the original manor, this was almost certainly the main hall in medieval times. You can still see the remains of the minstrels' gallery dating back to the Middle Ages and, in the evening when this charming room is lit by candlelight, it is the perfect setting for a romantic dinner with old glass and silverware on display around you.

Curiously, the size of print on the à la carte menu is the largest of any hotel I've ever visited, and, although many of the dishes have been cooked in a continental style, the menu has deliberately not been translated into French so that the management no longer needs to worry about 'puzzled looks appearing on our customers' faces'. A sensible enough policy as the detailed selection includes a good range of traditional and more original dishes.

A table d'hôte menu is available as well as the à la carte, and with refreshing honesty the management also admits the table d'hôte either contains local ingredients that have been spotted that day, or is being used to 'push a slow-moving item on the "carte" '. Starters include freshly Boiled Devon Crab in a Tomato Mayonnaise, dressed with Pink Grapefruit and Avocado, or an unusual mixture of Ham, Parsley and Garlic layered in a terrine, set in the meat jelly on a pool of Mustard Sauce.

Main dishes are rather more traditional, ranging from Steamed Fillet of Brill to a Baked Chicken Breast flavoured with Wild Mushroom, Meat Glaze, Pears and Cream. Two more original options are a speciality Hampshire Game Pie made from marinated local game and beef, cooked in Port, Red Wine and Juniper Berries, and Roast Duck Breast in a rich Orange, Soy and Ginger Sauce. All main courses are served with vegetables or side salad. The food, it must be said, is of the highest quality and beautifully presented.

There are a total of fifteen bedrooms in an assortment of sizes. All are simply furnished: those in the older part of the house are smaller and have a rather more traditional decor, whereas those in the younger extension are much more modern. All have private bathrooms, although those adjoining the smallest bedrooms are verging on the cramped. Colour television and direct-dial telephones come as standard in all rooms.

The manor's only leisure facility is the beautiful three-and-a-half acre garden, complete with a croquet lawn during the summer months. Fishing on the Rivers Test and Itchen and horse riding can be easily arranged through local instructors. For antique collectors, the nearby village of Stockbridge has at least a dozen antique shops with goods to suit most pockets and tastes. Other attractions within a short driving distance are Marwell Zoo, Longleat House and Safari Park, Beaulieu Palace, the cathedrals of Winchester and Salisbury, and the famous standing stones at Stonehenge, about fifteen minutes away by car.

99

GIDLEIGH PARK

Address Chagford, Devon TQ13 8HH
Tel: 0647 432367 Fax: 0647 432574

Nearest town Chagford.

Directions Find the centre of Chagford, facing
Webbers store with Lloyds Bank on your right,
turn right into Mill Street. After about 150 yards,
fork right and go downhill to factory crossroad.
Go straight across into Holy Street and follow the
lane for one and a half miles to the end.
A member of the **Relais et Châteaux** consortium.

Awards AA *** (red) and rosette; British Tourist
Authority commended; Michelin three (red)
turrets; Egon Ronay 81% and star for restaurant;
Egon Ronay Wine Cellar of the Year Award 1984;
Consumers' Association Country House Hotel of
the Year Award 1987; *Times* Hotel Restaurant of
the Year Award 1988; Egon Ronay Hotel of the Year
1990.

Open throughout the year.

Special breaks Winter Walking Weeks available.

Price for dinner, with wine, bed and breakfast for two – £200–£250.
Credit cards (In order of preference) Access and Visa.
The hotel is not suitable for the disabled; children 'are treated as adults, charged as adults and expected to behave as adults'; dogs are allowed in bedrooms.
Overall mark out of ten 9

Gidleigh Park is one of the half-dozen most expensive Country House Hotels in Britain and sits in an exceptionally beautiful part of the Devon countryside. It is located near the hamlet of Gidleigh, so named after King Harold's mother Gydda who settled here in the eleventh century. The foundations of her Saxon longhouse can still be seen near the thirteenth-century church. Gidleigh Park is considerably younger, having been built originally as a country retreat by the Australian shipping magnate C. H. C. MacIlwraith, although it is known that a manor house has stood on this site since the sixteenth century.

American proprietors Kay and Paul Henderson have run Gidleigh Park since 1978 with the avowed aim that it should function along the lines of a private home rather than a luxury hotel. The hotel is extremely comfortable and, although inside and out the old mansion is a delight, it could hardly be described as ostentatious. The staff are predominantly young, and their enthusiastic personal service is one of the many attractions of Gidleigh Park.

Apart from the main entrance hall and the bar loggia, the main public room is the large sitting room where a welcoming log fire generally burns on all but the mildest of summer evenings. It is a supreme luxury to throw off your walking boots at the main door and relax in here for a while after an afternoon's stroll across the moor, knowing that the most arduous task which still awaits you is a long bath before dressing for dinner.

Paul Henderson has had a secret desire to offer the best English breakfast of any Country House Hotel in Britain and, as one sharp *Good Food Guide* critic observed, the breakfast menu is already considerably longer than that offered by many small restaurants in the evening! A hearty English breakfast and the personal attention of the American proprietors are two of the key reasons why a quarter of the visitors to Gidleigh Park come from the United States.

Probably the principal attraction of Gidleigh Park, though, apart from the outstanding beauty of its situation, is the extremely high standard of cuisine offered by chef Shaun Hill. Each evening a set-price dinner of two cooked courses, followed by cheese, dessert and coffee, is offered for around £30 per person (including VAT). There is a clear preference for luxury ingredients, and each main dish is accompanied by an array of four or five lightly cooked vegetables whose presentation is a work of art. First courses are exquisite, and range from a Terrine of Duck Foie Gras, with Brioche Toast, to Calf's Brain on Brown Butter. One and a half ounces of Beluga Caviar, with a Potato Galette and Sour Cream, are also available for a supplementary charge. Fish and meat dishes include roasted Challans Duck Breast with Thyme and Garlic Sauce, Steamed Turbot with a Tamarind and Lemon Grass Sauce, and Calf's Fillet, Kidney and Sweetbread with Meaux Mustard and Shallot Sauces.

Whatever your choice, Gidleigh Park has easily one of the best wine lists of any Country House Hotel in England with over 400 bottles available, plus a 'bin end' list of 250 wines which you are advised to order by 5 p.m. because of the time it takes to search out a particular bottle from the cellars! The range of French wines is particularly strong (notably some of the better Alsace wines from the last couple of decades) and, understandably, there is a good choice of American wines as well.

Gidleigh Park has a total of fourteen bedrooms which, for a hotel of this calibre, vary quite considerably in size and price. All have recently been redecorated to a high standard. The best rooms are the ten which have expansive views over the Teign Valley; the other four face the forest behind the house, but, having said this, all rooms are beautifully decorated, have en suite bathrooms, colour television and direct-dial telephones.

The most obvious nearby attraction is Dartmoor, the largest National Park in the south of England, which lies all around the hotel. Gidleigh Park has forty acres of its own on the edge of

Dartmoor and facilities on the estate, and the National Park, for walking and horse riding are superb. Dartmoor also happens to be one of the richest areas in Britain for viewing prehistoric settlements and stone circles. The only other leisure facility of note offered by the hotel is an all-weather tennis court, although there are two croquet lawns, and guests have been known to enjoy a swim in the north Teign River which runs through the grounds and is said to be one of the best possible cures for a hangover!

100

GLENCOT HOUSE

Address Glencot Lane, Wookey Hole, near Wells, Somerset
Tel: 0749 77160 Fax: 0749 670210

Nearest town Wells.
Directions From Wells follow signs for Wookey Hole. On approaching the village look for a small sign on your left saying Glencot House first left. Follow this lane towards the hotel.
Open throughout the year.
Special breaks for two nights mid-week inclusive half-board accommodation are available all year.
Price for dinner, with wine, bed and breakfast for two – under £100.
Credit cards Access and Visa.
The hotel is not really suitable for the disabled; children and dogs are welcome.
Overall mark out of ten 7

Glencot Manor is a charming late Victorian house which was built to very high specifications by the famous artist and architect Ernest George. The manor was commissioned by the Hodgkinson family who were the nineteenth-century owners of the famous Wookey Hole caves and nearby paper mill. The style of the house is mock-Jacobean, and today the hotel stands amid eighteen acres of private garden and woodland close to the Wookey Hole caves.

This is not a large hotel and, having only been open since the end of 1985, has yet to attract much recognition from the guides of the leading tourist, consumer and motoring organizations. Its reputation is slowly building up on the basis of friendly, informal service, enhanced by the fact that a lot of the original Victorian character of the house has survived. The public rooms and the bedrooms are well proportioned and comfortably furnished, with many featuring oak and walnut wall panelling.

The main public room is the elegant dining-room, whose half oak-panelled Victorian decor makes a charming backdrop for residents to enjoy their evening meal. Seating capacity is only twenty-five so, regretfully, non-residents are not accommodated. All food is home-cooked using fresh local produce. The style of cooking is traditional British and is overseen by proprietor Mrs Jenny Attia. It is hoped that a full-time chef will be employed in the not too distant future.

A selection of at least five or six dishes is available for both the starter and the main course. Typical starters include Egg Mayonnaise, Rollmop, Garlic Prawns and a home-made Soup. Main dishes always include at least a couple of fish options, perhaps Grilled Trout or Fried Dabs, but you might prefer instead Lamb Chops in Red Wine, Sirloin Steak (sautéed or grilled as you prefer) in a Rich Red Wine Sauce, or Chicken Escalope. All main dishes are served with a selection of local vegetables and either a jacket potato or generous side salad.

Sweets include an enormous helping of Sherry Trifle, home-made Fruit Pie, or a Meringue Glacé Flan. Cheese and biscuits are available as an alternative. The restaurant is licensed, but the range of wines is unremarkable, so residents are well advised to look no further than the excellent house white or red.

All of Glencot's eleven bedrooms have been recently refurbished and decorated in a style of informal country elegance: comfortable chairs and pleasing chintzes. Many rooms have private bathroom facilities, colour television, telephone and tea-

and coffee-making facilities. All are accessible by a number of stairs, but there is one large bedroom with two double beds which is particularly popular with elderly visitors, or disabled persons with limited mobility away from a wheelchair. For that special romantic break, there are also two four-poster master suites available.

Glencot House has a number of leisure facilities available for residents. These include a jet stream pool, sauna, sun bed, snooker room, basic exercise equipment, and a table tennis room. A hairdresser and beautician work in the hotel five days a week. Fishing can be enjoyed on the private stretch of River Axe which runs through the hotel's estate, and the hotel is close to three major golf courses.

The estate surrounding the hotel is quite idyllic, not only because of the river running through it, but also because of features such as the waterfall and private footbridge which residents can appreciate during a relaxing pre-dinner or Sunday afternoon stroll. Other nearby attractions include Wells Cathedral, the Roman town of Bath, Glastonbury Abbey (where legend says King Arthur was once buried), the world-famous caves at Cheddar Gorge, and the popular coastal resort of Weston-super-Mare.

101

HOMEWOOD PARK

Address Hinton Charterhouse, Bath, Avon BA3 6BB
Tel: 0225 723731 Fax: 0225 723820

Nearest town Bath.

Directions From Bath, take the A36
Warminster/Salisbury road and continue for just
over five miles. Turn left towards the two villages
of Sharpstone and Freshford, and you will see the
hotel at the end of the first turning on the left.

Awards Egon Ronay Hotel of the Year 1987; AA ***
(red) graded and rosette; British Tourist Authority
commended; Michelin three (red) turrets and red
'M'; 1986 *Good Hotel Guide* César Award for 'classic
country excellence'.

Open throughout the year.

Mid-week winter breaks are available from
November until the end of March.

Price for dinner, with wine, bed and breakfast for
two – £150–£200.

Credit cards All major cards accepted.

*The hotel is suitable for disabled visitors; children are
welcome but dogs are not allowed.*

Under six miles from the centre of Bath, Homewood Park has built up its reputation by offering a much more informal type of luxury accommodation than comparable hotels in the town of Bath proper. The cellars are the oldest part of the house, dating back several centuries, although the hotel as it now stands was built in stages between the mid-eighteenth and mid-nineteenth centuries. Essentially, though, Homewood Park is an appealing Victorian-style house which remained a private residence until present proprietors Stephen and Penny Ross opened it as a hotel at the end of 1980.

The front porch is one of the most interesting architectural points of the house as it is certainly older than the rest of the building. A ruined abbey is near the hotel and it is known that, for many years, Homewood Park was the abbot's house. It is not inconceivable that the porch was transferred from the crumbling abbey to the house by an enthusiastic Victorian owner.

The main staircase rises from the public entrance hall and, apart from the comfortable bar, the main public area is the lounge with its large fireplace, soft armchairs and good views across the rambling gardens – look out for the unique bronzes created by a local artist. There are a number of smaller private rooms available for business meetings, including two more secluded dining rooms which are normally reserved for private functions, in addition to the main dining room.

As the rest of the hotel, the dining room is decorated in bright colours and has cut flowers everywhere, adding a special freshness to the whole room. Staff are predominantly young and enthusiastic to serve – although never inexperienced. The dining room overlooks the gardens and serves a two- or three-course table d'hôte menu each evening. Starters include Salmon and Scallops wrapped in pastry and bathed in a Sauce of Sherry and Tarragon, and a unique speciality of chef Stephen Ross, Turbot marinated with Limes and served with a Salad of Fennel and Orange. Main dishes display the chef/proprietor's desire to find distinctive and unusual flavours by using fresh local ingredients to create delicate and interesting meals. Choices vary seasonally, but there is always fresh fish, according to the market, and you are likely to find Duckling Roasted in a Sauce of Lentils and Smoked Bacon; Baby Guineafowl with Sauces of Shallot and Sherry Vinegar and Garlic Cream; and Stuffed Loin of Veal in pastry with a Sauce of French Mushrooms, Cream and Wine.

There are fifteen bedrooms at Homewood Park, all doubles and all individually styled and furnished. Each one is finished in a blend of soft colours – perhaps a pale yellow and pink with an apple-green carpet, or a soft honeysuckle-patterned wallpaper with a Victorian dressing table – and there are at least a couple of pieces of antique furniture in each room. Most of the beds are a luxurious six feet wide and all the bedrooms have spacious private bathrooms decorated with oak panelling (right down to the loo seats). In each bathroom you are likely to find at least one flourishing plant, and plenty of space to spread out your toiletries. All rooms have colour television, direct-dial telephone and radio.

The hotel offers facilities for tennis and croquet. Horse riding, golf, fishing and any number of beautiful walks in the surrounding Limpley Stoke Valley are available nearby. Tourist attractions within an easy drive include the towns of Bath, Avebury, Marlborough and Salisbury, the famous standing stones at Stonehenge, Ston Easton Park, Hunstrete House at Hunstrete, the Clifton suspension bridge, and the SS *Great Britain* in Bristol.

102

HUNSTRETE HOUSE

Address Hunstrete, Chelwood, near Bristol, Avon
BS18 4NS
Tel: 0761 490 578

Nearest town Bath.
Directions From Bristol, follow the A37, branching
on to the A368 towards Chelwood when you see
the signs. Aim for Hunstrete village and you will
soon see the hotel sign.
Part of the **Clipper Hotels Group**.
Awards AA *** (red) graded. RAC ****
Open throughout the year.
Winter breaks are available from November until
the end of March.
Price for dinner, with wine, bed and breakfast for
two – over £150.
Credit cards Visa and Access.

*The hotel is suitable for the disabled; children under nine
and dogs are not allowed.*
Overall mark out of ten 9

Set against the backdrop of the Mendip hills, Hunstrete estate
has a history that goes back several generations before the
Norman Conquest of England in 1066. For centuries a monastery
stood on the estate offering hospitality and shelter to weary
pilgrims making their way to or from the abbey at Glastonbury.
The abbey was completed in 1184 and flourished in the couple
of hundred years which followed.

Hunstrete House as it now stands dates from no earlier than
the eighteenth century, and although much of its honey-coloured stonework has weathered to a stately grey, it has lost little
of its Georgian charm. In 1988 the present owners, Clipper
Hotels, carried out a considerable programme of refurbishment
and renovation in order to convert the house into a Country
House Hotel.

Hunstrete's public rooms contain a collection of antiques.
Every room has an assortment of interesting oil paintings, and
both the library and the drawing room have shelves laden with
early pottery and fine porcelain. The library is a quiet, sunny
room with a small but beautifully ornate white fireplace that
contrasts well with the decorative frieze around the edges of the
ceiling. The main bookcase is an interesting Georgian style, with
a good selection of books that residents can enjoy during their
stay.

The main public room is the Terrace dining room. Its huge
arched windows look out on to an Italianate, flower-filled courtyard: the ornate fountain one would associate more commonly
with a bustling Italian square than an English Country House.
The three-course table d'hôte menu changes every five or six
weeks within each season. The proprietor takes pride in the
extensive wine list which is by no means one of the longest in
the country, but is certainly one of the most broad-based.

Head chef Robert Elsmore embraces the best modern British
techniques, and a choice of about four hot or four cold hors
d'oeuvres is available to start your meal each evening. Favourites

include Quenelle of Chicken Mousseline, and a Salad of Cornish Mussels, served with a chilled Vermouth Sauce. Main dishes range from Medallions of Pork, panfried and served on a bed of Spinach Leaves and coated with an interesting Sauce made from Creamed Stilton, to Saddle of (Scottish) Venison cooked pink and coated with a Juniper and Gin Sauce, garnished with fresh Cranberries, and Red Mullet served on a Coulis of Vegetables moistened with Butter and Rosemary.

The hotel has twenty-four bedrooms, all individually decorated in a variety of colours. Each room is named after a wild bird which is native to the British Isles and includes a framed print of the bird on the wall. Seven of the rooms are in a converted stable block, and they do vary quite a bit in size: from the spacious Dove Room with its eighteenth-century four-poster, right down to three small singles. For extra seclusion, the hotel offers the quaint Swallow Cottage, which comprises a double bedroom, bathroom and sitting room – perfect for a honeymoon. All rooms have private bathrooms, colour television, telephone and radio.

Hunstrete House has its own heated outdoor swimming pool, together with an all-weather tennis court and a croquet lawn during the milder summer months. Horse riding is available through riding stables in Hunstrete village; there is excellent trout fishing nearby, and there are a number of golf courses. For something completely different, hot-air ballooning can be arranged with prior notice from the hotel grounds.

Nearby attractions for the sightseer include the fine Roman remains and more recent Georgian architecture of Bath, Wells Cathedral, Stourhead Gardens, Longleat House and Safari Park, Berkeley and Sudeley Castles, Dyrham Park, Lacock Abbey, Sir Peter Scott's Wildfowl Trust at Slimbridge, Cheddar Gorge, and the ancient abbey of Glastonbury where King Arthur is said to have been buried.

103

LAINSTON HOUSE

Address Sparsholt, Winchester, Hampshire SO21
2LT
Tel: 0962 63588 Fax: 0962 72672

Nearest town Winchester.
Directions Travel south on the M3 following the
signs for Winchester city. Leave the motorway at
signs for Winchester city centre and follow the signs
for Stockbridge A272. Turn left after two-thirds of
a mile and you will see the hotel on your right.
A member of the **Prestige Hotels** consortium.
Awards AA *** graded and rosette for food; RAC
*** graded; British Tourist Authority commended;
Egon Ronay and Michelin recommended.
Open throughout the year.
Weekend breaks are available.
Price for dinner, with wine, bed and breakfast for
two – over £150.
Credit cards Amex, Access, Diners and Visa.
The hotel is ideally situated for the disabled with one or

two specially adapted rooms and toilet facilities within easy
access; children are welcome, as are dogs.
Overall mark out of ten 8

Two miles north-west of the old cathedral city of Winchester,
Lainston House stands in sixty-three acres of superb downland
Hampshire countryside. The first recorded owner of Lainston
estate is Simon de Winton, who died in 1316, although the
present house dates from the William and Mary period at the
end of the seventeenth century. For a single decade in the nineteenth century, the house was home to nearly a hundred luna-
tics, but thankfully this darker side to the history of Lainston
House came to an end in 1853.

Probably the most colourful person associated with the House
was Elizabeth Chudleigh, a flighty young girl of sixteen who
first came to stay when the house was owned by John Merrill,
a prominent local Whig (Liberal) politician. Elizabeth became
maid of honour to the Princess of Wales and met, fell in love
with and married the grandson of the Earl of Bristol in 1774. A
child was born but died soon after, and before very much longer
Elizabeth became the mistress of the Duke of Kingston, whom
she bigamously married. After her trial for the crime of bigamy,
she left Europe and set up a brandy factory in Imperial Russia
where, it is said, she was kindly received by the mighty Empress
Catherine the Great.

A large portrait of the wicked, but ultimately shrewd, Lady
Elizabeth still hangs in the main entrance hall to the hotel. The
public rooms are elegantly furnished, but none more so than
the Cedar Room. This finely panelled bar doubles as a small
library filled with leather-bound books, and a plaque on the wall
notes the fact that an enormous cedar tree, which fell to the
ground during a storm in January 1930, supplied enough wood
to panel the entire room.

The main restaurant is made up of two dining rooms, the
smaller of which used to be the nursery when Lainston House
was a private residence. The decor is eau-de-nil, restful on the
eyes and complementing the lawns which sweep away from
beneath the large windows. Up to thirty-five can be accommo-

dated on one side and twenty-five on the other, and as the restaurant is popular with non-residents, advance booking is advised.

The style of food prepared by head chef Frederick Litty is traditional English Country House, using a great deal of local produce, although his German origins help add a noticeable continental touch to many dishes. A delightful candlelit à la carte meal is available each evening. Starters range from Sautéed Scallops, tossed in a Lemon Dressing and served on a bed of mixed lettuce, to Dublin Bay Prawns on a bed of lettuce with Oyster Mushrooms and a Lemon Dressing.

Main dishes include a delicious Breast of Duck on a light Garlic Sauce, served with Apple and Celeriac Layers and a mixed Salad with a Truffle Dressing, and Fillet of Veal with a Cream and Armagnac Sauce served with Mange Touts, Sauté Potatoes and Wild Mushrooms. One recommended fish speciality, served usually as a main dish, is Roast Turbot on a bed of Wild Rice and presented with a delicate Saffron Sauce. A selection of popular wines is shown on the menu, according to what dishes are on offer.

Lainston House has thirty-two bedrooms, including a number of suites and the delightful Delft Room. Fourteen rooms are located in Chudleigh Court, a recently completed annexe which reflects the charm and elegance of the bedrooms in the main house. All rooms are individually designed and furnished, although the style of decor is modern throughout. Each one has en suite bathroom, colour television, private mini-bar, direct-dial telephone and a wall safe for that extra security.

Among the leisure facilities available for residents to enjoy are two all-weather tennis courts, a croquet lawn, clay pigeon shooting, and the possibilities for endless walks around the sixty-three-acre estate. In addition, golf, fishing on the River Test, horse riding and indoor pursuits including squash, sauna and solarium can be easily arranged through the hotel's reception.

Nearby attractions are detailed in an eight-page booklet given to all guests on arrival and, as you might imagine, there are a large number of places to visit and sights to see in this part of southern England. Among the more famous are Breamore House; Beaulieu (including Lord Montagu's famous motor museum); Wilton House; the public gardens at Exbury and Heale House (note these are only open during the summer); Salisbury and Winchester Cathedrals; Marwell Zoo, and the town of Portsmouth with its superb naval attractions – HMS *Victory*, the *Mary Rose* ship and museum, and the Royal Navy submarine museum.

104

LEWTRENCHARD MANOR

Address Lewdown, Okehampton, Devon EX20 4PN
Tel: 056 683 256

Nearest town Tavistock.
Directions Follow the A30 west from Exeter as far
as Lewdown village. Head south for one mile
towards Tavistock, on the Lewtrenchard and
Chilton Road, and you will see the hotel
signposted just before the church on the left.
A member of the **Pride of Britain** consortium.
Awards AA ** (red) graded; recommended by *Good
Food* and Egon Ronay guides.
Open February until just after New Year.
Special breaks Holiday Weekend and mid-week
winter breaks are available.
Price for dinner, with wine, bed and breakfast for
two – £150.
Credit cards Access, Visa, Diners and Amex.
*The hotel is not suitable for the disabled; children under
eight, and dogs, by arrangement.*
Overall mark out of ten 8½

Set in a little valley just off the north-west corner of Dartmoor, Lewtrenchard Manor is a secluded Country House Hotel which dates back to 1620. It was home for many years to the Baring-Gould family, and the most famous former occupant is probably the Reverend Sabine Baring-Gould who is best remembered for writing one of the greatest hymns of all time, 'Onward Christian Soldiers'. Two friendly family ghosts are reported to make the occasional check on their former home, but no complaints have been reported so far!

All of the public rooms and bedrooms have a number of pieces of antique furniture, and rich oil portraits adorn the walls. These are family pieces, built up over the last couple of centuries by the Baring-Gould family and acquired by present owners James and Sue Murray when they took over the hotel in 1988. The main lounge is a sumptuous old room, with one of the finest dark wood carved fireplaces in southern England, delicate stained glass windows and an ornate plaster ceiling.

Dark wood panelling is a feature throughout the hotel, and nowhere is this more striking than in the main dining room. The hotel has two dining rooms, both relatively small with a total seating capacity of thirty-five, and one enjoys particularly good views across the courtyard. Head Chef David Shepherd trained at the Inn on the Park in London and the Greenway, Cheltenham, and offers a table d'hôte Menu Gourmand or à la carte each evening. Home-grown herbs, fresh Devon cream and the best local produce will feature prominently in the preparation of your meal.

The five-course Menu Gourmand is restricted to a rich pre-set range of specialities, opening with something like a Puff Pastry filled with Fresh Scallops, Chicken Livers, Mussels and Courgettes in a Herb and Garlic Dressing, followed by a Tresse of Fresh Fish, then a Fruit Sorbet before your main dish, which could be anything from Fillet of Veal in a Chablis Sauce, to Wild Salmon.

Lewtrenchard Manor has a total of eight bedrooms, with another three suites being planned in space which is available across the leafy courtyard. Each room is quite unique, with good views through the old leaded windows. All rooms are furnished traditionally with a host of antiques, and little extras such as a

Victorian wash basin and jug as a charming reminder of the days before en suite bathrooms were standard. Most of the bedrooms have polished wood panelling covering at least part of the walls in keeping with the style throughout the rest of the hotel. In addition, all rooms have colour television and direct-dial telephone.

The hotel has a two-acre stocked trout lake within its grounds, and four miles of private fishing rights on the nearby River Lew, so this is a haven for keen fresh-water fishers. The other main leisure pursuit on offer is the opportunity to rough shoot on the thousand-acre estate, although nearby driven shoots are occasionally organized. Horse riding can also be arranged if you wish. Golf can be enjoyed at the famous St Mellion golf course which top professional Jack Nicklaus designed. Nearby attractions include the many historical places of interest throughout Devon and the beautiful Cornwall coast, plus the Dartmoor National Park about fifteen minutes' drive away, Lydford Gorge, and the city of Plymouth.

105

LUCKNAM PARK

Address Colerne, Wiltshire SN14 8AZ
Tel: 0225 742777 Fax: 0225 743536

Nearest town Bath.
Directions Exit the M4 at junction 17 on to the A429,
turning right before Chippenham on to the A420.
At Ford (three miles) turn left to Colerne. (Do not
take the road from the Shoe to Colerne.) At the
crossroads for Colerne turn right. The entrance is
on the right-hand side after 400 metres.
A member of the **Small Luxury Hotels of the World**
consortium.
Awards RAC **** graded; West Country Tourist
Board five Crowns commended.
Open throughout the year.
Price for dinner, with wine, bed and breakfast for
two – over £150.
Credit cards All major credit cards accepted.
*Children of all ages are welcome and the hotel is suitable
for disabled guests. Dogs are not permitted.*
Overall mark out of ten 8½

Lucknam Park is a magnificent Georgian Country House, situated in rural Wiltshire some six miles from Bath, and less than two hours' drive away from London. Set within nine acres of lawns and gardens, Lucknam Park is delightful to behold at any time of the year but especially so in autumn. During that season, one's approach to the hotel along its mile-long beech avenue is like travelling through a tunnel of colour. At one time the area was completely covered in trees: the history books suggest that before the eleventh century the site was a Saxon settlement cleared within a 'vast forest'. Farming provided the main activity for many generations until the seventeenth century when Lucknam Park ceased to be a single farm and instead became part of a landed estate. After being owned and managed by a succession of merchants and ship owners – each of whom left their mark on the property – it was eventually opened up as a luxury hotel in 1988 by international hotelier Christopher Cole. He spent £4 million in developing and transforming this Grade II listed building into one of the finest Country House Hotels to be found in England today, with highly comprehensive leisure and beauty facilities.

The building exudes a quality of finish and style quite outstanding for such a hotel. The impressive public rooms are all decorated with carefully chosen fabrics, furnishings and antiques. Lucknam Park exudes a Georgian 'feel', while sacrificing nothing of modern comfort, a combination described not inaccurately by its owners as 'restrained opulence'. If anything, however, one's impression of the public rooms is of their being almost too museum-like in their formality. That apart, the elegance of this hotel is unquestionably impressive, while the staff to room ratio of two to one ensures outstanding service.

The restaurant is adorned with porcelain, glass and silver, yet retains a discreet and restrained character. Its spaciousness and light – the latter afforded by a number of tall French windows – are complemented by rich brocades and pastel-shaded walls. Formal dress is stipulated for dinner. The catering is gaining a reputation as being one of the finest modern English cuisines in the country, providing well-balanced menus with the accent on fresh, natural produce. Game, fish, poultry, meat and vegetarian tastes are all well catered for. The six-course gourmet menu is changed every night, giving ample scope for Head Chef Michael Womersley to express his imaginative culinary talents. Particularly noteworthy is his Hot Pot of Cornish Fish and Vegetables in Vouvray White Wine, scented with garden herbs; and for dessert, the popular Hazelnut Box served with a Mocca Sauce and Cherries marinated in Armagnac. Lucknam Park's wine list is of a comparable standard to its cuisine, containing such outstanding selections as Château Latour 1970 and Champagne Brut Reserve Louis Roederer Crystal 1982.

There are ten suites and thirty-two bedrooms at Lucknam Park, individually designed by Peter Inston to provide generous accommodation inside, while giving superb views over the surrounding parkland outside. The presence of four-poster beds, tapestries and antique furniture underlines the attention to historical detail for which Lucknam Park justly deserves its high reputation.

One of the hotel's prize-winning features is its own leisure spa and beauty centre, situated across the quadrangle from the main house and available free of charge (with the exception of the beauty salon and solarium) to all guests. There is a heated indoor swimming pool, a whirlpool spa, saunas, a steam bath and gymnasium, while the beauty salon offers a wide range of treatments and indulgences. Leisure activities out of doors include all-weather tennis courts, a croquet lawn and a jogging path: indeed almost any activity can be arranged on request, from canoeing to trampolining.

Nearby cultural attractions include Bath, with its theatre (tickets can be arranged through the hotel), Castle Combe and the stately home Corsham Court. Special musical evenings and weekend entertainments are often provided within Lucknam Park itself.

106

MAIDEN NEWTON HOUSE

Address Maiden Newton, near Dorchester, Dorset
DT2 0AA
Tel: 0300 20336

Nearest town Dorchester.

Directions From Dorchester, take the A37 Yeovil
road for four miles, then fork left along the A356 to
Crewkerne. After a further four miles, fork right in
the centre of Maiden Newton, at the village cross,
and the hotel can be seen to the left of the war
memorial.

Part of the **Wolsey Lodge** consortium.

Awards RAC Highly Acclaimed; British Tourist
Authority Design Award for commended Hotels
1988; recommended by Ashley Courtenay, Michelin
and Egon Ronay guides.

Open February until just after New Year.

Winter breaks from November until the end of
March; also two-day half-board terms.

Price for dinner, with wine, bed and breakfast for
two – £150–£200.

Credit cards Access and Visa.

The hotel is not suitable for the disabled; children under twelve are not particularly welcome (except babies in cots); 'small, well-behaved' dogs are allowed.

Overall mark out of ten 8½

Maiden Newton House is one of those typical old English manor houses whose appeal to overseas and home visitors alike remains as strong now as it has ever been. It is therefore not difficult to appreciate why the village of Maiden Newton was immortalized by Thomas Hardy as 'Chalk Newton' in his classic *Tess of the d'Urbervilles*. Today Maiden Newton House stands in the beautiful valley of the River Frome and is easily accessible by all the main routes through Dorset.

The house was built of mellow stone in medieval style. It was originally built in the fifteenth century but was substantially altered in the early nineteenth century by the Hon. William Scott, younger son of the fourth Baron Polworth. Resident proprietors Bryan and Elizabeth Ferriss restored much of the ageing building before opening it as a hotel in Spring 1985 and, for both, it was the realization of a lifelong ambition to own and run a luxury Country House Hotel. The Ferrisses have deliberately set out to recreate the atmosphere and environment of a luxury private home rather than a hotel. There is undoubtedly no 'hotel' design scheme: the reception formalities are brief and all the public rooms are extremely well appointed. Fine porcelain, antique furniture, rich oil paintings and good books are all part of the decor which you find here, as, indeed, you would expect in a better private home. Guests are made to feel more like favoured friends than customers.

Dining arrangements at Maiden Newton are unusual, though not entirely unique. Dinner is served 'en famille' in the charming dining room whose long, narrow windows allow the evening sun to pour through during the long summer months. All guests sit around the same large table with Bryan and Elizabeth, who act as host and hostess, rather like at a proper dinner party. The maximum number dining is twelve, and particular attention is given to seating arrangements depending on how well guests know each other, whether they are foreigners with limited English, and so on. Non-residents can occasionally be accommodated when the house is not full, but are advised to ring well in advance.

Elizabeth Ferriss describes her style of cuisine as 'imaginative dinner party cooking'. Menus vary according to what's in season, and portions are just the right size to allow room for a helping of local cheeses (there's usually a selection of six or seven from which to choose). Guests are advised in advance what is likely to be on the evening's menu, but a typical dinner would open with a Smoked Salmon Pâté, and be followed by a main dish such as Fillet of Pork with Coriander and Vermouth. Sweets and local cheeses follow in that order.

All the hotel's six bedrooms are individually furnished in typical Country House style. They are better described as small suites as each one is remarkably spacious and furnished with traditional antiques wherever possible. The finest room is the William Scott Suite, a first-class room with a large four-poster bed and magnificent views far across the river. This is the largest bedroom and features a private dressing room. All the rooms have their own bathroom facilities and a colour television is available on request.

For fishing enthusiasts, Maiden Newton House offers some excellent private facilities for you to enjoy your sport while staying here. Both banks of a three-quarters of a mile stretch of the River Frome within the grounds of the house are ideal for game fishing; rods and flies are available through the hotel reception. The hotel stands in twenty-one acres of parkland, and the informal gardens around the house include a croquet lawn during the milder months. Golf, tennis and horse riding can be arranged locally.

Among the many nearby attractions are Maiden Castle, the Dorset coast ten miles away, the historic houses at Athelhampton, Montacute, Parnham and Kingston Lacy, and the large public gardens at Abbotsbury, Minterne Magna and Clapton Court. In addition, the towns of Dorchester, Yeovil and Bournemouth are a short drive away.

107

THE MANOR HOUSE

Address Castle Combe, Chippenham, Wiltshire
SN14 7HR
Tel: 0249 782206 Fax: 0249 782159

Nearest town Chippenham.
Directions The Manor House lies between the M4
and A420 just off the B4039, six miles from
Chippenham. If travelling here on the M4, leave at
junction 17 or 18. From junction 17 it is
approximately fifteen minutes' drive along country
lanes.
Awards AA and RAC **** graded.
Open throughout the year.
Winter breaks available.
Price for dinner, with wine, bed and breakfast for
two – over £150.
Credit cards All major cards accepted.
*Children and dogs are both welcome, by prior
arrangement.*
Overall mark out of ten 7½

Settled amid twenty-six acres of garden and parkland, the Manor House of Castle Combe has stood in the green Wiltshire countryside for over a thousand years. Earliest settlements have been traced to Roman times, although it is more plausible that those early visitors chose the site above the valley because of its great defensive position rather than the undoubted beauty of its surroundings.

The original Manor House was first built in the fourteenth century, when England was in one of its few peaceful phases during the medieval centuries, and the nearby Castle Combe fell into disuse. Most of the original building was destroyed by fire a couple of generations later, and only a grain-drying kiln and granary (which was not discovered until the 1970s) can be dated to the original fourteenth-century building.

Most of the front of the present building was completely rebuilt in the seventeenth century, although some alterations have been made right up to the present generation. The house's best-known former Lord of the Manor was the long-lived Sir John Falstaff who resided here from 1390 until 1460. A magnificent eighteenth-century Italian frieze, depicting Shakespearian characters, hangs in the public lounge next to the front hall, and it is generally believed that Sir John was the inspiration for Shakespeare's imaginative character, Sir John Falstaff.

Your first sight of the interior of the house will be the wide entrance hall, and the warmth of the welcome you are certain to receive when you arrive will be typical of the friendly, yet unobtrusive, care and attention which you can expect throughout your stay. Still in the entrance hall, look out for the intricately carved oak panelling all around you. The date 1664, with which it is inscribed, is rather confusing as the panelling was not commissioned especially for the Manor House but was 'borrowed' from another house nearby.

The main public room is the comfortable public lounge, with the Shakespearian frieze, and a rather odd assortment of deep armchairs and little antique tables for you to rest drinks or magazines on. An open fireplace, with white tiled surround, completes the distinctly period atmosphere of this room.

Easily the grandest room in the Manor House is the long

dining room, with its narrow rectangular windows overlooking the surrounding gardens and parkland. The room was added to the hotel in the 1970s, but nevertheless was constructed in a style in keeping with the rest of the hotel and decorated in an unobtrusive combination of browns and creams. The atmosphere is rather formal, but nevertheless welcoming, and the quality of the food most impressive.

The style of cooking is reasonably traditional, and the staff of twelve chefs aims to bring back some more classical dishes, plate-serving them in a lighter, less formal style. Continental and English specialities are available every evening: summer specialities include Wye Salmon and Devon Lobster, while favourite winter dishes include locally shot Pheasant and a Rich Game Pie. Vegetables are all cooked firm to the bite, sauces made by reducing stocks, and no bechamel or demi-glaze is ever used in the kitchen. An impressive wine list is also available.

The Manor House has thirty-six bedrooms, all recently refurbished to a high standard with private bathroom facilities, colour television, direct-dial telephone and, thoughtfully, baby-listening device. During the refurbishment process, many of the bedrooms' original features have been restored to their original condition, while the stable block has been converted into a further two bedrooms and suite. In addition, Archway Cottage – once the gateway to the ancient Manor House – has recently been restored and converted to provide two more luxurious bedrooms.

Leisure facilities are excellent: most outdoor activities – fishing, golf, tennis and so forth – can be arranged locally.

Nearby attractions include an inexhaustible range of walks and strolls through the surrounding grounds where, reputedly, there are anything up to seventy different varieties of trees to be seen; Castle Combe itself makes an interesting visit, and a booklet with details of the castle's history is on sale at reception; the ancient Roman town of Bath is only a short drive away and, a little further on, you can visit Bristol, Stroud or even South Wales quite easily.

108

PLUMBER MANOR

Address Sturminster Newton, Dorset DT10 2AF
Tel: 0258 72507 Fax: 0258 73370

Nearest town Sturminster Newton.
Directions The hotel is located half-way between
the towns of Sherborne and Blandford, just off the
A357.
A member of the **Pride of Britain** consortium.
Awards AA rosette.
Open from March until the end of January.
Bargain breaks are available during the months
between October and April.
Price for dinner, with wine, bed and breakfast for
two – £100–£150.
Credit cards Access and Visa.
*The hotel is suitable for the disabled; children under twelve
and dogs are not allowed.*
Overall mark out of ten 8

At the end of a long, winding chestnut tree-lined driveway, just
off the main A357 which connects Sherborne and Blandford,
you will find Plumber Manor. The house has been home to the

Prideaux-Brune family since the seventeenth century, but it has only been open as a Country House Hotel since 1972. Today it is still under the personal supervision of the family, and home to Brian and Richard Prideaux-Brune with his family.

A magnificent collection of family portraits lines the main gallery, which leads to the six bedrooms located in the main house. These really are fascinating to stand and admire for ten minutes or so before dinner, and give you a real sense of continuity and local history, all the more interesting once you have had the opportunity to meet one of the members of the family involved in the day-to-day running of the hotel now.

All the public rooms are elegantly furnished with family antiques and a rich period decor. Some of the accumulated family treasures are fascinating: the large stuffed and mounted Greenland falcon, for example, has to be one of the most intriguing ornaments in any British Country House Hotel! Fresh flowers are added to most rooms in the hotel and some of the displays are quite magnificent.

There are three dining rooms at Plumber Manor, all of which are furnished in typical English Country House style, and the main one (which seats forty) is extremely popular with residents and non-residents alike. Advance booking by at least two weeks is strongly recommended. Brian Prideaux-Brune takes charge in the kitchen, and his style of cooking is an excellent combination of English and French.

Two table d'hôte menus are available each evening, with a difference of a few pounds between them because of one or two more expensive base ingredients (like smoked salmon) on one of them. On both menus there are at least four or five choices for the main courses. Starters include Melon with Port, Moules Marinières, and a delicious combination of Avocado with Melon, Prawns and Crab Marie Rose.

Main dishes feature Roast Rack of Lamb, Breast of Duckling, and Calf's Liver with Onion, Sage and White Wine. One particularly enjoyable dish for two or more persons is Beef Wellington, which is served with an exquisite Madeira Sauce. There is a nominal supplement of about a pound for this dish, and you

375

will need to allow twenty-five minutes for it to be prepared, but it is, however, well worth the additional considerations.

Accommodation at Plumber Manor is divided between the main house, where there are six bedrooms facing south and west, and a converted natural-stone barn where another ten double bedrooms were opened in August 1982. The barn rooms are particularly appealing and they all have window seats overlooking the stream and garden. All sixteen bedrooms have private bathrooms, with no shortage of huge bath towels large enough to envelop most frames, colour television and telephone.

The only leisure facilities at Plumber Manor are a tennis court and croquet lawn, in keeping with a small comfortable hotel of this nature. Several golf courses, coarse fishing on the River Stour, horse riding and clay pigeon shooting are all available nearby. Other attractions in the surrounding area include the eighteenth-century model village of Milton Abbas, built by the Earl of Dorchester in 1770; Giant's Hill overlooking Cerne with its 1500-year-old chalk carved figure; the agricultural town of Sturminster Newton itself complete with its fine sixteenth-century bridge over the River Stour; the hilltop town of Shaftesbury where Alfred the Great founded a nunnery and placed his daughter there as Abbess, and the coastal towns of Lyme Regis and Weymouth.

109

RHINEFIELD HOUSE HOTEL

Address Rhinefield Road, Brockenhurst, Hants SO42 7QB
Tel: 0590 22922

Nearest town Brockenhurst.
Directions Leave M27 at junction 1 and follow signs to Lyndhurst. Take A35 to Bournemouth, turn left after about one and a half miles to Rhinefield.
Awards AA ***; winner of Ashley Courtenay prize for hotels with gardens.
Open throughout the year.
Special breaks Short breaks run throughout the year. Special programmes are available at Christmas and New Year.
Price for dinner, with wine, bed and breakfast for two – over £100.
Credit cards Access, Visa, Amex and Diners.

The hotel is not ideal for disabled guests. Children and dogs are accepted.
Overall mark out of ten 8

Rhinefield House Hotel is located in the heart of the New Forest, a conservation area not far from London. As one of the high points in the Forest, with good visibility over the surrounding area, it was a good defensive position and there were fortifications here as early as Saxon times. A royal hunting lodge was built by William the Conqueror on the Rhinefield estate, but was demolished and rebuilt three times during the six subsequent centuries. The lodge was a favourite retreat of several English kings and also of Oliver Cromwell's son, Richard. It is believed that Oliver Cromwell and Charles I had their last meeting at the lodge when the king was on his final journey from prison to his eventual execution.

In the mid nineteenth century the lodge was bought by Mrs Mabel Walker, goddaughter of Queen Victoria and one of the richest ladies in the country, who once again demolished the building and built a large Victorian country house with superb formal gardens.

An unusual feature of Rhinefield House is the Alhambra cocktail bar, originally built by Mrs Walker as a smoking room as a present for her husband's birthday. This mysterious room is based on the ruined Alhambra Palace in Granada, and the Moorish craftsmen brought over to achieve this are said to have taken two years to create it from imported onyx and gems.

The Armada dining room – the original dining room of the house – derives its name from a wood carving of the Spanish fleet above the fireplace. A wide-ranging à la carte menu features specialities from the locality while a less extensive businessman's menu is available for those with limited time.

Today, Rhinefield House offers thirty-two spacious en suite bedrooms in the new wing, all with colour television, direct-dial telephones and tea- and coffee-making facilities. The comfort and beauty of its rooms are enhanced by the backdrop of garden and forest views enjoyed from all the windows. The older part of the building houses six conference rooms which benefit from the natural light and beautiful surroundings. These rooms are distinguished by oak panelling, ornate ceilings and the grandeur of an occasional mini Westminster.

Situated underneath the main hotel the Atlantis Leisure Club provides a gymnasium, Roman-style pool, whirlpool, solarium and sauna, as well as table tennis and pool tables. Outside are another swimming pool, two tennis courts and a croquet lawn. Horse riding, sailing and clay pigeon shooting can be arranged through the Leisure Club.

Rhinefield's award-winning formal gardens have been restored to their original layout which was designed to maximize vistas across the Forest. This will come into its own as the garden gradually grows to maturity.

The local area provides a number of sites of interest for guests, including nearby Beaulieu Abbey and its renowned Motor Museum. Sailing at Lymington and other resorts is popular, as is simply exploring the New Forest itself.

110

STON EASTON PARK

Address Ston Easton, Bath, Avon BA4 4DF
Tel: 076 121 631 Fax: 076 121 377

Nearest town Shepton Mallet.
Directions Ston Easton Park is situated just off the
main A37 from Bristol to Shepton Mallet. It is six
miles from Wells and eleven miles from both Bath
and Bristol.
Awards AA *** (red) graded and rosette; British
Tourist Authority commended; Egon Ronay
recommended; Michelin recommended; Egon
Ronay Hotel of the Year 1982.
Open throughout the year.
A special **Christmas and New Year programme** is
offered each year.
Price for dinner, with wine, bed and breakfast for
two – over £150.
Credit cards All major cards accepted.
*Children under twelve are not allowed, nor are dogs
allowed in public rooms or bedrooms, although free
kennelling is available.*
Overall mark out of ten 9½

This outstanding old Georgian mansion first caught the public imagination in 1982. The hotel opened to the public on 1 June of that year and, remarkably, within a matter of months it was awarded the prestigious Egon Ronay Hotel of the Year Award, arguably the top honour which any British hotel can hope to achieve. Far from resting on their newly found laurels, proprietors Peter and Christine Smedley have sought to maintain, and if anything improve, the services and facilities on offer to guests since 1982.

A manor has stood on the site of the present hotel for centuries: indeed the estate was clearly recorded around the time of the Domesday Book, in the late eleventh century. In the eighteenth century, one John Hippisley-Coxe married Mary Northleigh of Peamore, a wealthy woman whose substantial means helped John begin building the manor as it now stands. Successive owners of Ston Easton distinguished themselves in social and political circles, and among the visitors to the house over the next couple of centuries were William Pitt the Younger, and Queen Mary – who insisted on arriving for afternoon tea one day during the last war, despite the fact that the interior of the house was covered in dust sheets.

The contents of the house were sold off at auction in 1956 and the future of Ston Easton looked bleak. Trees were felled on the estate, and a demolition order was signed in 1958 after lead had been stolen from the roof and much of the house vandalized. Thankfully it was saved, and successive owners since then (including a former Editor of *The Times*, Lord William Rees-Mogg) helped restore it to its present splendour.

The Palladian style and decoration of the house was restored in the late 1970s and early 1980s, supervised by Jean Monro, an acknowledged authority on eighteenth-century decoration, and today the hotel feels more like a stately home than 'just' a hotel. The first public room you enter is one of the more striking; with its coved ceiling and ornate plasterwork, the Entrance Hall truly is magnificent, and the eighteenth-century hanging lantern makes the perfect finishing touch. Other notable public rooms are the Saloon, with its main door flanked by Corinthian columns and its ceiling adorned with an elaborate ornamental plaster masterpiece; the delightful Library with its mahogany book-cases, and the Print Room with its unique decoration of eighteenth-century engravings.

The main dining room was originally the Old Parlour. It has a soft colour-scheme, recently refurbished, and blends well with the rest of the house. The style of cuisine is a combination of modern English and French, with the best local produce used wherever possible. A four-course table d'hôte dinner is available each evening, and opening selections from the detailed range of options (which are more typical of an à la carte menu) include Salad with Lobster and Avocado in a light Yoghurt Dressing, and Pan-fried Duck Livers on a bed of Caramelized Apple and Cider.

Main courses include Roast Rack of English Lamb Persillé, and Medallion of Venison with a confit of fresh fruit. At least one dish is included for vegetarian eaters and this might be something like Wholemeal Pasta with Local Mushrooms.

Ston Easton Park has a total of nineteen luxury bedrooms, all of which are of a good size, and several have four-posters dating from the Chippendale and Hepplewhite periods. All the rooms have one or two pieces of antique furniture and a selection of framed prints. The one suite available has an open fire, a crystal chandelier and a comfortable seating area off the double bedroom. All rooms overlook the surrounding parkland and have private bathroom facilities, colour television and direct-dial telephone. The recently converted seventeenth-century Gardener's Cottage within the hotel grounds provides either two separate luxury suites, or joint accommodation for four.

Nearby attractions include Dyrham Park; Castle Combe; the Elizabethan mansion Corsham Court; the medieval village of Lacock which is now owned by the National Trust; the prehistoric monument at Avebury, and the Georgian house of Bowood.

111

THORNBURY CASTLE

Address Thornbury, near Bristol BS12 1HH
Tel: 0454 418511 Fax: 0454 416188

Nearest town Thornbury.
Directions When you reach the town of Thornbury,
continue downhill to the northern edge where the
Castle lies behind the very prominent tower of the
parish church.
A member of the **Pride of Britain** consortium.
Awards AA *** (red) graded; RAC *** graded and
Blue Ribbon; Egon Ronay and Michelin
recommended; former Egon Ronay Best Restaurant
in Britain Award-winner; 1984 and 1989 Hideaway
Report Country House Hotel of the Year Award.
Open throughout the year, except early January.
Winter breaks are available from early November
until early March.
Price for dinner, with wine, bed and breakfast for
two – over £150.
Credit cards All major cards accepted.
*The hotel is not suitable for disabled visitors; children
under twelve, and pets, are not allowed.*
Overall mark out of ten 9

With an enviable location in the valley of the River Severn, Thornbury Castle is the only Tudor castle in England operated as a Country House Hotel. Although traces of a manor house on the present site go back to pre-Norman times, the present building was built by Edward Stafford, the third Duke of Buckingham, who received a special licence from Henry VIII in 1510 to 'fortify, crenelate and embattle Thornbury Manor'. Sadly, Stafford did not live long to appreciate his fine new property, as his former master, the king, had him executed in May 1521 for having spoken certain 'treasonous words'.

The Castle remained as a Royal territory for thirty-three years, arguably the most interesting period in its long history, and during this time Henry VIII himself stayed here for several days with his young queen, Anne Boleyn (who, coincidentally, was herself to die by the executioner's sword in 1536). Henry's daughter, Mary Tudor, lived at the Castle for some years, and once she became Queen in 1554 returned it to the descendants of the Duke of Buckingham.

Today Thornbury Castle is still surrounded by its own private vineyard, just as it was in the sixteenth century, and visitors to its high walls can enjoy the same fine views across the Severn Valley which have appealed to at least two English monarchs, and generations of nobility, ever since. All the public areas of the hotel are furnished in magnificent splendour with antique furniture throughout. The main lounge has a number of old family portraits, and its wide (narrow-pane) oriel windows overlook the large walled Tudor garden.

The Castle has two dining rooms, both decorated and furnished in traditional baronial style with solid oak-panelled walls, large open fires in ornate fireplaces, and heraldic shields all around. Although the hotel is constantly being refurbished, the character of the public rooms, and the dining rooms in particular, has changed little down the centuries since the building was first constructed: the first Duke of Buckingham could easily have felt at home among the tapestries and high ceilings and, above all, with the fine cuisine prepared in classic style by chef Derek Hamlen.

It is difficult to give more than a suggestion of what you might expect on the menu of a former Egon Ronay Restaurant of the Year, but whatever you choose you can be sure that it will have been prepared from the very best of local produce and that the presentation will be exquisite. Menus change daily, and starters are likely to include Salmon marinated in White Wine and Orange Juice, and Cornish Devilled Crab topped with Double Cream and a Parmesan gratinée. For your main dish, two recommended favourites are Veal Fillet Sauté, with assorted Mushrooms and Malaga, and Thornbury Castle's speciality Venison and Port Pie. One interesting fish choice, which is more usually served as a main course, is fresh Tay Salmon cooked in butter with Saffron and White Wine.

Thornbury Castle currently has eighteen luxury bedrooms, each carefully converted from the main apartments in the original castle. Each one is individually styled and furnished in a very traditional manner, with antique furniture and paintings, lavish drapes and fine fabrics. All the rooms have private bathrooms, colour television and direct-dial telephones.

Croquet is available at the Castle, and Thornbury Castle Shooting Club offers very good clay pigeon shooting facilities. Most popular indoor and outdoor leisure activities, including golf, tennis, horse riding, gliding and ballooning, can also be enjoyed locally.

Nearby attractions include the natural beauty of the West Country and, slightly further afield, the Wye Valley, south Wales, and the Cotswolds. Other attractions include Sir Peter Scott's famous Wildfowl Trust at Slimbridge, the Regency splendour and Roman remains in Bath, and countless towns and villages all around you including Bristol and Cheltenham.

112

WHATLEY MANOR

Address Easton Grey, Malmesbury, Wiltshire SN16
ORB
Tel: 0666 822888 Fax: 0666 826120

Nearest town Malmesbury.
Directions From the M4 leave at junction 16, 17 or
18. Whatley Manor is on the B4040 between the
village of Easton Grey and Malmesbury.
Awards AA *** RAC graded; Egon Ronay and
Michelin recommended.
Open throughout the year.
Special **weekend breaks** are available all year.
Price for dinner, with wine, bed and breakfast for
two – £100–£150.
Credit cards All major cards are accepted.
*The hotel is unsuitable for the disabled; children and dogs
are welcome.*
Overall mark out of ten 8½

The first thing that strikes many visitors to Whatley Manor is its
rather interesting geographical location. Lying almost halfway
between Bristol and Swindon, the hotel sits right on the border

between Wiltshire and Gloucestershire, near the town of Bath and on the fringes of the Cotswolds. It is not difficult to understand why, for miles around, the area is an officially designated place of natural beauty.

Set in extensive gardens which run down to the banks of the River Avon, the original Whatley Manor dated back to the seventeenth century. The architecture of the seventeenth-century mansion did not appeal to a wealthy English sportsman who bought the site in the early 1920s, as he proceeded to almost completely alter the house. Thankfully this was no more than a passing fit of vandalism and, like the phoenix, from the ruins of the first Whatley Manor arose the present Tudor-style buildings with a number of purpose-built public and private rooms which today can be appreciated in all their splendour.

All the hotel's public rooms have been tastefully upgraded to modern-day luxury standards without losing their original identity: the old Saddle Room still has its saddle and polo stick racks, but now includes a billiard table as well. The library still has shelves and shelves of nineteenth- and early twentieth-century tomes (including a long run of *Punch*) but is now an elegant little bar. The most attractive room, though, is the enormous – almost disproportionately large – lounge with its oak-panelled walls, deep armchairs and beautifully arranged bouquets of freshly cut flowers. There can be few more relaxing places in this part of England to enjoy an after-dinner coffee, or linger over the Sundays with absolutely no need whatsoever to rush for anything.

The restaurant has superb views across the gardens, and has been carefully furnished and decorated to create an atmosphere that feels both intimate and relaxed. It is a large room, decorated in soft pastel shades and has about twenty tables. More could be seated, but it is to the hotel's credit that they have not crammed the maximum number of tables and chairs into the room, as it means guests can sit back and enjoy a level of intimacy missing in so many British hotels which wrongly believe they have achieved it.

The style of food is modern English, with strong continental influences, and traces of *nouvelle cuisine* can be detected on the menu. Fresh local produce is used as much as possible, and the proprietor Peter Kendall is quick to point out that his kitchens *do* use lots of butter, cream and alcohol in the preparation of the menu each evening, so forget the diet and indulge!

A three- or four-course table d'hôte menu is available, representing superb value at under £25 per person. The hotel is understandably popular with local non-residents and holiday-makers looking for a good evening out, so advance booking, particularly for weekends during the summer, is essential. Whatever you select, there are just under a hundred wines to choose from, although the range of vintages is a little disappointing considering the amount of thought and presentation which has gone into the main dinner menu. Red Bordeaux are well priced, with the obvious highlight a 1970 Château Cantemerle at £32 a bottle.

Easily the highlight from the half dozen or so starters is a fine Game and Pistachio Terrine: a savoury pâté of venison, local game and pistachio nuts served with a brandy and pink peppercorn dressing. If that fails to appeal, then you may prefer to indulge yourself with some Fresh Quails' Eggs, or a platter of Frogs' Legs before venturing into your main dish. The presentation of all meals at Whatley Manor is superb, and one of the chef's speciality main courses is Chicken and Pork Choysan, served stir fried in sesame oil, with Spring Onions, Chinese Lettuce Leaves, Radish, Pineapple and succulent Waterchestnuts. The end result is finished with honey and rice wine – very oriental!

Whatley Manor has twenty-nine bedrooms, double the number here just a few years ago when the present owner took over the hotel. Recently three spacious bedrooms have been opened in the Tudor Wing. All are furnished to very high standards, with period furniture used throughout. All have their own bathroom facilities, colour television, fresh flowers whenever possible and great views over the surrounding estate.

The hotel has facilities for tennis, croquet, fishing, sauna, solarium, jacuzzi, table tennis and snooker, in addition to a large heated outdoor swimming pool. Nearby attractions include

Bristol, Bath, Cirencester and Cheltenham as well as Longleat stately home and safari park, and the magnificent standing stones at Stonehenge.

113

WOOLLEY GRANGE

Address Woolley Green, Bradford-on-Avon,
Wiltshire BA15 1TX
Tel: 02216 4705 Fax: 02216 4059

Nearest town Bath.
Directions From the M4 take the A429 at junction
17 to Chippenham. From here take the A350 to
Melksham, and continue through the village of
Holt. After one mile, look for the right hand turn
to Bath on the B3150. Follow this for a short
distance: a turning to the left (signposted Woolley
Grange) takes you to the hotel.
Open throughout the year.
Special breaks for stays of three days or more.
Summer break concessions.
Price for dinner, with wine, bed and breakfast for
two – over £150.
Credit cards Amex, Diners and Visa.

Children and dogs are welcome but there are no facilities for the disabled.
Overall mark out of ten 8

Without detailed directions, locating Woolley Grange within its backwater of rural Wiltshire can become an exercise in patience. But this very inaccessibility is part of the hotel's considerable charm: once discovered, its serenity, informality and quietness slowly envelop you and work their soothing and relaxing magic.

Woolley Grange has a long and well-documented history which is brought to life by a collection of documents relating to the property, displayed in the front hall and Long Room. The date over the front door reads 1665 and from this time until the early eighteenth century Woolley Grange was owned by the Randolph family. When the Baskervilles bought the estate they added two wings to the house and extended the garden: further embellishments were made by Captain Septimus Henry Palairet in the nineteenth century. The property was purchased by Nigel Chapman in 1988. Together with his wife Heather and their family, he has been able to fulfil a lifelong dream by transforming this rambling thirty-roomed house into a Country House Hotel. The look and atmosphere are chiefly seventeenth century, and although it has been run as a Country House Hotel for less than three years, its operation is efficient and well established.

The Long Room or library contains a television and well-stocked video library – a good place to curl up on a winter's day. For those who prefer a quieter atmosphere, the panelled withdrawing room has comfortable sofas and chairs; an open log fire completes the relaxing surroundings. On the west wing, a beautifully designed and plant-filled Victorian conservatory provides an 'al fresco' room for pre-prandial drinks or daytime meals.

One of the chief delights of the hotel is its 'glasnost' attitude towards children. The whole family is certainly made to feel welcome and there is a plethora of opportunities to occupy the younger generation. The Clock Tower Barn has a nursery (rejoicing in the name of Woolley Bears Den) staffed by a nanny between 10 a.m. and 6 p.m. The nursery is well stocked with toys and ideas for both indoor and outdoor activities. For older children there is a games room containing a snooker table, venerable juke box, pinball machine and other distractions designed to keep the children occupied and out of their parents' way for a few hours. If it's hot, sooner or later you'll probably gravitate to the swimming pool (which itself is heated). This has a protective surrounding gate, as a precaution against over-inquisitive young ones. It's not only the bespoke facilities which make Woolley Grange a special place to take children, however: here and there along passages and on landings you'll come across unexpected touches – a stuffed bear, a mermaid mural, even a wooden monkey suspended from a door.

The culinary expertise of Woolley Grange is unexpectedly high. Anand Sastry, the head chef, was a protégé of Raymond Blanc (see Le Manoir aux Quat' Saisons) and the menu – which is changed regularly – is reminiscent of Blanc's creative and distinctive style. The spring list includes such dishes as Salad of Oak-Smoked Duck Breast, Runner Beans and a Truffle Oil dressing or Oak-Smoked Magret Duck served with a delicate White Truffle dressing for starters, while the pot roasted Guinea-fowl and the turbot are particularly recommended as main dishes. A selection of excellent and in some cases unusual cheeses complements the main menu: the Beenleigh blue, Milleens and Tornegus are certainly worthy of sampling. The overall emphasis of the culinary fare is on freshness, and since most of the vegetables and herbs are grown in Woolley Grange's impressive walled garden, this quality can be almost guaranteed. And of course children are not forgotten when it comes to catering: special meals are available to keep them – and therefore their parents – happy.

There are twenty spacious bedrooms, fourteen within the house itself and a further six bedrooms in the adjoining stone courtyard cottage. Each is decorated simply but stylishly, with antiques sitting happily alongside contemporary works of art or the odd Victorian eccentricity, and most enjoy the cheerful glow of a gas 'coal' fire. En suite bathrooms have been designed to incorporate nineteenth-century architectural features, while at the same time sacrificing none of the comforts of twentieth-century luxury.

Woolley Grange can arrange a number of leisure pursuits to occupy guests. Apart from its own bicycles and tennis and croquet lawns, there is scope for riding (including tuition), shooting, fishing and even ballooning nearby. The spa city of Bath is eight miles away, while the cathedral cities of Wells and Salisbury are within easy reach.

The Channel Islands

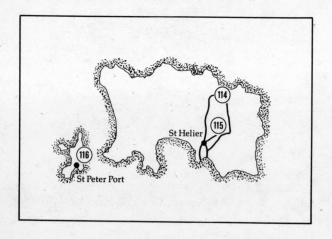

Channel Islands

114 Chateau La Chaire
115 Longueville Manor
116 La Sablonnerie

CHATEAU LA CHAIRE

Address Rozel Bay, Jersey, Channel Islands
Tel: 0534 63354 Fax: 0534 65137

Nearest town St Helier.
Directions Château la Chaire is situated six miles
north of St Helier.
Awards AA ***; Egon Ronay 73%; Jersey Food
Festival Gold Award 1986–9.
Open throughout the year.
Special breaks Three-night winter breaks,
November through January.
Price for dinner, with wine, bed and breakfast for
two – £100–£150.
Credit cards All major credit cards accepted.
*No children under seven allowed. The hotel is not suitable
for the disabled.*
Overall mark out of ten 8

Situated on the north-eastern tip of Jersey, Rozel Bay qualifies as one of the island's most beautiful and secluded corners. The Kew Gardens botanist Samuel Curtis had a hand in fashioning the valley here, and his legacy survives to this day in a profusion of floral colours, especially beautiful during the spring and summer months. Château La Chaire nestles on the valley's sun-drenched slopes within its own seven acres of grounds and terraced gardens, only a short walk from the beach. The hotel was built in 1843, a gracious and elegantly proportioned testi-mony to the art of Country House architecture. More recently it was acquired by the Hatton Hotel group who have, if anything, enhanced this Victorian elegance by transforming the building into a first class Country House Hotel. Today, Rozel Bay is one of the island's foremost beauty spots, with the added attraction for guests keen to 'get away from it all', of guaranteed peace and quiet.

Château La Chaire's external Victorian elegance is comp-lemented internally by its splendid rococo drawing room, with its original antiques, beautifully ornate ceilings and restful atmosphere. To visitors, Jersey is a sometimes unexpected mix-ture of English civility and French flair. This Gallic influence is strongly manifest in Château La Chaire's restaurant – La Chaire. Here, in the traditional oak-panelled setting with its attached conservatory, one can enjoy a superb cuisine which is strongly represented by seafood choices. For example, a typical starter might consist of Jellied Shellfish and Saffron Terrine with a Dill dressing, or Casserole of Shelled Mussels, Tagliatelle and fresh Tomato bound in a Basil and Cream Sauce. Main course options include Fillet of Sea Bass encrusted with Pine Nuts and Herbs served on a Cider Vinegar Sauce, or the ever-popular Local Lobster, either served chilled with a seasonal Salad, or grilled and glazed with Garlic butter or coated with Thermidor Sauce. As well as the comprehensive fresh seafood options, the hotel's extensive menu lists several meat and fowl choices. Not surpris-ingly, in view of the proximity of France, the wine list is particu-larly strong on French vintages, although other wine regions of the world are well represented.

The hotel has thirteen luxurious bedrooms, all with en suite facilities and half of them boasting their own private jacuzzi. Such touches as colour television, in-house video, direct-dial telephone, hair dryer and bathrobes come as standard, while frequently varied little gifts add that touch of individuality so important in giving good impressions to guests. All the rooms are distinctively decorated, many in pastel shades, and the views from the balconies over the Rozel Valley are charming, whatever the season.

Jersey is just a short flight from the UK mainland, and one of its attractions is the distinctly continental flavour, though without the problems of a language barrier or the need for a passport. The island has plenty of interesting places to visit, including nearby Rozel Bay, which is a bustling fishing harbour, or the capital St Helier only six miles away and ideal for duty-free shopping. If you prefer the scenery there are plenty of beautiful coves and safe beaches for which Jersey is famous, not far from the hotel. Local tours, golf, fishing and riding are all available nearby, and if you want to 'hop over' to France, there are plenty of flights.

115

LONGUEVILLE MANOR

Address St Saviour, Jersey, Channel Islands
Tel: 0534 25501

Nearest town St Helier.
Directions Jersey can be reached by air or ferry from
the UK mainland. From the airport, follow the B36,
then A12, and finally A1 to St Helier. Near the
harbour follow the sign indicating Tunnel and East
A17 to Georgetown. Then take the A3 (Longueville
and Gorey road) for about half a mile and the hotel
is signposted on your left.
A member of the **Relais et Châteaux** consortium.
Awards AA **** (red) and rosette for food; RAC ****
(blue ribbon) graded, Egon Ronay recommended.
Open throughout the year.
Special winter breaks are available from November
to March.
Price for dinner, with wine, bed and breakfast for
two – over £150.
Credit cards Access, Visa, Amex and Diners.
*The hotel is unsuitable for disabled visitors; children under
seven are not allowed.*
Overall mark out of ten 9

An enthusiastic American reporter described this tranquil manor house as 'a Queen with a French accent'. The hotel instinctively feels French, yet there is a touch of English charm which prevails in all the spacious public rooms, and in the quality of service which never quite lets you forget that you are still on British soil, despite Jersey's close proximity to the French coast.

There are few serious challengers to Longueville Manor's claim to be one of the best hotels on the Channel Islands. Certainly it is the only red-star-graded AA hotel on any of the Channel Islands and, after the recent completion of their new half-million-pound West Wing, probably the most popular luxury hotel on Jersey.

The earliest recorded mention of Longueville Manor dates back to 1309 when it was recorded in the local Assize Poll as 'Lungevill'. The manor changed hands in 1367 when it was sold by Phillippe de Barentin to one Raoul Lemprière, and just prior to this date the Great Hall, which is now the hotel's dining room, is believed to have been built. The original fourteenth-century arched entrance to the manor also remains, forming the hotel's main gateway today. Longueville's fortunes improved considerably after 1480 when the island's Bailiff, John Nichol, bought the manor and surrounding grounds. His great grandson also became Bailiff of Jersey and owned Longueville for many decades. Evidence of his family's long association with the house can still be seen by the coat of arms above the fireplace in the drawing room.

The manor remained in private hands until 1948, when the present owner's parents bought the rather run-down old building and began the slow process of renovation. A year later, in July 1949, Longueville Manor finally opened its doors as a Country House Hotel with just thirteen bedrooms.

The hotel today has thirty double bedrooms in addition to a couple of luxury suites, for which advance booking is essential during the peak summer season. All 32 rooms are individually decorated and styled, and have full private bathroom facilities together with colour television, in-house videos, and direct-dial telephone. The standard of furnishing and decor is very high and the rooms here are the best on Jersey. One bedroom still retains a touch of medieval charm with an authentic eighteenth-century four-poster bed, one of the oldest antique hotel beds in any British hotel. If you are planning that special romantic break then few bedrooms could offer a more idyllic atmosphere – but book early.

The centrepiece of the hotel and the undeniable highlight of a stay here is the time you spend in the magnificent dark wood-panelled dining room which has lost little of its charm since it was built as the Great Hall six centuries ago. There is seating for up to sixty-five people in a relaxed atmosphere, and recently a new Chef de Cuisine, Andrew Baird, was recruited from Hambleton Hall to maintain the hotel's traditionally high standards of international cooking. A set menu is available every evening alongside an impressive à la carte choice. Half-board guests are allowed a reasonable deduction off the à la carte menu if that is their preference over the set menu on any particular evening.

Local seafood features prominently on both menus, as you might expect, and whatever your choice, presentation is exquisite. A sorbet precedes your main course, and is likely to be a variation like Spiced Tomato Sorbet, or Melon and Sauternes, rather than the standard orange or lemon dish. Main course specialities include Steamed Fillets of Dover Sole with Langoustine Tortellini, and Roast Breast of Duck with Mushroom and Foie Gras Jus. A full wine list is available, but half a dozen suggested vintages are listed alongside the set menu on any given evening.

Nearby attractions include a wealth of sporting and leisure facilities. There are two excellent eighteen-hole golf courses in addition to two nine-hole courses. The hotel itself has a heated outdoor swimming pool, but the opportunities for sea-bathing and sunbathing are superb throughout the island. St Helier, the island's capital, has a wide range of shops offering the best of British and continental goods without the standard VAT (currently seventeen and a half percent) which is normally added on the UK mainland. Another alternative is a boat trip round the island, or a day trip by ferry or hydrofoil to Guernsey, the next largest of the four main Channel Islands. Marine trips are generally available to Herm and Sark as well, particularly during the summer months.

LA SABLONNERIE

Address La Sablonnerie Hotel, Sark, Channel
Islands
Tel: 0481 83 2061

Nearest town St Peter Port.
Directions You must first travel by air or ferry to
Guernsey. A regular boat service from White Rock
pier in St Peter Port operates to Sark and tickets can
be purchased on board or from the Isle of Sark
Shipping Company at the pier. Alternatively, a
hydrofoil service operates from St Malo to Sark, or
occasionally from Jersey to the island. If you advise
the hotel of your ferry time you will be picked up
and driven the short journey to the hotel.
Awards Ashley Courtenay and *Gourmet* magazine
recommended; *Good Food Guide, Good Hotel Guide*,
Egon Ronay and Michelin Guide commended.
Open from the end of April until the beginning of
October.
No **special breaks** available.

Price for dinner, with wine, bed and breakfast for two – around £100.
Credit cards Access, Visa and Amex.
Children over the age of eight are welcome, but dogs are allowed only at the hotel's discretion.
Overall mark out of ten 8

La Sablonnerie is a modest little hotel located on Sark island, the smallest of the four main Channel Islands. The island itself lies just over seven miles away from Guernsey and about twenty-two miles west of the French coast. It is approximately three and a half miles long by one and a half miles wide, and offers a glimpse of what rural English life was like several decades ago; there are no traffic lights, no pedestrian crossings, very few roads and no cars to interrupt the tranquillity of your stay.

Sark is almost cut in two where la Coupée runs along the top of the ridge linking Big Sark and Little Sark. The Channel Islands were the only part of Great Britain occupied by Germany during the Second World War, and Sark did not escape the invasion. The single-track road which connects Big Sark and Little Sark – where the hotel is located – was constructed by German Prisoners of War in 1945, shortly after the island's liberation. The steep 200–foot drop on either side is an interesting sight as you cross this narrow ridge towards la Sablonnerie.

Wherever you go on this lovely island, you can be assured of relaxed tranquillity and a genuine feeling of 'getting-away-from-it-all'. This is obvious from the moment you reach Sark Harbour and, provided you have informed the hotel of when you plan to arrive (afternoons are preferred), then your first taste of the island's beauty will be from the horse and carriage which is sent to meet all guests. The drivers are well versed in the island's history and environment.

The hotel itself is, in fact, a discreetly modernized old Sark farmhouse. It is a credit to the present owner Elizabeth Peree that she has succeeded in achieving the blend of welcoming farmhouse atmosphere with the comfort of a modern hotel. La Sablonnerie's first tenants had a rather grim past. Jean Nicolle was found guilty of sorcery at a Guernsey trial in 1620. For his sins, he was severely whipped and banned from the island for life. As a parting gesture, he had one of his ears cut off. The stern Guernsey judges were not so lenient seven years later when his wife, Rachel Alexandre, was found guilty of witchcraft – she was burned alive. An interesting reminder of the days when witchcraft was rife on the lonely Channel Islands can still be seen if you look closely at the hotel's original chimneys. The builders were careful to include the all-important overhanging ledges of flat stones as a precaution against tired witches landing on the roof and coming down into the house to rest!

La Sablonnerie does not pretend to offer itself as a hotel in the luxury bracket, but instead offers traditional Sark courtesy combined with the attraction of modern-day comforts. The atmosphere is relaxed and unhurried, and the public rooms are cosy and tastefully furnished. Duty-free bar prices are a pleasant plus. The hotel flanks a well-tended garden on two sides, and an appealing sun lounge is the perfect spot to admire the garden on the occasional summer day when the weather is not kind enough to sit outside in the Tea Gardens, located just a few yards from the hotel.

The dining room is small and intimate, and the old-fashioned decor enhances the 'olde worlde' feel of the rest of the hotel. Thirty-eight can be seated at any one time, of whom two-thirds are generally residents. This is one of the best eating-out spots on Sark, so advance booking for non-residents is recommended. Local produce is used throughout, with much of the fruit and vegetables grown in the hotel garden. Fresh local fish is a speciality, and a popular starter is Fresh Oysters served on a bed of Crushed Ice. Two recommended favourites from the small selection of main dishes are Scampi in a superb Pernod and Cream Sauce, and Lobster Thermidor.

The hotel has a total of twenty-one rooms, including a beautiful Honeymoon Suite and a good selection of double, twin, single and family rooms. All bedrooms have recently been refurbished. Only six have private bathroom facilities, while another six have private shower rooms. If you book ahead you should be able to ensure private facilities.

Nearby attractions include countless lovely walks around the island, or boat trips arranged through the hotel reception to see the coastline at its best. The flora and fauna of the island of Sark are fascinating, and the island is a bird-watcher's paradise. This is particularly the case during early spring and autumn when large numbers of migrating birds use the island as a resting place. An old silver mine, which closed in 1845, is near the hotel and an interesting reminder of the island's nineteenth-century economy. Day excursions are possible to the larger Channel Islands of Guernsey and Jersey.

INDEX

Abbotsbury Gardens and
    Swannery 330, 370, 376
Abbotsford 26, 50, 75
Airds Hotel 3–5
Aldeburgh 197
Alnwick 82
Alston Hall 311–13
Althorpe 162, 223
Ardanaiseig 6–8
Arisaig House 9–11
Armathwaite Hall 79–81
Arundel Castle 271, 290, 302
Ascot 257, 299
Ashford 275, 278
atmosphere xvi
Auchterarder House 12–14
Avebury 316, 341, 354, 382
Aviemore 17
Avoncraft Museum of
    Buildings 226

Bailiffscourt 269–71
Bakewell 170
Ballathie House 15–17
Balmoral 20, 53, 65
Banchory Lodge Hotel 18–20
Barrington Court 330
Bass Rock 38, 50
Batemans 274, 287, 296
Bath 316, 323, 351, 352, 354,
    356, 357, 365, 367, 373, 385,
    388, 390, 393
Battle 294, 296
Beamish House 82–4
Beamish Museum 96

Beaulieu 326, 334, 344, 361,
    379
Beauport Park 272–4
Belton House 163, 166, 178
Belvoir Castle 162, 166, 178
Ben Nevis 42
Beningborough Hall 116
Berkeley Castle 233, 323, 357
Berkshire Vinery 299
Berrington Hall 215
Beverley 122
Bicton Park 338
bird-watching 23, 28, 38, 50,
    140, 323, 357, 385, 407
Birmingham 159, 226
Bishopstow House 314–16
Blair Castle 14, 29
Blenheim Palace 233, 241, 248,
    323, 341
Bodiam Castle 274, 296, 305
Bodysgallen Hall 133–6
Bolton Castle 119
Border Forest Park 105
Bournemouth 334, 370
Bourton-on-the-Water 232,
    245
Bowes Museum 119
Bowhill 26, 75
Braemar Castle 20, 65
Breamore House 361
Brierly Crystal factory 226
Brighton 265, 271, 284
Bristol 354, 373, 385, 388
Broadlands 326, 334
Brockenhurst 377
Brookhouse Inn 157–9

Broughton Castle 233
Buckland-Tout-Saints 317–20
Buckland Manor 207–09
Budleigh Salterton 338
Burghley House 163, 178
Burrell Collection 35
Burton-on-Trent 157, 159

Caernarfon Castle 136, 153
Calcot Manor 321–3
Cally Palace 21–3
Cambridge 184, 188, 204, 223, 257
Cannizaro House 251–3
Canterbury 278, 287, 305
Cardoness Castle 23
Careys Manor 324–6
Carlisle 81, 88, 90, 126
Castle Bolton 96
Castle Combe 367, 372, 373, 382
Castle Douglas 23
Castle Fraser 53
Castle Howard 96, 102, 116
Cawdor Castle 32
Cerne 376
Chartwell 265, 274, 281, 287, 296, 302
Chastleton House 233
Château La Chaire 397–9
Chatsworth House 166, 169, 172
Cheddar Gorge 352, 357
Chedington Court 327–30
Cheltenham 208, 227, 231, 237, 385, 388
Chepstow Castle 143
Chester 136, 153, 175
Cheviot hills 84
Chewton Glen 331–4
children welcome xviii, 4, 8, 9, 15, 18, 21, 23, 33, 36, 41, 45, 51, 54, 57, 60, 63, 66, 73, 80, 85, 88, 92, 94, 97, 103, 106, 121, 138, 147, 151, 161, 164, 170, 176, 190, 198, 211, 214, 220, 231, 247, 251, 254, 263, 272, 276, 288, 291, 294, 298, 301, 306, 324, 336, 339, 343, 349, 352, 359, 365, 371, 378, 386, 391
Chippenham 372
Chirk Castle 153
Cirencester 388
Clapton Court 330, 370
Cleveland Hills 86, 87
Cliveden 254–7
Colchester 188, 194
Combe House 335–8
Conway Castle 136, 153
Corsham Court 367, 382
Cotswold Hills 228, 229, 248, 323, 385, 387
Cottage in the Wood 210–12
Craigievar Castle 20, 53
Crathes Castle 20, 53
Crathorne Hall 85–7
Crieff glassworks 14
Cringletie House 24–6
Croft Castle 215
Cromlix House 27–9
Crosby Lodge 88–90
Culloden House 30–2
Culloden's Moor 31, 32

Dartmoor 313, 337, 347–8, 363, 364
Dartmouth 313, 337
decor xvi
Dedham 189, 191, 201, 204
Derby 159, 169, 172
disabled, provision for 15, 16, 21, 33, 36, 45, 54, 66, 72, 80, 92, 94, 145, 151, 161, 174, 181, 190, 198, 202, 208, 220, 228, 231, 247, 251, 283, 288,

301, 306, 315, 322, 324, 343,
352, 356, 358, 365
Diss 195, 197
Doddington Hall 166
dogs welcome xix, 15, 18, 21,
28, 33, 36, 45, 51, 54, 57, 60,
63, 66, 73, 80, 82, 85, 88, 94,
97, 100, 103, 106, 121, 128,
138, 145, 151, 157, 161, 177,
198, 231, 251, 254, 263, 270,
272, 291, 298, 301, 324, 336,
339, 343, 349, 359, 365, 371,
378, 386, 391
Dorchester 330, 368, 370
Doune Motor Museum 29, 68
Dover 278, 287, 305
dress xvii
Drum Castle 20, 53
Dunblane Cathedral 29
Dundrennan Abbey 23
Dunkeld 17, 56
Dunottar Castle 20
Durham 96
Dyrham Park 357

East Lambrook Manor 330
Eastbourne 271, 284
Eastwell Manor 275–8
Edinburgh 26, 29, 38, 48, 50,
75, 90
Eigg 11
Elcot Park 339–1
Elms, The 213–15
Erddig Hall 153
Eton 253, 299
Ettington Park 216–19
Exeter 320, 337
Exmoor 337

facilities xvi
Farne Islands 84
Faversham 278
Fifehead Manor 342–4

fishing 8, 17, 19, 28, 53, 56, 62,
68, 71, 75, 84, 87, 93, 102,
108, 122, 140, 149, 159, 162,
172, 175, 178, 187, 200, 237,
261, 277, 281, 284, 296, 299,
316, 323, 334, 337, 344, 351,
357, 360, 364, 370, 376, 393
Fitchingfield 204
Flatford Mill 187, 201
Flitwick Manor 220–3
Floors Castle 26, 74, 84
Folkestone 278, 287, 305
food xvi
Forde Abbey 330
Fort William 3, 5, 9, 17, 40, 42,
43
Fountains Abbey 96, 102, 116

Galloway coast 23, 90
gardens 20, 81, 136, 153, 278,
287, 296, 299, 302, 316, 326,
330, 334, 357, 361, 370, 376
Gatehouse of Fleet 21
Gidleigh Park 345–8
Glamis Castle 14
Glandon Park 293
Glasgow 29, 33, 35
Glastonbury Abbey 351, 357
Gleddoch House 33–5
Glen Coe 5, 8, 47
Glencot House 349–51
gliding 140, 385
Gliffaes 137–40
Gloucester 212, 237, 245
Glyndebourne Festival
Opera 281, 302
golf 14, 23, 35, 37, 38, 50, 53,
62, 65, 68, 71, 75, 84, 87, 93,
96, 99, 108, 115, 122, 140,
146, 149, 159, 162, 172,
183–4, 187, 200, 209, 215,
229, 237, 248, 253, 257, 261,
265, 274, 281, 284, 293, 296,

299, 302, 308, 326, 333, 337, 341, 351, 360, 364, 370, 376, 385, 402
Goodwood 290, 302
Grafton Manor 224–6
Grange-over-Sands 127, 129
Gravetye Manor 279–81
Great Malvern 210
Greenway, The 227–30
Greywalls 36–9
Guernsey 402, 406

Hackness Grange 91–3
Haddo House 20, 53
Haddon Hall 169, 172
Hadrian's Wall 105, 126
Hambleton Hall 160–3
Hampton Court 253, 299
Hanbury Hall 215
Hanbury Manor 181–4
Hardwick Hall 169, 172
Harewood House 102
Harlech 136, 144, 146, 149
Harrogate 96
Hartlebury Castle 215
Harvington Hall 215
Hastings 272, 274, 287, 296
Hatfield House 184
Hawes 117
Hawick 84
Haworth 99
Hay-on-Wye 143
Heale House 361
Henley Regatta 257, 261
Hereford 143, 212
Hever Castle 265, 278, 281, 287, 302
Hexham 103, 105
Hintlesham Hall 185–8
HMS *Victory* 326, 334, 361
Holker Hall 129
Holy Island 84
Homewood Park 352–4

Horsted Place 282–4
hot-air ballooning 341, 357, 385, 393
Hull 120, 122
Hunstrete House 354, 355–7

Ilkley 99
Inveraray Castle 47
Inverlochy Castle 40–3
Inverness 17, 65
Ipswich 185, 194, 198
Isle of Eriska 44–7
Isle of Iona 47
Isle of Skye 11

Jedburgh 75
Jersey 398, 399, 401, 407
Jervaulx Abbey 96, 119
Jervaulx Hall 94–6
Johnstounburn House 48–50

Kelso 72, 75, 84
Kendal 81, 129
Kennel Holt 285–7
Kersey 201
Keswick 79
Kew Gardens 253
Kildrummy Castle 20, 51–3
Kildwick Hall 97–9
King's Lynn 192, 194
Kingston Lacy House and Gardens 334, 370
Kinnaird 54–6
Kirkby Fleetham Hall 100–2
Knockinaam Lodge 57–9

Lainston House 358–1
Lake District 81, 90, 99, 110, 112, 129
Lammermuir hills 39
Langar Hall 164–6
Langley Castle 103–5
Leeds Castle 265, 278, 287, 296, 305

leisure facilities *see* sports and
  leisure facilities
Leith Hall 20, 53
Levens Castle 129
Lewtrenchard Manor 362–4
Limpley Stoke valley 354
Lincoln 163
Little Thakeham 288–90
Littlecote House 341
Littlehampton 269
Llandudno 133
Llangoed Hall 141–3
Loch Awe 8
Loch Etive 8
Loch Linnhe 3, 4
Loch Lomond 29, 35, 68
Loch Ness 32
Long Meg 126
Longleat House 316, 334, 344,
  357, 389
Longueville Manor 400–3
Lords of the Manor 231–3
Lowther Wildlife Adventure
  Park 81
Lucknam Park 365–7
Lydford Gorge 364
Lyme Regis 338, 376
Lymington 379
Lythe Hill 291–3

Maes-y-Neuadd 144–6
Maiden Castle 370
Maiden Newton
  House 368–70
Maidenhead 254, 261
Maison Talbooth and Talbooth
  Restaurant 189–91
Mallory Court 234–7
Mallyan Spout 106–8
Manoir aux Quat' Saisons,
  Le 238–41
Manor, The 242–5
Manor House, The 371

Marlborough 354
Marlow 261
Marwell Zoological Park 326,
  344, 361
Mary Rose 326, 334, 361
Matlock 167
Medmenham Abbey 261
Mellerstain 75
Mendip hills 356
Michaels Nook 109–12
Middleham Castle 96, 119
Middlethorpe Hall 113–16
Minsmere 201
Montacute House 330, 370
Moorfoot hills 26
Morecombe Bay 129
Muirfield 37
Mull of Kintyre 8
Murrayshall 60–2
Museum of Army
  Transport 122

National Motor Museum 326,
  361, 379
Netherfield Place 294–6
New Forest 378, 379
New Forest Butterfly Farm 326
Newby Hall 96, 116
Newstead Abbey 166
North Yorkshire Moors 92,
  102
North Yorkshire Moors
  Railway 93
Northumberland National
  Park 105
Norwich 188, 194, 197
Nottingham 164, 166, 169
nursery 391–2

Oakley Court 258–61
Oban 3, 5, 8, 44, 47
Old Rectory, The 192–4
Oxford 184, 219, 223, 238, 241,

245, 246, 248, 257, 308, 323, 341

Packwood House 237
Palé Hall 147–50
Parnham Park 290, 293, 302, 370
Peak National Park 168, 169, 171, 172
Peebles 24
Pennyhill Park 297–9
Penrith 123, 126
Perth 15, 17, 54, 56, 60
Petworth House 290, 293
Pevensey 274, 296
Pilsdon Pen 330
Pitlochry 56
Pittodrie House 63–5
Plumber Manor 374–6
Plymouth 311, 313, 320, 364
Polesden Lacey 265
Port Appin 3, 4
Portsmouth 271, 326, 334, 361

Raglan Castle 143
Rhinefield House Hotel 377–9
Rhum 11
Riber Hall 167–9
Richmond 96
riding 28, 35, 65, 75, 81, 84, 96, 108, 115, 140, 149, 162, 178, 187, 200, 209, 216, 229, 237, 248, 253, 257, 274, 281, 293, 296, 302, 316, 326, 334, 337, 341, 344, 357, 360, 364, 370, 376, 379, 385, 393
Ripon 96
Riverside 170–2
Roman Camp 66–8
Rookery Hall 173–5
Rookhurst 117–19
Rowley Manor 120–2

Royal Naval Museum, Southsea 326
Royal Tunbridge Wells 284, 287
Ruthin Castle 151–3
Rutland Water 161
Rye 274, 296

Sablonnerie, La 403–6
St Albans 184
St Helier 397, 399, 400, 402
St Peter Port 403
Salcombe 313
Salisbury 316, 334, 341, 344, 354, 361, 393
Salisbury House 195–7
Sark 403, 404
Scarborough 91, 93, 108
Scone Palace 14, 56
Scotney Castle 287
Seckford Hall 198–201
Seldon Park 262–5
service xvi
Severn Valley 211, 384
Shaftesbury 330, 376
Sharrow Bay 123–6
Shell Island 150
Shepton Mallet 380
Sherborne Castle 330
Sherwood Forest 166
Shieldhill 69–71
shooting 8, 28, 56, 62, 71, 75, 87, 102, 149, 162, 172, 178, 191, 248, 271, 284, 299, 302, 323, 334, 360, 364, 376, 379, 385, 393
Sissinghurst 278, 287, 296, 305
Skidby Windmill 122
Skipton 97, 99, 119
Slimbridge 323, 357, 385
Snape Maltings 197, 201
Snowdonia National Park 136, 150

South Downs 289
South Lodge 300–2
Southampton 271, 308, 334
Southwell Minster 166
sports and leisure facilities 8,
    14, 17, 23, 28, 32, 35, 38, 56,
    62, 65, 75, 81, 87, 93, 99, 111,
    115, 140, 149, 162, 175, 178,
    183–4, 187, 200, 204, 209,
    215, 218–19, 229, 237, 239,
    244, 248, 257, 260, 265, 271,
    274, 277, 284, 290, 293, 296,
    299, 302, 308, 313, 316, 325,
    326, 333, 341, 351, 357, 360,
    367, 373, 379, 388, 393, 402
    see also names of individual
    leisure pursuits
Stapleford Park 176–8
Stirling 27, 29, 68
Stockbridge 344
Ston Easton Park 354, 380–2
Stonehenge 308, 316, 323, 334,
    341, 344, 354, 389
Stourhead House and
    Gardens 316, 357
Stratfield House 308
Stratford-upon-Avon 208,
    209, 216, 219, 223, 226, 237,
    245
Strathallan Aircraft
    Museum 14
Stuart Strathearn
    glassworks 29
Studley Priory 246–8
Sturminster Newton 374, 376
Sudbury Hall 169
Sudeley Castle 233, 323, 357
Sulgrave Manor 222
Sunlaws House 72–5
Sunningdale 261, 265
Sutton Place 299

Tantallon Castle 38, 50

Tanyard 303–5
Taunton 330
Tavistock 362
Tetbury Manor 321–3
Tewkesbury 237, 245
Thames, River 257
Thaxsted 204
Thirlestane Castle 26, 75
Thornbury 383
Thornbury Castle 383–5
Tintern Abbey 143
Tor Castle 42
Traquair House 26, 50
Trossachs 14, 35, 68
Tweed, River 71
Tylney Hall 306–8

Uckfield 282
Uplands 127–9
Upper Slaughter 232, 245

Waddesdon Manor 222, 248
walking 28, 38, 56, 65, 68, 84,
    105, 172, 187, 212, 323, 337,
    348, 373, 406
Warwick Castle 219, 233, 237
Wells 349, 351, 357, 393
Wentworth 261, 265
West Highland Museum 42
Westonbirt Arboretum 323
Weston-super-Mare 351
Whatley Manor 386–9
Whipsnade Zoo 184
Whitby 87, 93, 106, 108
Whitehall 202–4
Wilton House 316, 334, 361
Wimbledon 252, 253
Winchester 299, 308, 334, 341,
    344, 358, 361
Windemere Steamboat
    Museum 81
Windsor 223, 253, 257, 258,
    261, 299, 308

Woburn 222
Wookey Hole 350
Woolley Grange 390–3
Worcester 209, 212, 213, 215,
    226, 237
Wordsworth Museum 112
Wye Valley 212, 385

Yarm 85
Yeovil 330, 370
York 93, 96, 108, 113, 114, 115,
    122
Yorkshire Dales 94, 99, 102,
    119
Yorkshire Wolds 121